Film Sequels

For Jared, Melody and Phoenix, with much love

Film Sequels

Theory and Practice from Hollywood to Bollywood

Carolyn Jess-Cooke

Edinburgh University Press

© Carolyn Jess-Cooke, 2009

Edinburgh University Press Ltd
22 George Square, Edinburgh

Typeset in Ehrhardt
by Servis Filmsetting Ltd, Stockport, Cheshire, and
printed and bound in Great Britain by
CPI Antony Rowe, Chippenham and Eastbourne

A CIP record for this book is available from the British Library

ISBN 978 0 7486 2603 8 (hardback)

The right of Carolyn Jess-Cooke
to be identified as author of this work
has been asserted in accordance with
the Copyright, Designs and Patents Act 1988.

Contents

Preface

'[I]n a sense no sequel is as good as its predecessor:
sequels inevitably seem to fail us in some obscure
yet fundamental way.'

Terry Castle, *Masquerade and Civilization*, 133

'Sequels equal money!'

Mr Dresden, Orange Film Board advertisement (2007)

This book explores the film sequel from its origins in silent cinema to its phenomenal popularity in contemporary Hollywood and beyond with a view to challenging the two chief assumptions of this category, as indicated by the quotations above: that sequels are always disappointing, and that they always mean big bucks at the box office. Such broad assumptions may explain why film sequelisation has been largely overlooked by academic studies and scholarly research; despite a century of film sequels, this book provides the first sustained account of this structure. Existing accounts of the film sequel tend to describe it as no more than a vampirish corporative exercise in profit-making and narrative regurgitation. Why, then, is sequel production on the rise? What exactly is the sequel, and how does it differ from other categories of repetition, such as the remake, serial and trilogy? By exploring the practice of film sequelisation throughout a range of relevant contexts and critical approaches – including intertextuality, genre, industrial transitions, the impact of new technologies, the independent film marketplace, cross-cultural dialogues and psychoanalytic theory – *Film Sequels* defines the sequel as a framework within which formulations of repetition, difference, history, nostalgia, memory and audience interactivity produce a series of dialogues and relationships between a textual predecessor and its continuation, between audience and text, and between history and remembrance. Such a consideration of these relationships offers a much more intimate understanding of some the most important contexts of film production and consumption in the twenty-first century, and it is precisely these broader contexts that motivate the intellectual enquiry of this book.

Film Sequels was born of an abiding interest in how and why the sequel dissatisfies. Contemporary film production is dominated by varieties of textual repetition and commercial products, including adaptations, remakes, series, franchises, trilogies, appropriations, spin-offs, parodies, pastiches, homages and genre films. Yet none of these tends to receive the same volume and timbre of disappointment as does the sequel. Many remakes fail critically and commercially, as do 'original' productions, genre films, independent pictures, and so on. The reason why a sequel disappoints – and why the very concept of sequelisation is often met with a collective groan – seems to do with how the sequel re-imagines and extends its source in ways that impose upon our memories and interpretation of the previous film. In creating a second ending of an 'original', the sequel conjures a previous viewing experience, and it is precisely this imposition of spectatorial memory, or this kind of enforced retro-interpretation and continuation, that appears to underline the sense of dissatisfaction that the sequel often creates. Such dynamics are explored here with a view to understanding the contexts within which the film sequel is produced and consumed. No book is produced in isolation, and *Film Sequels* was no exception. I was fortunate enough to receive help, insight and nods in the right direction from the following people, to whom I owe debts of gratitude: Dominic Alessio, Barry Ardley, Jonathan Auerbach, Peter Burt at the University of Sunderland, Jennifer Cunico, Elizabeth Ezra, Jennifer Forrest, Rosemary Hanes at the Library of Congress, Scott Higgins, Joe Kember, Coonoor Kripalani-Thadani, Jessica Langer, Aditi Menon-Broker, Claire Perkins, Simon Popple, Ben Singer, Sanjay Sood, Colin Young and Josh Yumibe. A special word of thanks goes to Constantine Verevis for his collegiality and helpful discussions on sequelisation; to David Hancock for providing me with a copy of his Screen Digest Sequels Report and for regular sequel updates; to Glenda Pearson at the University of Washington for helping me access some tricky film databases and indexes; to my sister Michelle for initiating me into the world of online social networking (which facilitated Chapter 3); and to Evita Cooke for help and assistance of a much more fundamental nature.

I am grateful to the University of Sunderland and for an award from the Arts and Humanities Research Council, both of which provided me with research leave to complete this book. Thanks to the British Academy for a travel grant which facilitated a very productive visit to the Library of Congress in Washington, DC. I was also lucky to discover the diverse range of films stocked at my local book/film lender, the Gateshead Public Library, which proved most helpful to my research.

I began this project while I was pregnant with my first child, Melody Angel, and finished it after the birth of my second child, Phoenix Jared. Much of my sequels research has eclipsed time spent with both of them; one positive outcome of an otherwise guilt-laden routine was that I was compelled to think harder and work faster than ever before. It is therefore necessary to dedicate this book to my own bright little 'sequels', and to my husband Jared, for his love, encouragement and patience, and for his consolation when my computer wiped an entire draft of Chapter 1.

Acknowledgements

A version of Chapter 6 appears as 'Virtualizing the Real: Sequelization and Secondary Memory in Steven Spielberg's *Artificial Intelligence: A. I.*, *Screen* 47: 3 (Autumn 2006), pp. 347–66.

The Age of the $equel: Beyond the Profit Principle

Contemporary cinema is infused with recycling and repetition. From video game tie-ins to McHappy Meal toys, the new horizontally integrated Hollywood continues to create ways of engaging the spectator within a network of remembering and re-enacting scenarios that are designed to recycle a film's narrative and repeat the spectatorial experience as far as possible. In accordance with these commercial practices, sequential filmmaking has developed in recent years into several formats that internalise forms of repetition and continuation within narrative structures, such as sequels, remakes, series, trilogies and adaptations.

The most profitable of these structures is the film sequel.[1] A regular attraction in cinemas around the globe since the early twentieth century, the sequel has developed into a major intertextual framework with carefully controlled predictive elements to guarantee audience turnouts. In the twenty-first century, the sequel is a frequent box-office earner, reaping $683 million in the US across two sequels in the summer of 2004, and over $1 billion worldwide from a single sequel in 2006.[2] Now creeping into world cinemas and independent film festivals, the sequel is also a burgeoning element of the video game industry, and often corresponds with technological efforts to improve the spectatorial experience and interactivity, such as online video games, DVD 'behind the scenes' specials and 'deleted scenes', and revamped theme park attractions. Yet despite its prevalence throughout many quarters of film culture, the sequel is largely denounced – or ignored – by media commentaries. Although a healthy amount of scholarship exists in the areas of film remakes, intertextuality and adaptation, there is very little on sequelisation.[3] Available literature tends to condemn the sequel as a rip-off, a fundamentally inferior exercise, a kind of cinematic virus, or a cannibalistic re-hash designed to milk a previous production for all its worth.[4]

Why, then, does the popularity and success of the sequel continue from strength to strength? How do we account for emergent experiments with the sequel's structure, and how might this structure be considered critically? What is the relationship between sequelisation and narrative developments, such as transmedia storytelling? In what ways does the sequel differ from other sequential categories, such as remaking, adaptation and serialisation? What cross-cultural effects does this Hollywood format have upon world cinemas, and how can these be measured? In answering these questions, this book takes the approach that views of the sequel as a wholly commercial venture ignore its important registers of continuation, nostalgia, memory, difference, originality, revision and repetition in a range of formal, cultural, industrial, technological and theoretical contexts. In a rather rigorous study of sequels conducted in 2004, the *Screen Digest Cinema Intelligence Briefing Report*, David Hancock observed that recent film production indicates 'more an experimentation with sequels than a flogging to death'.[5] The film sequel's frequent appropriation as an 'experimental' structure within the contexts above therefore demands more scrupulous critical attention than has been accorded to this form in the past. This challenging task is the main occupation of *Film Sequels*. By exploring sequel production beyond box office figures, *Film Sequels* aims to account as much as possible for some of the major critical contexts within which sequelisation operates, and to consider sequelisation as part of a new critical vocabulary that is necessary to contend with a host of emergent practices and formats in digital culture.

Persistently encountered across various media, the sequel has its origins in literary culture. As Paul Budra and Betty A. Schellenberg's *Part Two: Reflections on the Sequel* (1998b) makes clear, the sequel has developed as a sequential literary format throughout the history of narrative, and can be traced back to oral narratives dating as far back as Homer's *Iliad* in the eighth century BC. With the rise of print culture, sequelisation increased in the form of off-shoots and variations on the theme of plagiarism, but also developed rapidly as a framework by which authors began to define narrative continuation, authorship and originality. For example, the term 'sequel' is used in Shakespeare's *Hamlet* to describe 'what comes next', or the 'sequel at the heels' of related gossip. In *Love's Labour's Lost* – for which Shakespeare wrote a sequel, *Love's Labour's Won*, which is now, somewhat ironically, lost – a character remarks 'Like the sequel, I' in response to a request to follow his companion. On each of these occasions, the sequel rather casually denotes continuation. Yet more progressive uses of the sequel were in store. While Shakespeare was busy scribing his sequels to *Henry VI Part One*, Christopher Marlowe wrote two plays known as *Tamburlaine Parts One and Two*, using the sequel format to investigate the complex relationship(s) between originality and repetition, and to suggest the impossibility of total originality and 'pure, utterly identical, repetition'.[6]

These early modern uses of sequelisation indicate its semantic registers of following and, more importantly, its articulations of intertextual relations and originality as highly problematic. In the twenty-first century, however, these 'problems' are inherent elements of screen media. Film audiences are well versed in the assortment of quotations, parodies, derivatives and narrative exploitations that make up what is essentially an intertextual medium. Also, the emergence of digital technologies, virtual/cyber realities, user-generated content and interactive gaming has shaped reception and storytelling practices far beyond the sequel's literary origins, to the extent that the historical concepts of intertextuality and originality often cannot sufficiently address the more complicated relationships created by cross-cultural exchange and intermediality. While my use of the sequel does not aim to endorse the bout of 'labelitis'[7] which has purportedly infected Hollywood, I argue that sequelisation offers a critical 'lens' through which we can identify such intermedial relationships and their impact on the viewing experience. The sequel's commercial operations also provide key starting points for considering the increasingly repetitious forms of contemporary film production. Rather than look to the sequel in terms of its (often tendentious) taxonomic instances, I aim to consider the sequel as a trope of repetition, difference, continuation and memory.

DEFINING THE SEQUEL

Deriving from the Latin verb *sequi*, meaning 'to follow', a sequel usually performs as a linear narrative extension, designating the text from which it derives as an 'original' rooted in 'beforeness'. Previous systems of classifying the sequel have tended to ignore its distinct narrative properties. This has contributed to misreadings of sequelisation and of the modes of appropriation in general. Thomas Simonet, for example, points out the problems of classification at the same time as he supports *Variety*'s definition of the 'sequel' as comprising one-third of the 'recycled-script film' category. According to this definition, the primary difference between a sequel, a remake and a series film is that the sequel 'repeats the characters of another film, taking up the action where it left off; the characters' history in the earlier film is mentioned, understood or otherwise significant in the later one'. Employed to categorise 3,490 films reviewed in *Variety* between 1940 and 1979, this description is severely lacking in scope and precision. Other texts that look to the sequel include a limited number of studies on serial novels, nineteenth-century sequence narratives, and a somewhat narrow account of cinema sequels and remakes between 1903 and 1987.[8] Amongst more recent contemplations are a dismissal of the sequel as 'self-explanatory' (in contrast with the much more narratologically complex series),[9] the sequel as 'a self-referential allusion to an earlier work',[10] or as one of several mechanisms (including, of course, the remake and series) which 'send cinema back to its origins, to an atmosphere of fascination with the working of machines, with the spectacle of the commodity, with the metropolitan setting'.[11] These studies indicate the tendency to conflate sequelisation with conceptualisations of the series, the remake and sequence narratives, each of which have separate ideological registers and discrete generic, performative and textual functions.

To be fair, the differences between these categories are not often crystal clear. A primary reason for this is that they are hybrid structures, premised on the dialogue and occasional marriage between media and modes. The prequel, for instance, is often mistaken for the sequel, and vice versa. But although the prequel is concerned with the origins of a narrative or character – or what Gérard Genette described as an 'analeptic' continuation, a 'backward continuation (i.e., what came *before*), meant to work its way upstream'[12] – it is usually released after an original production (such as *Batman Begins* [Christopher Nolan, 2005], the prequel to *Batman* [Tim Burton, 1989]), thus generating assumptions that it is a sequel. A recent Hollywood trend is sequels of remakes (such as *Ocean's 12* [Steven Soderbergh, 2004] and *The Brazilian Job* [F. Gary Gray, 2009]), as well as 'Sequel A meets Sequel B' productions (such as *Atom Man Vs. Superman* [Spencer Gordon Bennet, 1950], *King Kong Vs. Godzilla* [Ishirô Honda, 1962], *Godzilla Vs. the Sea Monster* [Jun Fukuda, 1966], *Freddy Vs. Jason* [Ronny Yu, 2003] and *AVP: Alien Vs. Predator* [Paul W. S. Anderson, 2004]) – some of which have resulted in sequels of their own.

There is also the matter of separating sequels from series and trilogies when a third filmic instalment is released. For instance, *Shrek 2* (Andrew Adamson, Kelly Asbury and Conrad Vernon, 2004) is a sequel, but does *Shrek the Third* (Raman Hui and Chris Miller, 2007) make a trilogy? Would a fourth production make a series? What are the differences between these, and how do we account for exceptions to the rule? Again, definitions are easily misconstrued. As explored in Chapter 4, the trilogy expands the Aristotelian concept of a three-act structure – comprising a beginning, middle and end – across three texts. The film trilogy generally refers to a body of three films that operate coherently within a tripartite narrative framework that concludes with the final instalment. However, the trilogy is often convoluted by the issue of balancing a film's singular three-act structure with the larger three-acts of the trilogy. In other words, the third film chapter is required to have its own discrete beginning, middle and end, at the same time as each of these acts must wind down, conclude and tie up the concerns of the previous two films. The director must be careful not to introduce too many new characters or events, and must negotiate expectations of how the trilogy will end. In addition, the weight of the trilogy must be evenly distributed across all three films, but most often – as in the case of *The Godfather III* (Francis Ford Coppola, 1990), *Terminator 3: Rise of the Machines* (Jonathan Mostow, 2003), *The Matrix Revolutions* (Larry and Andy Wachowski, 2003), and *X-Men: The Final Stand* (Brett Ratner, 2006) – the third film sinks under the bulk of many disparate endings, dead characters and forced conclusions that audiences would rather have been left to imagine themselves.

The narrative complication posed by the film trilogy appears to have given birth to a 'mid-way' derivative category that takes on some of the attributes of the sequel, the series and the trilogy. This category is the threequel.[13] Defined by the anonymously penned online encyclopedia Wikipedia as 'a sequel to a sequel', the threequel can be distinguished from a trilogy by its refusal to end a sequential narrative, and by the implicit suggestion that a fourth instalment might be possible. Threequels such as *Alien 3* (David Fincher, 2003) and *Mission: Impossible 3* (J. J. Abrams, 2006) closely respond to a previous film sequel and indicate the continuation of the narrative into possible fourth, fifth and even sixth episodes without the burden of bringing an overarching trilogy-narrative to a close.

This brings us to the difficult task of distinguishing between sequels, series and serials, which formed a major part of early film production. In any discussion of film taxonomies, much controversy surrounds the exact definitions of each. As Chapter 1 of this book argues, however, the practice of each precedes critical understanding and/or theorisation, and in many cases terminology is not altogether accurate. In this regard, it is imperative that I make my chief distinction between three fairly similar categories crystal clear: whereas seriality and series defy change, the sequel champions difference, progress and excess. Think of popular animated TV series *The Simpsons* (Mark Kirkland, Jim Reardon *et al.*, 1989–2007), the *James Bond* films (Terence Young, Irvin Kershner, *et al.*, 1962–present) or *The Perils of Pauline* (Louis J. Gasnier *et al.*, 1914) – in each case, the protagonists never age, never (re)marry, never switch jobs. Other genre-driven series – such as *Star Wars* (George Lucas, 1977), *Star Trek: The Motion Picture* (Robert Wise, 1979) and Sergio Leone's spaghetti westerns – are less character-driven than they are interested in extrapolating characters and narratives across a number of films that contribute to the unfolding of particular genre codes and ideologies. This kind of series is strictly devoted to the playing out of a 'narrative scheme that remains constant'.[14]

Conversely, what each of these categories has in common is a shared investment in circularity and continuation, and, as I go on to argue, one commonly grows out of another. Aljean Harmetz, for instance, has observed that 'in the 1940s and 1950s sequels were usually B movies elongated into a series, e.g. Dr. Kildare, Andy Hardy, Ma and Pa Kettle, Francis the Talking Mule',[15] whilst the *James Bond* series was a natural progression from the box-office success of *Dr No* (Terence Young, 1962) and its sequel, *From Russia With Love* (Terence Young, 1963). Such progressions from one form to another move according to a complex network of socio-political affairs, shifting reception practices, industrial transitions, new technologies and cross-cultural dialogue. It is precisely these factors in practice that contributes to the textualisation of film categories. For instance, the early twentieth-century 'serial queen phenomenon' noted in Ben Singer's *Melodrama and Modernity* (2001) is a fascinating case of gender-politics played out according to the serial format, which in turn was devised to bring audiences – predominantly women, who had much leisure time on their hands and could take advantage of the availability of crèches at most local theatres – to the cinemas on a regular basis. In the current era, merchandising, film franchising and cross-media narratives play a massive part in film production, and the resulting homogenisation of blockbusters and film sequels plays a key role in the textualisation of the sequel, in many cases, as a formulaic retread.

Suffice it to say that none of the appropriational modes encountered throughout this book lends itself easily to straightforward definitions. It is often necessary to unpack these forms and examine their points of overlap and confluence. For example, to consider the processes of and relationships between translation, commercialism and cross-media relations which occur in the event of the film sequel, I draw upon various sub-categories of intertextuality – in particular Genette's theory of 'paratextuality', one of five sub-categories of his transtextuality theory. As an example, Genette's definition of a paratext as a 'secondary signal' of a text, which includes subtitles, footnotes, intertitles, prefaces and other textual marginalia, can also be assigned to films in terms of movie posters, trailers, DVD extras, that similarly surround the film text.[16] In so far as it operates as an ancillary narrative – by developing plotlines and characters, moving in diverse narrative trajectories from the original, repeating key themes, characteristics, gags and shots, and generally acting as a commentary upon the original – the sequel can also be seen as paratextual. Yet this model only works so far, and only for a select number of sequels. Many film sequels offer examples of sequelisation as – to borrow another of Genette's types of intertextuality – hypertextual, which describes 'any relationship uniting a text B [the hypertext] to an earlier text A [the 'hypotext'], upon which it is grafted in a manner *that is not that of commentary*' (my emphasis).[17] As I go on to show, it is not entirely possible to define every sequel according to such neat categories of intertextuality. For instance, Francis Ford Coppola's *The Godfather Part II* (1974) is both a prequel and a sequel of *The Godfather* (Coppola, 1972), which in turn was adapted from Mario Puzo's 1969 novel of the same name. But which of these sources is the hypotext? How can we fully define the relationship between Coppola's sequel and its precursors – as well as its generic inheritances – when hypertextuality refers to '*any* relationship' between an original and derivative? And, as Genette admits, 'there is no literary work that does not evoke . . . some other literary work, and in that sense all works are hypertextual.'[18] Although very much an intertextual structure, the sequel in its current forms is not always accessible solely through the channels of intertextual theory.

CONTINUATION: A CORPORATIVE STRATEGY?

It is for this reason that I investigate the sequel's industrial contexts in my tentative construction of a 'theory' of sequelisation, in recognition of the burgeoning impact of transnational media corporations (or TMCs) – commercial entertainment monopolies – upon the way in which sequels are produced and distributed across the globe. Indeed, many of the studio giants of Hollywood's Golden Age are now owned and operated by international entertainment conglomerates – for instance, both MGM and Columbia Pictures are now owned by Sony, a multi-million dollar Japanese corporation which also manufactures a multitude of electronic products and lists music production, financial services and marketing amongst its commercial output. Accordingly, film production is affected by this new corporate structure. Perhaps the greatest impact is in the form of media franchising. Media franchises are generated by TMCs and often entail numerous film sequels that are shot back-to-back and simultaneously granted release at cinema theatres worldwide, as in the case of *Matrix Revolutions*, to combat video pirating.[19] Every element of consumer activity – including exploitative activity – is cautiously controlled by these media giants. 'Event movies',[20] as their film packages are also known, are planned and packaged to distribute entertainment around the world in as many ways and forms as possible to expand the spectatorial experience of the film's theatrical release – and its commercial potential – across myriad cultural events.

This is achieved in part by media/merchandising tie-ins. Gore Verbinski's film sequel *Pirates of the Caribbean: Dead Man's Chest* (2006) provides an excellent example of this. Reaching $1 billion at the box office in just sixty-three days, the film's release coincided with a hailstorm of merchandise and movie memorabilia, ranging from car dealerships, a world ocean race, MSN messenger and breakfast cereal, to related media events such as an updated version of the musical, *Pirates of Penzance*, an entirely new musical called *The Pirate Queen* by the creators of *Les Misérables*, a number of video games and a mobile phone game, all of which no doubt contributed to the film's history-making box-office success.[21] Originating as a fairground attraction at Disneyland, *Pirates of the Caribbean* made its initial film appearance in the form of Verbinski's *Pirates of the Caribbean: The Curse of the Black Pearl* (2003). Alert to the successful reception of Johnny Depp's performance as the intoxicated pirate Captain Jack Sparrow, which he claimed to be inspired by Rolling Stones rocker Keith Richards, Disney signed up the film's stars for a further two sequels and enlisted Richards to play Depp's father. Depp's performance in *Pirates 2* – which was critically regarded as buoying up an otherwise soggy storyline – underlined the creation of a video game named *Pirates of the Caribbean: The Legend of Jack Sparrow* (Buena Vista Games, 2006). This game allows players to 'be' Jack Sparrow, retells the events of the first movie from Sparrow's perspective, and even features Depp's voice.[22] Paramount to the film's success is the creation of a participatory spectatorship and the correspondence of previous or related narratives and paratexts.

The importance of existing narratives or related texts to a film's success is indicated perhaps even more strongly by Michael Bay's *The Island* (2005). Unlike *Pirates 2*, *The Island* took less than a tenth of its $235 million budget across US theatres in its opening weekend.[23] Film showings at 3,200 theatres across the US soon ground to an abrupt halt, achieving about a third of the film's costs in total box-office revenue. As a summer blockbuster, the film was expected to return its investment with considerable profit like its lucrative sci-fi comparables, *I, Robot* (Alex Proyas, 2004) and *Minority Report* (Steven Spielberg, 2002). Every measure had been taken to ensure a box-office smash. DreamWorks had invested $35 million in marketing the film. *The Island*'s stars had proved a draw in films of the past – Ewan McGregor as poetic love interest in *Moulin Rouge!* (Baz Luhrmann, 2001), Scarlett Johansson in the critically acclaimed *Lost in Translation* (Sofia Coppola, 2003), and Sean Bean as Boromir in *The Lord of the Rings* trilogy (Peter Jackson, 2001, 2002, 2003). And the film wasn't bad, as blockbusters go. So why did it flop? Arguably, *The Island*'s failure was the result of a lack of 'built-in awareness' possessed by sequels and remakes. Although it combined a number of previously successful ingredients, *The Island* was still a new recipe for audiences who were used to re-digesting their favourite storyline or star in a part-two blockbuster. As Edward Jay Epstein points out, *The Island* had to compete against other films which, although new releases, were already familiar to audiences in the form of video games, prequels and sequels, classical films or comic books.[24] Conversely, *Pirates 2* paraded a host of familiar scenes, stars, fashions, genres and narratives to audiences who were eager to experience Disney's fairground attraction on-screen. And the studio promised opportunities to sail with Captain Jack as far as the media horizon extended. Myriad instruments and paratexts of popular culture enabled consumers to engage with the *Pirates of the Caribbean* narrative again and again, with the storyline of the third filmic instalment visible in the near future, replete with its own forms of participation and repetition. As I go on to discuss in Chapter 3, merchandising, marketing and deferred narrative endings underline the key theoretical principles of sequelisation. Sequels are transitional, not conclusive. By definition, the sequel has no end; it is a perpetual diegesis with which consumers can engage as many times in as many ways as possible.

SEQUELS, IDEOLOGY AND VIEWING PLEASURES

The prevailing focus of this book is on the sequel's latent registers of 'afterwardness' which informs many filmic representations of gender, cultural transitions and identities, history and national disasters as both coming after and repeating to some extent an 'original' entity or activity in some film sequels. Departing from a range of existing theoretical positions, sequel theory emerges as an autonomous discourse on industrial, textual and cultural practices of reproduction and repetition. Rather than dwell upon the value of film sequels, or consider whether sequels are 'better' than their originals or not, I prefer to spend time examining the critical issues and assumptions beneath these categories of judgement, particularly the ways in which sequels transmit and circulate sexual, political and cross-cultural ideologies.

My idea of the 'profit principle' of the sequel paraphrases Sigmund Freud's essay, 'Beyond the Pleasure Principle' (1920),[25] which marked a major turning point in his psychoanalytic theories of pleasure and instinct by looking closer at the forces which drive us to pleasure and action, or the 'compulsion to repeat'. Here, Freud examines the process by which subconscious forces compel individuals to repeat events over and over again regardless of how painful or traumatic these events may be. It appears to me that a similar repetition-compulsion underlines sequelisation, in so far as the sequel taps into a particular cultural urgency to memorialise, interact with and perhaps alter the past, an issue I examine at length in Chapter 6. Sequelisation as a form of repetition-compulsion is evidenced by the way sequels are designed to keep audiences coming back to cinema theatres, to re-experience the film across a host of tie-ins, and generally make cinema-going a habit.[26] Profit is thus dependent on generated patterns of repetition-compulsion.

Freud's thoughts on repetition-compulsion similarly prove vital in considering the memorialisation of a source text as a major part of sequelisation. The film sequel functions as the belated ending of the original, and, for the spectator, offers a protracted reconstruction of a previous viewing experience. Like the concept of *déjà-vu* presented in *The Matrix* (Larry and Andy Wachowski, 1999) which 'happens when they change something', the sequel is often a 'glitch' in the reception and memory of an original film. Remakes and adaptations offer comparable methods of retrospective interpretation, but whereas each of these usually departs from the source text to create alternative contexts and updated interpretations, neither tends to alter the original ending. The sequel, however, completely changes the ending of the original by continuing the narrative towards a possibly less satisfactory conclusion; we are never left to imagine that everyone lived happily ever after, but instead are subjected to the revivification of a previous ending, only to watch it end all over again. Post-performance interpretive activity is enforced and mediated in the event of the sequel. Several reasons for the sequel's bad press are its tendency to impose upon interpretation, to infringe upon the memory of the original, and because it prescribes a memory in replacement of that memory. More on that in Chapter 6.

For better or for worse, film sequels turn the spectator into an active participant. They offer the 'ability to foresee' and 'make forecasts'[27] about a narrative
by inviting the audience to engage and predict the narrative in new (yet highly
familiar) contexts, each of which generates dialogue amongst audiences and
establishes interpretive communities, such as chat rooms, web blogs, fandoms
and 'fanfic' efforts to create sequels to existing sequels and/or originals.[28] The
sequel's citational nature continually opens up a host of textual trajectories and
directions, not only towards the original but in many narrative directions. Like
Noël Carroll's description of film allusion, the sequel invariably involves all or
some of the following: 'quotations, the memorialisation of past genres, the
reworking of past genres, homages, and the recreation of "classic" scenes,
shots, plot motifs, lines of dialogue, theme, gestures, and so forth from film
history'.[29] Calling upon the spectator to draw upon or speedily acquire a
working knowledge of film history and dredge up memories of the original, the
sequel is founded upon the (somewhat false) sense of spectator interactivity.

This interactivity is based on the marketing of the sequel as a 'textual commentary',[30] or as a structure which invites and enables the spectator to make
connections and associations with cinema trends, genres, and popular culture
in general, such as the *Scream* trilogy (Wes Craven, 1996, 1997, 2000) and its
offshoot series, beginning with *Scary Movie* (Keenen Ivory Wayans, 2000).
Sequels necessarily address fans of the original, and are usually highly self-
conscious of audience expectations. Unlike remakes, the time frame between
sequels is usually short, which can be regarded as an attempt to continue and
feed into fan cultures generated by a recent film instalment, and additionally
to produce films that have sequel logic 'built in'. Films are now rarely made
without containing the possibility of a sequel within the primary narrative.
The dialogue that is created between an original and its potential derivatives
revises the notion of originality and, in turn, redefines 'originals' as 'origi-
naries' – or productions that are geared to spawn narrative offspring.
Audiences are alerted to these possibilities for future film episodes via
cliffhangers or other gestures towards continuation, and are able to access the
larger global process of 'media convergence',[31] whereby video games, online
gaming sites and message boards make the sequel available for both discussion and repetitive interactive engagement. But, as Henry Jenkins puts it,
'fans lack direct access to the means of commercial cultural production and
have only the most limited resources with which to influence entertainment
industry's decisions'.[32] Jenkins's later discussion of 'participatory culture'
points to trends and media practices which 'encourage the flow of images,
ideas and narratives across multiple media channels and demand more active
modes of spectatorship'.[33] Correspondingly, the sequel's modes of allusion
and reflection not only create a 'flow' of familiar images, ideas and narratives,
but additionally encourage the discussion and re-interpretation of these at all

levels of consumer culture. Where spectatorial interactivity comes into full effect in the sequel is chiefly at the level of engaging with a text that appears unfixed due to the prevalence of many open-endings, re-interpretations and repetitions. Although industrial production is rarely (if ever) affected by fan activity, the production of the sequel as an interactive text is created by developing methods of textual interpretation and transformation.

SEQUELS AND GLOBALISATION

The above works under the assumption that all sequels are made in Hollywood, but this is not always the case. Sequels are fast and furiously becoming regular occurrences outside Hollywood. Bollywood – the name given to Indian cinema in general, but which strictly refers only to the Hindi film industry based in Mumbai – offers a striking example of this. Once very much a culturally specific industry, Bollywood has recently demonstrated a move towards a 'new internationalism' which includes stabs at sequelisation. In 2006 alone, Bollywood sequels include *Dhoom 2* (Sanjay Gadhvi, 2006), the sequel to *Dhoom* (Sanjay Gadhvi, 2004), Rakesh Roshan's *Krrish* (2006), which follows his earlier *Koi . . . Mil Gaya* (2003), *Lage Raho Munna Bhai* (Rajkumar Hirani, 2006), which continues on from where *Munnabhai MBBS* (Rajkumar Hirani, 2003) left off, and *Phir Hera Pheri* (Neeraj Vora, 2006), part two of Priyadarshan's *Hera Pheri* (2003). Previously perceived as box-office poison, these sequels have enjoyed tremendous box-office success with Bollywood audiences but, more importantly, are saturated with the hallmarks of Hollywood blockbusters, such as bigger budgets, the appearance of Bollywood megastars, and 'babes, boys, and bikes'[34] – ostensibly in anticipation of a profitable global reception. For the most part, however, Bollywood's move towards sequelisation appears inexplicable. As one of the world's largest film industries, Bollywood is perpetuated and supported by a devoted domestic fan base. As Faiza Hirji comments, 'roughly ten million people a day purchase tickets to see a Bollywood movie, and some of these will return repeatedly [commonly ten to fifteen times] to view a favourite movie.'[35] With such a committed home audience, why the sudden desire to utilise a film format that had previously crashed and burned at the Bollywood box office?

One argument is that Hollywood casts the dark shadow of Western values over world cinemas, Bollywood included, to the extent that domestic audiences are no longer satisfied with home-grown movies. Consequently, if indigenous film industries are to survive, their productions must cater to the tastes of home audiences. Global media giants have worked hard to penetrate Bollywood's billion-strong audience. In 1991, Rupert Murdoch took News Corporation, his £30 billion vertically integrated global media company, to Asia and created

STAR (Satellite Television Asian Region). To a vastly impoverished home entertainment network Murdoch brought 300 digital TV channels to over 390 million viewers by 2004; many of these channels introduced American media to the Indian community for the first time. Other TMCs leaped at the 1998 trade liberalisation measures, distributing films into previously closed territories and creating eager new audiences around the world. The result is a series of cultural and industrial conflicts and compromises between Hollywood and world cinemas, evidenced by films that replace previously enshrined cultural values with those of a global superpower. And in terms of Hollywood's influence on narrative structures, there is an evident structure of repetition currently in development. Claims Prathamesh Menon, 'If you point to any new Bollywood release, you can bet that there existed a Hollywood original somewhere down the line.'[36]

On the other hand, of course, globalisation is never entirely a one-way street. Bollywood has in turn made its mark on the filmic *mappa mundi*, enjoying enormous critical success and cultural recognition with films like Gurinder Chadha's *Bhaji on the Beach* (1993), *Bend it like Beckham* (2002) and *Bride and Prejudice* (2004). Other films have brought to Hollywood an unprecedented taste for Asian cinema with a box-office tally to match.[37] Many world cinemas have been reshaped in recent years by the infiltration of US popular culture, but Hollywood also continues to engage in cultural awareness and diversity to the extent that the so-called 'Hollywoodisation' of foreign industries is no longer an entirely fitting description of the forces of hegemony and cultural imperialism at work. Such arguments for and against globalisation inform my discussion in Chapter 5, but for now it is sufficient to note the sequel as one instance in a series of ideologically charged Hollywood structures that brings about (often controversial) conversations between cultures.

THEORY VS. PRACTICE: THE FINAL CONFLICT

The following chapters look to sequelisation in theory and practice within and outside the domain of Hollywood. My study of sequelisation ranges from sequels in recent mainstream cinema, art-house and 'indie' sequels, sequels on TV, the impact of the domestic market on sequelisation, and the impact of the video game industry on Hollywood. Issues of genre, gender, cross-cultural identities and narrative frameworks in the post-millennial moment are foregrounded in these explorations as necessary ports of call. The following chapters aim to encounter the practice of film sequelisation throughout a range of contexts, yet my theory of sequelisation is constructed first and foremost through an understanding of the sequel's related reception practices. As Chapter 2 identifies, the sequel is essentially a response to a previous work, a rereading and rewriting of an 'original' that additionally calls upon an audience to reread and rewrite their memories of a previous text. Like *xushu*, the Chinese literary equivalent of the sequel which bloomed during the mid-seventeenth century, 'sequelling' always involves both the act of authoring and reading. The sequel involves, as Martin W. Huang puts it, 'a reception process of the precursor work(s) as well [as a writing process] in the sense that the *xushu* are a continuation of and commentary on the earlier work(s)'.[38] It is the reception process as both an originating and a continuing process that I will focus on in the following book.

NOTES

1. Six of the ten highest-grossing films of all time are sequels, according to data compiled by the Exhibitor Relations Company. See http://www.ercboxoffice.com/erc/reports/top10oalltime.php. Of the ten highest openers, eight are sequels. See http://www.ercboxoffice.com/erc/reports/top500openers.php

2. http://news.bbc.co.uk/1/hi/entertainment/film/3630616.stm; http://www.themovieinsider.com/previews/upcoming-movie-sequels.php?y=2008&field=year. The two 2004 sequels are *Mission: Impossible III* (J. J. Abrams) and *X-Men: The Last Stand* (Brett Ratner); the 2006 sequel is *Pirates of the Caribbean: Dead Man's Chest* (Gore Verbinski). For box office information see http://www.the-numbers.com/movies/series/Sequel.php and http://www.boxofficemojo.com/movies/?id=piratesofthecaribbean2.htm

3. See Verevis, *Film Remakes*; Mazdon, 'Introduction'; Forrest and Koos, *Dead Ringers*; Horton and McDougal, *Play It Again, Sam*; Druxman, *Make It Again, Sam*; Durham, *Double Takes*.

4. Castle, *Masquerade and Civilisation*, 133; see also Berliner, 'The Pleasures of Disappointment'; Greenberg, 'Raiders of the Lost Text: Remaking as Contested Homage in *Always*'; Hoberman, 'Ten Years That Shook the World'.

5. Hancock, *Screen Digest Cinema Intelligence Briefing Report*, 9.

6. See Harraway, *Re-citing Marlowe*, 94. See also Leggatt, 'Killing the Hero', 53–67.

7. Simonet, 'Conglomerates and Content', 156.

8. See Nowlan and Nowlan, *Cinema Sequels and Remakes 1903–1987*; Morris, *Continuance and Change*.

9. Delamater, ' "Once More, from the Top" ', 80.

10. Greenberg, 'Raiders of the Lost Text', 137.

11. Casetti, *Theories of Cinema 1945–1995*, 280.

12. Genette, *Palimpsests*, 177.

13. No critical account currently exists for this term nor its development, but its employment in critical film discussion can be found at http://archive.thenorthernecho.co.uk/2001/7/27/164301.html; http://www.ctnow.com/movies/hce-summerflix.artapr30,0,580787.-story?coll=hce-utility-movies; http://www.austin360.com/movies/content/shared/-movies/stories/2006/05/threequels.htm, and http://en.wikipedia.org/wiki/Threequel

14. Eco, *The Limits of Interpretation*, 86.

15. Harmetz, 'The Sequel Becomes the New Bankable Film Star', 15.

16. Genette, *Palimpsests*, 3.

17. Ibid., 5.
18. Ibid., 9.
19. http://whatisthematrix.warnerbros.com/rv_cmp/rv_press_09_29.html
20. See Dobler and Jockel, 'The Event Movie'.
21. Andrews, 'Pirates Tale Captures Fans to Become £1bn Treasure Trove'. Bringing in $135 million in its first weekend, the film succeeded *Spider-Man*'s (Sam Raimi, 2002) box-office achievement in 2002 as the most successful opening weekend ever.
22. http://uk.xbox.ign.com/objects/746/746932.html
23. http://www.boxofficemojo.com/movies/?id=island05.htm
24. Epstein, 'The End of Originality'.
25. Freud, 'Beyond the Pleasure Principle', 30.
26. Elsaesser argues a similar case for early film serials. See Elsaesser, 'Fantasy Island', 145.
27. Eco, *The Limits of Interpretation*, 86.
28. This includes Timothy Burton Anderson's attempt to get his script, *Rocky III*, produced, which led to a lawsuit on the part of Sylvester Stallone, which Stallone won. See http://www.kentlaw.edu/e-Ukraine/copyright/cases/anderson_v_stallone.html
29. Biguenet, 'Double Takes', 131; Carroll, 'The Future of Allusion', 52.
30. Jenkins, *Textual Poachers*, 202.
31. Jenkins, 'Interactive Audiences?'.
32. Jenkins, *Textual Poachers*, 26.
33. Jenkins, 'Interactive Audiences?'.
34. http://www.bbc.co.uk/worldservice/arts/highlights/010628_bollywood.shtml
35. Hirji, 'When Local Meets Lucre: Commerce, Culture and Imperialism in Bollywood Cinema'.
36. Menon, 'Bollywood Undressed'.
37. For example, *Crouching Tiger, Hidden Dragon* (Ang Lee, 1999), which reaped $100 million at the US box office.
38. Huang, 'Introduction', 3.

CHAPTER I

Before and After the Blockbuster:
A Brief History of the Film Sequel

The title card of D. W. Griffith's 1911 film *His Trust: The Faithful Devotion and Self-Sacrifice of an Old Negro Servant* provides some insight into early conceptualisations of the sequel:

> "His Trust" is the first part of a life story, the second part being "His Trust Fulfilled" and while the second is the sequel to the first, each part is a complete story in itself.

The notion of a 'complete story' is clearly pitted here against the concept of the sequel. Although both *His Trust* and *His Trust Fulfilled* have a clearly defined narrative trajectory involving the resolution of conflict, the sequel re-stages the conflict/resolution situation of the first production, drawing upon spectators' knowledge of the action of the first film to stimulate engagement with the second. In *His Trust*, a black slave named George (Wilfred Lucas) is instructed by his master to take care of the master's wife and child while he goes off to war. News of the master's death soon reaches home. A mob burns the house to the ground, despite George's brave efforts to stop them. Saving the young child and the master's sword from the burning wreckage, George tenderly takes the woman and child to live in his run-down shack while he sleeps outside. Griffith's sequel operates as promised as a 'complete story' that, implicitly, can be enjoyed without having seen the first film. But the level of enjoyment brought to the viewing experience is enhanced by applying one's knowledge of the first film. Plot points are recalled and recapitulated in Griffith's sequel, such as the death of another parent (the mother) and the effect this has on the new 'family' unit, as well as George's greater sacrifices to live up to his promise (using his life savings to pay for the girl's education), and the return of the sword at the end as a symbol of valour and victory – both extremely important in fortifying the film's political context (the Confederate

War), and in signifying continuation, completion and narrative coherency.[1]
The sequel capitalises upon an intimate knowledge and recollection of the first
film.

Tom Gunning has noted the 'enormous economic reorganisation' of film
industries worldwide just two years before Griffith's film was released. This
period also corresponded with major changes in copyright law, which had previously failed to recognise narrative works as commercial property. The effect
of this law, in tandem with the economic shifts Gunning describes, played a
part in establishing 'fictional narrative as the major genre of film and storytelling'.[2] These industrial developments provide an important context through
which Griffith's use of sequelisation must be understood. The particular
reception practices generated by these developments are inseparable from the
storytelling techniques and economic imperatives by which films were being
produced, and in fact the 'cinema of reference',[3] as Gunning calls it, or the
'culture of copying',[4] as Jane M. Gaines prefers to describe it, belies the vigorous dependency of early film on predictability and mechanisms of audience
response as offered by the sequel.

This chapter considers the film sequel from its origins in cinema's early
years throughout the developments of the twentieth century to understand
some of the historical forces that shape our understanding of sequelisation
today. Beginning with an examination of sequel production during the years
1895–1920, I identify several major characteristics that may be contrasted and
compared with the contemporary film sequel. First of all, the sequel during the
early period champions audience foreknowledge of a narrative or theme, and
was used alongside the film serial to satisfy demand for the continuation and
development of popular productions. Secondly, the sequel during this period
did not usually continue one text, as is common in the blockbuster era, but was
commonly defined by its 'promiscuous intermingling'[5] and continuing of many
source texts. Whilst a host of usages and methods of sequelisation emerge
across the gamut of early film sequels, these characteristics suggest the sequel
as a mode of production that means and results in different things at various
historical junctures, and is always relevant to and reflective of greater industrial
contexts at any moment in cinema's history. Going on to examine sequelisation
across a variety of case studies at key moments of cinema history, I view the
sequel as it develops historically throughout and in parallel to narrative structures, reception and marketing practices, industrial relations and cross-cultural
dialogues. The intent here is to dislodge the sequel from its blockbuster
moment in order to consider those historical contexts and functions of the
sequel that impact our contemporary understanding of this category.

Throughout the period of 1906 to approximately 1936,[6] film serials formed
the chief mode of production, and were designed to carry a narrative across 12–
16 episodes. Although feature films or 'features' became a regular occurrence

at cinema theatres around 1911, serials continued to draw large audiences until about the end of the 1930s. Although film sequels *were* made during this period – and noticeably of serials – the practice of film serialisation dominated the market. However, the industrial measures initiated by serialisation, such as marketing strategies and literary tie-ins, perceivably informed sequelisation. Whilst there are distinct differences between seriality and sequelisation, as discussed later in this chapter, the early practice of serialisation forms an important basis of a critical understanding of the sequel phenomenon that emerged towards the end of the century.

A major reason for the early practice of film serialisation lies in the proliferance of serials in the literary world. As many of the reading masses in the nineteenth century could not afford to purchase novels but could manage the monthly shilling for a newspaper or magazine, literary serials proved highly popular. Literary serialisation during this period was perpetuated by an eager readership that discussed the latest serial with friends, family, and apparently anyone on the street who would listen. Historical accounts report crowds waiting at the docks in New York to query immigrants and tourists from England – who received Dickens's serial novel *The Old Curiosity Shop* before American readers – whether the character Little Nell was dead or not. When Dickens's serial reached New York, Little Nell's death was mourned in the streets.[7]

Scholars have rejected ideas of literary serials being produced purely for profit, deciding instead that their 'collective resistance to closure', of which sequels are shown to have played a major part, 'suggests that something important is at work culturally, and perhaps formally'.[8] Linda K. Hughes and Michael Lund argue for the serials' popularity as founded in the Victorian philosophy of causality and linear progress, whilst the dramatic, cliffhanger endings of each serial instalment offered a predominantly working-class readership a glimpse at improvement and bettered circumstances.[9] By lengthening the life-span of a novel across the period of a year or more, the serial format reflected Victorian notions of change and development occurring over time – and no doubt the monthly turnaround between episodes permitted enough time for new readers to join the fray once word of mouth had spread. In short, the serial novel capitalised upon particular ideologies of the modern era, evolving from a source of popular entertainment into a cultural force that generated contemporary ideas of episodic storytelling and, more importantly, an interactive fan base whose enthusiasm, grief or downright boredom could score success or doom for the serial publisher.

The literary serial did not so much die out, but rather switched mediums at the end of the nineteenth century. Early cinema was perceived as a novelty that would soon wear thin with zealous audiences. Just as the heyday of the serial novel had waned, so was the so-called 'cinema of attractions'[10] perceived even by its founding fathers as a gimmick without financial promise or longevity. To some extent, cinema's early critics were right; the early silent thirty-second 'actualities' and 'What the Butler Saw' peepshows soon withered from popularity. Although Auguste and Louis Lumière's hand-cranked scenes from all over the world were well received, their massive film output of over 500 'actualities' contained little perceivable narrative structure. Shortly after the Lumières' first film screening in 1895, Georges Méliès, a magician and former theatre owner, began experimenting with the new cinematic technology. Cinema had at last been 'born'. But it was not the cinema of the Lumières that rose in popularity, rather the cinema that transposed the episodic narrative format of the Victorian serial novel.

Adaptations of literary works proved highly popular throughout cinema's silent years. This practice perceivably influences aspects of filmmaking from notions of readership to the presentation of narrative – and, subsequently, episodic, sequential or serial narrative. The system of copying that quickly came into play across the new cinematic landscape resulted in most films deriving from at least one other text as filmmakers fought to produce the most popular film. And, as companies sought to improve upon other imitations and demonstrate the latest filmmaking techniques and technological upgrades, sequelisation became a method of showcasing progress, of which more later.

More generally, however, sequelisation was used as a method of generating audience response and repeated viewings. Thomas Elsaesser claims that early film's 'institutional function' was to 'bind the spectator to a particular mode of entertainment, to make going to the cinema a habit'. The result was apparently a 'psychological fixation' with formulaic film narratives which filmmakers traded upon by developing, continuing and repeating productions across a number of open-ended instalments.[11] Bombarded with a choice of up to 300 films per week and endowed with much more leisure time than contemporary audiences, early viewers were passionate about the film experience.[12] As a result of such dedicated film viewing and discussion amongst family and friends, audiences became cine-literate in an astonishingly short period of time. And because its survival depended entirely on methods of engaging and re-engaging cinema audiences, early cinema developed within this short period of time as a vastly intertextual, repetitive and self-reflexive medium.

A number of examples demonstrate some of the methods used to keep audiences coming back for more. For instance, *The Diamond from the Sky* (Jacques Jaccard and William Desmond Taylor, 1915) originated as a public competition worth $10,000 for the best outline for a new film serial. A further reward of $10,000 was then offered for the serial's ending, ostensibly 'to motivate moviegoers to stick with the serial over its unusually long run of seven and a half months'.[13] If that wasn't enough, $10,000 was later offered for the serial's sequel, which was produced and titled *The Sequel to the Diamond from the Sky*

(Edward Sloman) in 1916; the competition proved a big draw, as apparently 'thousands and thousands of people' entered (and would necessarily have needed to see the first instalment to compose its sequel).[14] Likewise, a prize of $10,000 was also offered for the winning suggestion for a sequel to the successful twenty-three instalment serial *The Million Dollar Mystery* (Howell Hansel, 1914), resulting in *Zudora* (Howell Hansel, 1914), which was released the same year. Although no such offers are made to the cinema-going public today, alternative and much more lucrative mechanisms of attracting and retaining audiences have been painstakingly developed over the duration of the twentieth century. What these early examples insist upon, however, are the economic strategies underlining reception practices at cinema's outset.[15]

Reception practices and economic strategies are explored across the following comparative study of the film sequel throughout two dominant moments in its history. However, the focus of this chapter rests upon broader cultural forces at two historical junctures; namely, modernity and postmodernity, during which the impact of emergent technologies, and ways of thinking about temporality, copyright and reproduction, appear as determinants in the ways in which sequelisation came to be a virtual phenomenon by the 1970s with many different (and conflicting) meanings and purposes. The importance of such forces to the film sequel is visible in the sequel's treatment of the passing of time. Unlike the film serial, which tends to concentrate on similar events occurring over a shortened period of time (or at the very least resists change), the sequel encourages us to meditate upon the past and upon the gulf of time that has separated one event from another. The sequel further urges comparisons between each temporal juncture, as if the future/present is both a natural progression from and return to the past. As I go on to show, the sequel in the early era offered distinctive conceptualisations of 'new' temporalities. Its critical offerings towards the end of the twentieth century function in a similar way but, as temporality and past-ness come to take on radically different meanings, so too does the sequel.

MODERNITY AND THE CATEGORISATION OF FILM 'KINDS'

'Not to be new in these days is to be nothing.'

H. D. Traill (1892)[16]

Films during the period from 1895 until approximately 1906 were not self-contained units for interpretation, but rather self-reflexive cultural products without a discernable beginning or end. Because film catalogues did not begin until around 1897 – and took another six years to formulate specific film categories – many remakes, serials and sequels are not classified as such, though many films subscribe to the particular textual interactions defined by these modes. In the post-1906 era, film classifications still did not follow a strict taxonomic definition, and many filmmakers tended not to cite their sources or, as Mikhail Iampolski argues of D. W. Griffith, repressed their sources 'like the perpetual regress of a mirror reflected within a mirror'.[17] Strategies of repetition and imitation are identifiable in films from England, France and America from which materialised generic formulas. Writing in 1926, Terry Ramsaye locates this moment at the Biograph film company in a box-office report from an arcade which showed that a film titled *Girl Climbing Apple Tree* made over three times the revenue of its competitors. Biograph's response? 'I think we had better have some more of the Girl-Climbing-Apple-Tree kind.'[18] Although 'kinds' of film existed from cinema's outset (largely as a result of the pilfering and reproduction of a successful film trait, technique or trick), the economic machinery by which films became classified did not come into practice for quite some time.

The 'kinds' of film that were produced during cinema's early years – whether demonstrative of a perceivable narrative form or not – were most often imitations of a previous model. Birt Acres's *Rough Sea at Dover* (1895), a one-minute film of waves crashing into the surf, appears again five years later in the form of G. A. Bamforth's *Rough Sea* (1900). No less than ten copies of the Lumières' *L'Arroseur arrosé* (1895) appeared during the years 1896 and 1900 in France, England and the US.[19] Thomas Edison repeated the controversial kissing scene from his short film *May Irwin Kiss* (1896) four years later in a longer version titled *The Kiss* (1900), but not before other transatlantic filmmakers had imitated his original scenario, such as the Bamforth Company's remakes (no less than three: *The Kiss in the Tunnel* [c. 1898], *Youthful Impudence* [c. 1898] and *Lover Kisses Husband* [1900]) and G. A. Smith's rip-off of Bamforth's remake, *The Kiss in the Tunnel* (1899). Richard Brown detects a 'prequel' of Edison's *The Kiss* in the form of a film titled *The Honeymoon* (c. 1902), which depicts a newly married couple embarking on their honeymoon aboard a train, and which appears in the Hepworth 1903 film catalogue immediately before *Kiss in the Tunnel*, offering a contextualisation for the kissing scene and a 'causal relationship between the couple'.[20] Georges Méliès's portrait of a homosexual kiss between the sun and moon (both apparently male) in *L'Éclipse du soleil en pleine lune* (*The Eclipse*) (1907) could be argued as recapitulating the famous scenario to controversial ends.

Filmmakers copied their own work, too. Edwin S. Porter capitalised on the success of his film *The Great Train Robbery* (1903) – inspired by Frank Mottershaw's *A Daring Daylight Burglary* (1903) – with *The Little Train Robbery* (1905), a spoof version featuring children and miniaturised sets. Porter also followed the successes of Selig's *Life of a Fireman* (1901), G. A. Smith's four-film sequence *The Big Fire* (1898), and Lubin's *Going to the Fire and Rescue* (1901) with his *Life of an American Fireman* (1903), which he then followed up with *The Life of an American Policeman* (1905) and *The Life of a Cowboy* (1906). The title of Porter's *The Burlesque Suicide, No. 2* (1902) implies it as a continuation to a previous instalment (which has apparently not survived); and *The Heavenly Twins at Odds* (1903) followed his film *The Heavenly Twins at Lunch* (1903) – which also resembles an earlier production by R. W. Paul, *The Twins' Tea-Party* (1897), which was a remake of Paul's popular 1896 version. Reasons for plagiarism and auto-citation are unclear, and therefore cannot accurately be relegated to profit. What is known, however, is that amidst this mass tendency for remaking, a gradual procession emerged away from repetitions towards variations of a popular theme.

Perhaps due to the introduction of (less than stringent) copyright laws in 1906, films after this period tend to shift away from flagrant plagiarism towards a slightly more subtle form of hybridisation.[21] Titled in reminiscence of Porter's *The Great Train Robbery*, George Bitzer's *The Hold-Up of the Rocky Mountain Express* (1906) meshes various sub-genres, including the travelogue, the western and the crime genre. More importantly, the move towards hybridisation or intertextual referencing can be seen as a method of addressing audiences that were, as I suggested earlier, absolutely immersed in cinema culture. Miriam Hansen observes that this 'new' system of imitation-by-hybridisation, at least in the case of Bitzer's film, was not understated but very much on display.[22] As with contemporary modes of appropriation, the allure of such films was grounded in the history of trends, texts and events created by a list of references and gestures to previous (and contemporaneous) productions, which prompted audiences actively to assemble the film's narrative by guessing the other narratives to which it referred. Instead of merely watching new (or copied) scenarios on-screen or listening to a lecturer's description of the film as it spooled before their eyes, audiences now participated in an activity larger than the film itself.

Other approaches include references not only to other films but to the spectatorial experience. R. W. Paul's *The Countryman and the Cinematograph* (1901) shows the reaction of a country simpleton to a film of an approaching train – a cheeky reference to the well-documented audience reactions to the Lumières' film, *L'Arrivée d'un train en gare de La Ciotat* (*Arrival of a Train at La Ciotat*) (1895), during which spectators reportedly ducked and fled from the theatre as the train reached the station on screen. Hansen notes the 'spectacle' of Rudolph Valentino's body 'half-stripped' and 'tortured at length' in the sequel, *The Son of the Sheik* (George Fitzmaurice, 1926), staged specifically for a rapidly devoted female audience.[23] These examples show that intertextuality and reflexivity were an important part of early cinema culture. Within a short period of time, audiences knew what to expect when they went to see a film. The influences of classical literature (such as Shakespeare and Charles Dickens), comic strips and popular songs, vaudeville and theatre, and historical events are felt in many early productions in terms of a competitive intertextuality, as films persistently borrow and blag from cinema's multimedia relatives to create a profitable commodity. Charles Musser explains it as follows:

> When films were based on well-known stories . . . this meant a different relationship between audience and cultural object than in most contemporaneous literature and theatre, where it was assumed that audiences had no fore-knowledge of the narrative's plot, characters, etc.[24]

This relationship was developed so that audiences had an increased level of expectation and awareness of the film's context. What is also clear, however, is that the boundaries separating one cultural object from another took many years to define, and that although 'originality' was (and remains) a worthy goal for any serious filmmaker, the 'kinds' of film that emerged during cinema's formative stages were simply methods of negotiating the virtually impossible feat of creating a 'new' piece of work.

Much scholarship across the twentieth century persuades that originality is impossible. However, film historians tend to point to the culture of copying in the early period as precipitating progress in the form of works that departed from prior productions to create something truly innovative. Although not unprecedented, therefore, such works indicated an emerging form of 'originality' amongst film culture in the form of 'new' ventures, or rather productions that reflected that which was deemed 'new' in modernity. A time of massive industrial, urban, social, scientific, economic and technological revolutions, modernity was also an era in which cinema's birth played a central role in reflecting the impact of such revolutionary developments on the life of the individual. In this regard, it appears that the culture of copying in early cinema was rooted in a collective endeavour both to capitalise on popular trends, themes and productions, and to articulate the ever-changing modern experience. In addition, as copyright laws began to define the legal boundaries of authorship, commercial property, and 'films' as distinct from photographs, a somewhat fluid set of production practices and narrational modes began to take shape.[25] There is further evidence that the practice of copying others' works and remaking one's own was a means of artistic improvement. As Jay Leyda claims,

> Just as the original films bred copies, the copies sped the true inventions . . . The pressure of repetition becomes a positive factor of progress almost as weighty as the urge to invent.[26]

Charting the copies and dupes noted above and across numerous film catalogues, an argument can be made that 'progress' is apparent in terms of repetitions with variations that seek to improve upon previously popular
productions, and which increasingly utilise forms of difference, not repetition,
in an attempt to keep audiences returning to theatres. It is within this environment that the film sequel emerged as a form that could effectively manage both
repetition and difference, primarily by offering a *context* for repetition. Sequels
such as *The Rookie's Return* (Jack Nelson, 1920), *Twenty Three and a Half
Hours Later* (Henry King, 1919) and *Der Golem und Die Tänzerin* (*The Golem
and the Dancer*) (Paul Wegener, 1917) successfully returned audiences to a previous character and plot because the emphasis in each case is on differences
from the original.

But why should 'difference' be a reason to return to theatres? Why was it
championed, and what were the reasons for its success? A number of trade
journal and magazine reports from the time point to difference in terms of
improvement and 'more of', such as the description of *The Sequel to the
Diamond From the Sky* (1916) as 'more dramatic – more powerful than the
original', whilst *Excuse my Dust* (Sam Wood, 1920), the sequel to *The Roaring
Road* (James Cruze, 1919) is described in terms of its 'thrilling auto race,
exceeding the one in the other picture'.[27] No such descriptions appear for
serial episodes. Although serials were designed to ensure a steady flow of
returning customers each week and exploited an already popular trend in the
literary market, sequels were marketed most often as improvements on an
already popular production. Serials, however, tended to be advertised in terms
of their repetition of whatever plot, theme or stock character was fashionable
at the time. Unlike serials, sequels offered film-savvy audiences the ability to
apply their knowledge of a previous production in a much more evaluative
manner. As Richard Dyer notes in his study on pastiche, 'all imitation must
imply an evaluative attitude.'[28] The comparative logic inherent in the sequel
registered the transitions and changes experienced by modern society within
a very brief period of time, such as the presentation of speed – 'I'm doing fifty
miles per hour!' in *Excuse my Dust*, which gestures towards advancements in
automobile manufacturing and, in the year of the film's release, the mass production of cars.

The examples noted previously in terms of their treatment of the sequel as
an improvement on a predecessor are taken from a period in which film categories were becoming comparatively more secure, yet there is also evidence of
the sequel as a demonstration of improvement and 'newness' at the turn of the
century amongst many films which are never categorised as sequels, serials, or
as pertaining to a particular genre. One very famous production, however,
offers a seminal example of sequelisation in ways claimed above, and it is to this
'sequel' and its predecessor that I now turn my attention.

FROM THE EYE OF THE MOON TO THE MOUTH OF THE SUN: GEORGES MÉLIÈS AS CASE STUDY

Pioneer, originator, father of film – across the history of cinema, Georges Méliès has become synonymous with its origins. Remembered for his ambitious endeavours with special effects and persistent interest in all things fantastical, Méliès's contribution to cinema is still marked today in terms of his development of a rather sophisticated form of narrative spectacle. Méliès returns frequently to themes (fantasy, science fiction), techniques (stop-motion, the tracking shot), genres (the *féerie*, science fiction) and characters (Satan) to re-explore their cinematic potential. Amongst his 500-strong film canon, one production in particular seems to operate as an unmarked 'sequel' to a previous film, with important results. Méliès's 'sequel' arguably departs from a very successful earlier work to showcase his improvements both technologically and artistically within an increasingly progressive and competitive market.

Méliès's 1902 film, the fourteen-minute *Le Voyage dans la Lune* (*Trip to the Moon*) was inspired by Jules Verne's novel, *De la Terre à la Lune* (*From the Earth to the Moon*) (1865) and H. G. Wells's *The First Men in the Moon* (1901). *Le Voyage dans la Lune* depicts a group of astronomers landing on the moon. Finding themselves in conflict with the moon's residents (or Selenites, as Méliès calls them), they kill the King of the moon people[29] and return home to celebrations in their honour. The film – Méliès's 400th production – cost him an extravagant 10,000 francs, his most expensive project to date. It became a hit around the world almost instantly, largely because of its pioneering special effects and innovative filmmaking techniques, which included double exposures, dissolves and fades, and elaborate sets contrived to depict extraterrestrial spaces. Audiences had never seen anything like it before. It was the 'newest' thing in town, playing at some venues for months.

A number of images and moments throughout the film indicate its investments in the modern experience, or in the modern emphasis on 'newness', suggestive of Méliès's intent to produce something quite different from the imitations and remakes that were prevalent at cinema theatres. Méliès's depiction of an extraterrestrial journey – and specifically cinema's ability to convey this – readily subscribes to what Vanessa R. Schwartz describes as 'fin-de-siècle *panoramania*', or a pre-eminence of panoramas (predominantly in Paris) at the turn of the twentieth century that offered 'armchair tourism', and which differed significantly from earlier panorama 'by an increasing attention to their technology' and an enhanced verisimilitude.[30] Schwartz notes the ways in which 'panoramania' impacted the new cinematic aesthetic, going so far as to claim its success as residing 'neither in its originality nor in its innovative technology, but rather in the way it materialised the inherently cinematic culture of the Parisian *fin de siècle*.[31] Capitalising on an already popular trend, Méliès combined the notion of the panorama with modern ideas of speed (the rocket journey), scientific exploration and theories (the moon as a human face), and the potential of the cinematic apparatus in depicting scenes far beyond the realms of ordinary experience. Méliès's reappraisal of features and images of the modern moment with which audiences were very familiar is conducted in this film throughout a variety of new contexts and images, and it is arguably such a combination of new and old that contributed to the film's popularity.

Film companies moved quickly to produce their own copies despite Méliès's Star Film trademark stamped on every scene, which imitators simply erased. Ever the brazen pirate – and at the time engaged in one of many court cases initiated by Edison for copyright enfringement – Siegmund Lubin reportedly tried to sell one of his copies of Méliès's film to Méliès himself. Prior to *Le Voyage dans la Lune*, Lubin had caused much confusion when he pirated Méliès's *The Astronomer's Dream* (1897) and re-titled it *Trip to the Moon*. Despite the worldwide fame this film brought Méliès, rampant piracy ensured he saw little of the proceeds. Other filmmakers, including Edison, followed Lubin's lead in copying the film. A host of films similar to *Le Voyage dans la Lune* appeared on screens around the world, such as *The Voyage of the Arctic* (Walter Booth, 1903), W. A. Smith's 1906 film *The '?' Motorist* (remade as *The Automatic Motorist* in 1911) and Segundo de Chómon's *Voyage au planète Jupiter* (1909). Such was the interest in making 'dupes' and imitations of *Le Voyage dans la Lune* that Méliès sent his brother, Gaston, to New York where he issued a catalogue of Méliès's productions under the title 'Star Films'. Most important, however, is the note of caution in the catalogue's foreword:

> A great number of French, English and American manufacturers of films who are searching for novelties, but lack the ingenuity to produce them, have found it easier and more economical to advertise their poor copies as their own original conceptions. This accounts for the simultaneous appearance in several issues of a well known New York paper of advertisements of the celebrated *Trip to the Moon* by four or five different concerns, each pretending to be its creator. All these pretensions are false . . . In opening a factory and offices in New York we are prepared and determined energetically to pursue all counterfeiters and pirates.[32]

With the films unprotected by copyright, however, no amount of energy or pursuing could deter the imitators. It is significant, then, that in such a brashly plagiaristic environment Méliès made his own 'copy' of *Le Voyage dans la Lune* in the form of *Le Voyage à travers l'impossible* (*Journey Across the Impossible*) (1904). Unlike his imitators, however, Méliès did not simply remake the film in another form. Rather, *Le Voyage à travers l'impossible* operates as a sequel, marking differences from and improvements of his previous production, arguably in a move to reclaim authorship and authority of an original work, the 'originality' of which had of course been marred by imitation.

Again based on work by Jules Verne (this time a play by the same name), which was in turn a sequel to one of Verne's novels, *Voyages et aventures du capitaine Hatteras* (*Journeys and Adventures of Captain Hatteras*) (1867), *Le Voyage à travers l'impossible* recapitulates the driving notion behind *Le Voyage dans la Lune* of extraterrestrial travel, although this time it is the sun, not the moon, to which a group of scientists travel. Flying into space on a train suspended from two dirigible balloons, the scientists land in the sun's mouth, and are 'swallowed'. Landing on solar ground, the travellers soon find the heat overwhelming. After some gags involving a fridge (into which the travellers cram to cool down, but soon become frozen and are thawed by a remaining traveller), the team launches a submarine (contained inside the train) and fall into an ocean. The team makes for the shore, and celebrations are held in their honour.

Plot similarities exist between the two films in terms of the framing concept of scientific exploration and the progression from an extraterrestrial journey to home-coming and celebrations. Similar filmmaking techniques are used, such as the tracking shot towards the moon/sun, and the depiction of a human face (provided in both cases by Méliès). The use of a train as a vessel of extraplanetary transport cunningly references the importance of the train in modernity as a symbol of ventures into new terrain[33] (symbolised previously by the reception of the Lumière production, *L'Arrivée d'un train en gare de La Ciotat*). The landing in each film is very similar, but in *Le Voyage à travers l'impossible* the previous landing on the surface of the moon is spun on its head when the travellers are eaten by the sun. The new territory is found to be uninhabitable in each film, but the second film differs from *Le Voyage dans la Lune* in its comical portrait of the team being frozen and thawed (instead of killing off an indigenous people). The shot of the team leaving the planet is virtually identical in each film, as is the underwater scene – but, as Elizabeth Ezra points out, the underwater scene in *Le Voyage à travers l'impossible* takes a more prolonged interest in oceanic scenery than did its predecessor. Whilst both films conclude with celebrations, Ezra finds in the conclusion to the second film a sense of continuation, or the suggestion that 'a similar adventure is about to begin.'[34]

Notably, both films are composed according to a symmetrical pattern of leaving and returning to earth, and conversely of arriving at and departing from a foreign terrain. In each case, Méliès's narrative symmetry contributes to a sense of progression and continuation. Of the shots of the rocket returning to earth in *Le Voyage dans la Lune*, for instance, Richard Abel notes a technique that 'matches, if not surpasses, the earlier comic surprise of the lunar landing', while the film as a whole is observed as 'a culmination' of and 'an advance' on Méliès's earlier work, which is achieved 'by means of narrative continuity'.[35] If advancement and continuity were shaping forces in the creation of the first film, *Le Voyage à travers l'impossible* is defined by its starkly self-reflexive effort to demonstrate Méliès's own ability not only to produce a repeat of his prior success, but also to improve upon the previous film in terms of new tricks and techniques. Méliès boasted of his 'well-wrought pictures' that, he claimed, 'are the most expensive of all'.[36] Taking pains to produce films that stood out from the rest for their quality and hard graft, Méliès hand-coloured the print of *Le Voyage à travers l'impossible* with four hues in ten shades.[37] Although hand-coloured prints were not rare, the procedure was reserved for special productions that screened as the last attraction of the evening. A process that added considerable value to a print, it also increased the film's price beyond what exhibitors normally paid, and studios eventually overtook Méliès's method by developing a cheaper and less time-consuming industrial stencil process.[38] None the less, *Le Voyage à travers l'impossible* was rendered distinct by this artisanal technique. Abel notes two further markers of distinction in the film – rendering it distinct not only from *Le Voyage dans la Lune* but from Méliès's competitors – namely, the development of spatial contrast in the second film, and, most importantly, 'a strict orchestration of repeated movement' that also plays out the symmetry of return and arrival noted above in terms of right to left action, suggestive of travel, reversed by the final journey which plays out from left to right. 'It is here,' Abel asserts, 'that Méliès' practice intersects with and yet diverges from the chase film as it is soon to be developed by Pathé, Gaumont, and others',[39] many of whom were already copying (and being sued by) Méliès, and to whom Méliès brings attention through the self-conscious technical flair demonstrated in *Le Voyage à travers l'impossible* as inferior. That the Star Film Catalogue further claims the film as 'Jules Verne outdone'[40] suggests an additional imperative to improve upon the film's textual source, thus marking the film as an 'original' in a marketplace of copies.

The rather complicated conjugations of original, copy and sequel arising in the film marketplace – many due to the success of *Le Voyage dans la Lune* – imposes on *Le Voyage à travers l'impossible* a similarly complex interpretive framework. Arguably made to champion Méliès's originality and to drown out the clamouring copies emerging from studios around the world, *Le Voyage à travers l'impossible* departs from and continues the methods of production that informed *Le Voyage dans la Lune* and its conceit. Although both films were preceded and followed by a number of Méliès's productions based on the concept of travel (*A Wandering Jew* [1904]), new technologies of speed (*An Adventurous Automobile Trip* [1905]), astronomy (*The Eclipse* [1907]) and even underwater adventures (*Under the Seas* [1907]), the contexts of copying informing the production of *Le Voyage à travers l'impossible*, in tandem with its massive budget – 37,500 francs, almost four times that of its predecessor[41] – suggest Méliès's investment in this film was an attempt to recoup much of the revenue generated by his imitators; indeed, he had seen little of the proceeds for *Le Voyage dans la Lune*. The use of the sequel framework here demonstrates significant interactions between notions of imitation and improvement within equally vital contexts of production, industrial survival and aesthetic development – all of which inform sequel production today.

SEQUELS IN THE SERIAL ERA

The contexts in which films were distributed and exhibited during the early period are crucial in investigating the currency of the sequel at this time. A hugely under-researched area,[42] distribution practices nonetheless tell us much about the factors informing the consumption of early films, and how this contributed to the development of certain modes of production and consumption, and, in this case, film sequelisation.

Before 1911, films were sold, not rented, to exhibitors (including the necessary projection equipment). Films were generally 'one-reelers' of around 10–15 minutes in duration, and were exhibited as part of a daily programme of films. Serials were released weekly to exhibitors, but continuity (or the screening of one episode after another) could not be guaranteed, and therefore proved detrimental to narrative linearity and coherency. The methods by which films were viewed were therefore determined by exhibitors, who drummed up a number of narrational methods that can be perceived as impacting the interpretive contexts of the spectatorial experience. Film exhibitors often arranged theatres in such a way as to integrate with the film's narrative and with the viewing experience (such as Hale's Tours, who arranged their theatre as a train carriage 'with a conductor who took tickets, and sound effects simulating the click–clack of wheel and hiss of air brakes').[43] Film lecturers – known as *benshi* in Japan – played a key role in assisting audiences' overall engagement with a (silent) film by describing what was happening on screen and employing a variety of contextualising and storytelling techniques – including impersonation of the characters on-screen, ranging from adults to animals – to construct a narrative format from a series of images shown to the audience.[44] Beyond these issues, however, is the more general problem posed by the one-reeler in producing a self-contained, well-developed narrative in so short a space of time.

The sequel appears in some early productions to offer a way of getting round this problem. Griffith's *His Trust* is one of many one-reelers that dominated film production until approximately 1911. Griffith's two-part production is also one of many films to use the concept of the sequel to present a longer film across more than one reel that did not lose its narrative coherency. Released in 1903, Biograph's *Wages of Sin: A – Murder* and *Wages of Sin: B – Retribution* operate in a similar way, but unlike Griffith's film, no title cards precede or

conclude the action in either film. Here, the titles serve to depict a clear beginning and end across two reels. The first reel offers a one-shot scene of a man
beating and killing a young woman. The second film continues immediately
after the first – indeed, it is the same shot – and shows the man being shot and
killed by police, apparently in retribution for the murder of the dead woman.
Wages of Sin demonstrates the necessity of the sequel in achieving *both* continuity and a more developed, coherent narrative than was permitted by one reel.

Films have repeatedly used the sequel in this manner across cinema's
history. In China, Zhengqiu Zheng's *Huo shao hong lian si* (*Burning of the Red
Lotus Monastery*) (1928–30), based on Shang K'ai-jan's newspaper serial, was
released as eighteen sequels instead of the impossibly long twenty-seven-hour
marathon that was originally produced. As I go on to show, Fritz Lang's four-
hour *Dr Mabuse, der Spieler* (*Dr Mabuse, the Gambler*) (1922) was released in two
parts, each titled separately to mark their operation simultaneously as single
narrative units and parts of a 'complete' story. This method is still in operation
today. A century after *Wages of Sin* was released, Quentin Tarantino chopped
his *Kill Bill* (2003, 2004) into two parts to avoid the problem of presenting a
production that was too long for a single screening. Like *Wages of Sin*, however,
the sequel here also serves as an extremely suitable framework for the presentation of return, revenge and retribution.

It was the film serial, however, that rose in popularity as a way to present a
narrative over more than one film. A massive offshoot of what Ben Singer
identifies as the 'commercialisation of amusement' in early cinema,[45] the serial
used cliffhangers, publicity, literary tie-ins and, in the midst of emerging feminism, female heroines, all with the intent of keeping audiences coming back
for more. The sequel's earlier provision of narrative coherency and continuation reached a commercial boiling point in the form of the serial. Beginning in
the US with the *Nick Carter* series (Victorin Jasset, 1908) and Biograph's *The
Adventures of Dolly* (D. W. Griffith, 1908),[46] the film serial spread rapidly as a
popular format throughout all corners of the world. Victorin Jasset followed up
his *Nick Carter* series with serial adaptations of Leon Sazie's novel, *Zigomar*, in
1911. Subsequently, *Zigomar* was imported to Tokyo by the Fukuhodo
Company in November of that year. *Zigomar*'s Japanese reception was not
merely successful; as A. A. Gerow points out, this serial had 'a major impact on
Japanese film culture and created a series of shock waves that would begin to
alter the ways in which cinema was discussed and defined'.[47] *Zigomar* imitations
and sequels spread throughout Japanese popular culture to the point that
'Zigomar' entered local slang as a by-word for enigmatic heroism. Authorities
fretted that the sudden public worship of a criminal figure – fictional or not –
would lead to widespread anarchy. As a result, *Zigomar* was banned from
cinema screens. But by the time of its censorship, the film text finally came to
be regarded in Japan 'as [a] visual object, not just as a written story'.

Other corners of the world experienced similar serial phenomena. In 1913, French director Louis Feuillade directed his highly successful serial *Fantômas*, followed by a number of equally successful serials including *Les Vampires* (1915–16), the success of which hastened the development of US serials, such as *The Exploits of Elaine* (Louis J. Gasnier *et al.*,1915), *The Perils of Pauline* (Louis J. Gasnier *et al.*, 1914), *The Hazards of Helen* (J. P. McGowan *et al.*, 1915), *Lucille Love, The Girl of Mystery* (Francis Ford, 1914) and *What Happened to Mary?* (Charles Brabin, 1912), all of which contributed to the development of celebrity, fan cultures, cross-media tie-ins and melodrama.

Characterised by an obvious formulaism, serials were, first and foremost, commercial vehicles.[48] A 1919 article in *Motion Picture News* notes the film serial as 'business insurance' which also contains the benefit of reaping revenue across fourteen episodes from 'heavy advertising' spent on a first episode.[49] Very similar to contemporary practices of merchandising and cross-media tie-ins, the use of 'heavy advertising' to generate substantial returns on a film's investment underlines the commercial strategies behind serialisation. Within an increasingly competitive marketplace, the sequel achieved a renewed position as a way in which a previously successful product could be re-launched, such as *Who Will Marry Mary?* (1913), the sequel to *What Happened to Mary?*, as well as *The New Exploits of Elaine* (Louis J. Gasnier *et al.*, 1915) and *The Romance of Elaine* (George B. Seitz *et al.*,1915), both sequels to *The Exploits of Elaine*. Effectively serving in such productions as a commercial strategy, the sequel is also figured as a method of renewal and response, particularly in terms of its incorporation of audience response into a continuation of a previously popular production.

This is apparent in Thomas Dixon's film, *The Fall of a Nation* (1916). Now lost, this film is claimed throughout a series of trade journal articles and advertisements from the time as a 'sequel' to D. W. Griffith's racist Ku Klux Klan narrative, *The Birth of a Nation* (1915), which was based on Dixon's book, *The Clansman*. The racist sentiment in both Dixon's book and Griffith's film continues to court controversy, and rightly so; Griffith presents the Ku Klux Klan as the positive good and protector of the American South against the African-American community, which is presented unanimously as evil and degenerative. Hailed as an epic worthy of a screening at the White House, *The Birth of a Nation* none the less sparked riots in many major cities across the US. Critics were (and continue to be) divided by the film's technical mastery and its supremacist ideology. A flurry of counter-films ensued, such as Emmett J. Scott's *The Birth of a Race* (1919) and Oscar Micheaux's *Within Our Gates* (1919), which memorably subverts Griffith's portrait of lecherous black men by presenting lecherous white men, one of whom assaults a black woman.

In the aftermath of such flagrant public response, Dixon's *The Fall of a Nation* sets out to redefine the skewed interpretation of history portrayed in both his novel and Griffith's film. The film's title deliberately contrives a 'sequel' connection to *The Birth of a Nation*, yet its narrative structure wanders far from the sequel format of the period. Continuing none of the narrative exposition of *The Birth of a Nation*, Dixon's sequel follows the same ideology of white supremacy as its predecessor within the context of a 'call to arms' tale in the mid-War epoch. Made both to capitalise on its successful predecessor and as a follow-up to the issues of American invasion and race as portrayed in *The Birth of a Nation*, *The Fall of a Nation* demonstrates the sequel's early grounding in profit and politics. Perhaps more importantly, Dixon's sequel articulates the cultural landscape of a particular historical moment, additionally proving the sequel as a reactionary format of significant cultural value.

Marked by its relationships to the serial and commerciality, the sequel developed during this period as a format with a wide range of possibilities for response and audience engagement. Although the serial had generated its own ways of engaging audiences and reflexively incorporating audience response into its framework, the agenda of the sequel includes renewal, return and difference, in contrast to the serial's emphases on repetition and sameness. As the serial went into decline during the late 1930s and 1940s, both forms appear to absorb many of the cultural transformations and technological developments of the period, materialising across a range of productions in starkly altered forms.

SERIAL KILLING AND THE PERILS OF SEQUELISATION: *DR MABUSE* AS CASE STUDY

Both serialisation and sequelisation are marked in one production as separate entities with discrete narratological and social implications. In Lang's *Das Testament der Dr Mabuse* (1933), these concepts may be seen to interact specifically to articulate huge shifts in ideological terrain and their effects brought about by World War II. Lang's sequel to his 1922 film, *Dr Mabuse, der Spieler, Das Testament der Dr Mabuse* returns Dr Mabuse (played by Rudolf Klein-Rogge), an evil psychiatrist whose influence turns otherwise innocent individuals into serial murders, to re-explore his terrifying villainy in ideologically charged scenarios. Lang was reluctant to sequelise this serial killer, but was apparently motivated by the rise of fascism to use the sequel as a method of confronting the Nazi takeover. For its too-close-for-comfort depiction of an evil dictator broadcasting propaganda across the radio, the film was banned by Joseph Goebbels, Nazi minister of propaganda and one of Hitler's closest associates. Over the course of many interviews Lang recounts a meeting with Goebbels, during which Goebbels apologised for pulling *Testament* from German screens and offered Lang the position of, no less, chief of the Third

Reich's film industry. 'He told me that, many years before,' recalls Lang, 'he and the Führer had seen my picture *Metropolis* in a small town, and that Hitler had said at that time that he wanted me to make pictures for the Nazis. Then Goebbels actually offered me the job of heading the Nazi film effort.'[50] The details of this meeting are increasingly obscured across Lang's various accounts, and a lack of evidence amongst his personal files suggests that the conversation between Goebbels and Lang never actually took place. Lang claims to have accepted Goebbels's offer before fleeing the country for the US the same day; his passport dates this move some months later. Although Lang's political sympathies remain unclear, the *Mabuse* films offer compelling commentaries on the abuse of power. Of the film's depiction of Mabuse as less a human being than an evil voice that turned its listeners to acts of torture and murder, Lang states that 'I put all the Nazi slogans into the mouth of the ghost of the criminal.'[51] Notably, the German version is free of direct Nazi references; only the English subtitles capture the Nazi slogans of Mabuse's diatribes. Whether Lang intended his film as an anti-Nazi commentary in retrospect or at the time of production may never be known.

More important, however, is the film's treatment of serialisation and sequelisation in what are unmistakable efforts to trace the regenerative nature of evil. Similarly, the serial's contexts of production are not forgotten – indeed, *Dr Mabuse, der Spieler* was based on Jacques Norbert's serialised novel – but serve as informing factors in terms of the film's generic preoccupations, specifically the detective or crime film, the formative stages of which occurred across the *Nick Carter* serials of Victorin Jasset and, of course, Feuillade's serials, *Les Vampires* and *Fantômas*. Lang was inspired by these productions to produce his own serials in the form of *Die Nibelungen* (1924), shown as *Siegfried* and *Kriemhild's Rache* (*Kriemhild's Revenge*), and *The Spiders* (1918–19), a two-part serial. Like *The Spiders*, *Dr Mabuse, der Spieler* was shown in two parts, and drew upon Lang's previous explorations of the detective genre and, particularly, his development of cinematic portraits of criminal psychology.

In *Dr Mabuse, der Spieler*, Lang portrays Dr Mabuse as a criminal mastermind who has the power of hypnosis and telepathy, which he uses to influence others to carry out his plans of total destruction and social ruin. Reminiscent of hyperinflation throughout 1921–4 and the resulting exploitative strategies employed by black markets and racketeers, *Dr Mabuse, der Spieler* shows Mabuse conjuring a variety of scams and fraudulent activities designed to bring the stock market crashing down. Assuming a variety of disguises and, after death, possessing the body of his own psychiatrist, Dr Baum (Oscar Beregi Sr), Mabuse is portrayed as less a human being than a self-replicating and regenerative presence that is effectively 'sequelised' throughout the actions of Mabuse's victims. Confined within an asylum for the mentally ill, Mabuse writes his manifesto for the spread of vice and debauchery – nothing more than

a bunch of scribbles that eventually prove potently hypnotic to the reader –
until he dies. As Tom Gunning notes in his study of Lang's films, the compulsive manner in which he 'writes' shows Mabuse in 'the grip of compulsive repetition'.[52] Mabuse's frantic writing is argued by Gunning as suggestive of
Mabuse's body as nothing more than the tool of writing, whilst the act of
writing here appears as 'an act of pure transmission, rather than expression'.[53]
In tandem with the film's investments in various textual forms (documents,
notes, letters, newspapers) as both evidence and methods of manipulation, the
portraits of deception, manipulation and transmission throughout this film
construct the persona of Mabuse as a 'text' that is appropriated and continued
in the form of secondary manifestations of its meaning.

   As the sequel's title suggests, *Das Testament* focuses on Mabuse's manifesto.
The ideological significance of serialisation to Lang's work resonates throughout *Dr Mabuse, der Spieler* and Lang's later film, *M* (1931), about a real-life
serial killer, the so-called 'Vampire of Düsseldorf', in depictions of the repetitious, 'serial', nature of a particular kind of murder. In *Das Testament*, however,
the doctor's influence not only continues to cause compulsive repetition of his
will, but also manifests a mortal 'successor' in the form of Dr Baum. Here, it
seems, sequelisation takes on particular significance and distinction from serialisation. Lang's use of double exposure to portray Mabuse's possession of
Baum's body is highly evocative of the continuous nature of Mabuse's manifesto, which is intended not only to provoke evil but also to be rewritten in the
form of a continuous cycle of murder and corruption. Later revealed as 'the
man behind the curtain', or the perpetrator of verbal instructions to Mabuse's
henchmen, Baum's embodiment further reinforces the notion of Mabuse as a
personification of a form of influence, or an insistently reproducible entity,
rather than a human being. Symbolic of the human body, the curtain also
recalls the disguises and masks behind which Mabuse operated in the previous
film. But whereas Mabuse's influence is shown in the first film to 'infect'
numerous individuals with his anarchic dogma, leading in some cases to murder
and suicide, the construction of a Mabuse 'successor' in the sequel offers a
much more serious kind of threat: a second generator of influence. Baum is not
only influenced, but also becomes the secondary source of influence. As suggested by a shot of not one but two ghostly Mabuses visiting Baum in his study,
Mabuse here is doubled; he is both shadow and flesh. Having already generated
repetitions of his own evil deeds, he is now able to generate further, much more
terrifying, continuations of the plans outlined in his manifesto, having 'regen-
erated' through Baum's possession.

   It is well documented that Lang adhered to Nietzschean and Freudian
thought in the creation of his *Mabuse* pieces. By describing Mabuse as a
'Nietzschean superman',[54] Lang indicates Mabuse as executioner of the
'advent of nihilism' and the 'catastrophe' towards which, Nietzsche claimed,

the 'whole European culture has been moving', as outlined in his *Will To Power*.[55] Freud's theory of repetition-compulsion is also registered in Mabuse's frantic scribblings in his cell, whilst the apparitions of Mabuse's victims that drive him to insanity, as well as his own ghostly double-ness later on, invoke Freud's writing on 'the uncanny', or 'the return of the repressed'.[56] Lang's depiction of the dispersal of terror is *both* in terms of its repetitious progression, like the Will to Power, towards a particular end, and in terms of the return of terror, its invincibility. In this regard, the duality of the concepts of serialisation and sequelisation serves to convey the particular brand of terror as paraded by the Nazi regime – just like the specific type of murder perpetrated in *M* – which is both serial and sequelising in nature. In terms of the repetitious and regenerative logic of both forms, Lang succeeds in identifying the real terror as founded not in one man, but in the potency of ideology.

Both forms are situated in new contexts, however, in terms of the effects of the reproductive technologies foregrounded in the film. Mabuse's regeneration and repetition are shown to be enabled by technologies of transmission, such as the telephone, the camera and the radio; later, in Lang's third *Mabuse* production, *Die Tausend Augen des Dr Mabuse* (*The Thousand Eyes of Dr Mabuse*) (1960), another technology, CCTV, is portrayed as a dangerous mechanism whereby the Mabuse mentality can again be reproduced in terms of surveillance, control and transmission. In all cases, Lang seeks to identify the methods by which a particular consciousness is transformed into individual action, and subsequently a dominant ideology and form of social control. Exploring the possibilities afforded by emergent technologies and psychological affect in achieving this control, the *Mabuse* films re-imagine serialisation and sequelisation far beyond their previous narratological and industrial purposes as concepts charged with the ideological, social and psychological complexities created by Hitler's reign.

SEQUELS, RETURN AND RETALIATION: THE CASE OF *GODZILLA*

From the 1930s to the 1960s, both the sequel and the serial served predominantly to achieve economic objectives as the major Hollywood studios attempted to grow financially. Through a gamut of productions featuring stars such as Charlie Chan and Abbott and Costello, the sequel performs a range of economic functions, at once serving as a vehicle for a popular star or character, and also operating in conjunction with the serial as it re-emerged in the form of new TV serials and televised repeats of earlier serials, low-budget sci-fi serials that featured stock characters and scenes (such as *Flash Gordon's Trip to Mars* [Ford Beebe *et al.*,1938]), and Republic's massive serial output (everything from

Darkest Africa [B. Reeves Eason and Joseph Kane, 1936] to *Adventures of Captain Marvel* [John English *et al.*, 1941]). The sequel's association with the serial throughout its heyday ensured its employment by studios as a commercial tool. As a result, critical responses to the sequel became less and less favourable. A 1936 article in *The New York Times* compares the film sequel to the 'practice of Shintoism', or ancestor worship, calling not for the demise of the form, but rather for a separation of continuation from formulaism:

> If producers could only turn out sequels [that show] a hero and a heroine unmarried at a picture's end, still with some obstacles in the path of their romance and with a glint in their eyes betokening their willingness to set out upon some new adventures before consigning their characters into the limbo of shelved celluloid . . . we are quite sure they would find a public waiting as eagerly for them as it waits now for the next instalment of a Faith Baldwin novel, a Tugboat Annie short story or bank night at the neighborhood movie house.[57]

The sequel, it seems, was all too eager for an ending – and one that was most predictable. By mid-century, both the sequel and serial were becoming worn out by industrial practices.

However, one sequel-series emerged during this period as an instance of the sequel as an important context in which to explore cross-cultural relations, national fears of retaliation, and complex notions of repression and return. Spanning over fifty years, Ishirô Honda's 1954 *Gojira* (*Godzilla*) and its sequels play an important role in charting cross-cultural relations between the USA and Japan after the US attack on Hiroshima. Jennifer Cunico, who devotes an entire undergraduate course to the study of the Godzilla phenomenon at the University of New Mexico, observes that the

> variety of directions the Godzilla series takes over its half-century track record [charts] contemporary attitudes toward the military, the media, government, corporate culture, popular perceptions of science (and science fiction), environmental issues, a changing global world order, terrorism, and nuclear catastrophe.[58]

Significantly, the sequel provides a way throughout the Godzilla lifespan to navigate the troubled waters of US–Japan relations, and later global relations, in terms of its contextualisation of the rather tricky dynamics of retaliation and repression. Honda's original apocalyptic portrait of the radioactive Jurassic monster named Gojira – a combination of the Japanese words *gorira* (gorilla) and *kujira* (whale) – focused on the historical and tragic events of the morning of 1 March 1954, when the US dropped a 15 megaton hydrogen bomb on the uninhabited Pacific archipelago of Bikini Atoll. The Bikini Atoll bomb was the biggest ever man-made explosion, and over a thousand times greater than the bomb dropped on Hiroshima and Nagasaki just nine years before. Despite the US taking precautions against human causalties, they did not count on the massive fallout, which exposed 264 people to radiation. Amongst those affected were a group of Japanese tuna fishermen aboard the *Lucky Dragon*, who were within 100 miles of the test zone. One of the fishermen, Aikichi Kuboyama, died six months after the blast despite intensive hospitalisation. The rest of the crew was hospitalised for over a year and lived at high risk of cancer and a shortened life-span.

Honda's film is deeply embedded in the contexts of war. Those most responsible for the production of *Godzilla* played important roles in war-related efforts. Honda served eight years in Japan's Imperial Army and over a year in China as a prisoner; the film's director of special effects, Eiji Tsuburaya, directed and produced the special effects for a number of propaganda films during the war, the footage of which was so convincing that it was used in later films as newsreel footage of the attack on Pearl Harbor; and the film's composer, Akira Ifukube, had previously composed marches for the Imperial Army and Navy.[59] *Godzilla* additionally imagines the war launched by the beast upon the people of Tokyo and the war they wage in return. The film begins by portraying the fishing boat and moves swiftly on to imagine the horrors of radiation in the form of Godzilla, whose radioactive fire breath incinerates everything it reaches. Moral debate pivots in the film on the weapon designed to kill Godzilla. The scientist Dr Daisuke Serizawa (Akihiko Hirata) is shown to have developed a weapon called the 'Oxygen Destroyer', which is more destructive than an H-bomb and is the only defence against Godzilla's wrath. But Serizawa is also quick to identify its much more destructive potential. Here his comments are pointed:

If the Oxygen Destroyer is used even once, politicians from around the world will see it. Of course they'll use it as a weapon. Bombs versus bombs, missiles versus missiles, and now a new superweapon to throw upon us all. As a scientist – no, as a human being – I cannot allow that to happen.

If Godzilla represents war, Serizawa articulates a reluctance to contribute to a continuous chain of retaliation and destruction.

Godzilla embodied national fears of a 'sequel' to Hiroshima and Nagasaki – the US's retaliation for the Japanese attack on Pearl Harbor – as well as the more general threat posed by the US in terms of its development (and careless use) of weapons of mass destruction. Compounded by the US government's refusal to take responsibility for the fallout at Bikini Atoll, as well as the US

Atomic Energy Commission's refusal to respond to Japanese letters asking for details of the chemical elements contained in the H-bomb (which might well have proved helpful in the course of radiation treatment), and the rather cool attitude of US officials to the prospect of poisoning faced by many Japanese people who had purchased the tuna carried by the *Lucky Dragon*, the already tense relationship between the US and Japan became much worse. The Japanese press criticised the US and called for greater protection against further bomb tests, whilst the Japanese fishing industry – a national economic stronghold – almost ground to a halt.

Godzilla was not the first film to present radiation fears. Films like *Them!* (Gordon Douglas, 1954), *It Came From Beneath the Sea* (Robert Gordon, 1955), *The Monster That Challenged the World* (Arnold Laven, 1957) and *Attack of the 50 Foot Woman* (Nathan Juran, 1958) pivoted on radiation mutations that threatened the world in both scale and venom. *Gojira*, however, responded quickly and directly to the Bikini Atoll disaster and, in turn, to each of the cultural crises that had developed and re-emerged in its wake. Honda's film was a smash hit, and its fire-breathing character quickly became a major icon in Japanese popular culture. The film concluded with the assumption that, although Godzilla had been killed, it was uncertain as to how many such creatures were in existence, thus paving the way for many sequels.

Godzilla's success took the Japanese film industry by surprise, and plans for a sequel were quickly rushed through. Less than a year later, the first sequel, *Gojira no Gyakushu* (*Godzilla's Counterattack*) (Motoyoshi Oda, 1955), followed a strict set of narrative 'rules' established by its predecessor, with a number of notable variations – the reflection on a national tragedy and its socio-political aftermath (this time, Nagasaki); the interaction of three people (two of whom are again romantically involved, but this time in a cross-cultural relationship) and the triangulation of their fates; the discovery of Godzilla, as well as another less powerful creature, known as Angilas; and the search for a weapon to destroy Godzilla, as the 'Oxygen Destroyer' developed by Serizawa in the previous film is no more. A great deal of attention is paid this time to Japan's preparation for war and the aftermath of destruction. With its overtones of the destruction of Nagasaki, the film shows the efforts of reconstruction, rebuilding and retaliation. When Godzilla returns for another round of chaos, the Japanese military is shown to be capable of bringing him down, using a force of nature in place of man-made weaponry to bury the beast. But, like the particular brand of evil explored in Lang's *Dr Mabuse* films, Godzilla is not kept down for long.

Whilst Godzilla's reprisal across Japanese popular culture and a series of low-budget B-movies increasingly turned the monster into a thing of parody, the rather unexpected appearance of the monster on American screens brought an interesting dimension to the cross-cultural dialogue present within the series.

Just two years after Honda's film broke Japanese box-office records, American director Terry Morse's adaption, *Godzilla, King of the Monsters!* (1956), made a similar impact on the Hollywood industry. The film is at once a remake and a sequel of Honda's original. Instead of remaking the original from scratch, Morse re-edited and dubbed Honda's version and introduced new footage, even reshooting some scenes shot-for-shot using Japanese doubles in place of Honda's characters. Perhaps the most important element was the integration of a new protagonist, an American reporter named Steve Martin (Raymond Burr), who we learn is a good friend of the original film's moral leader, Serizawa. Morse's seamless integration of new material into the old is key to the film's success. The result, however, is a dimming down of the original's allegorical and political contexts. Focus is shifted instead to the spectacle of the fire-breathing monster and the ensuing action. Aiding, to large extent, the reconfiguration of Honda's original cross-cultural commentary as an action movie, the US remake set the standard for subsequent 'sequels' which increasingly turned to stock footage and the use of spectacle in their portrait of Godzilla.

Later *Godzilla* sequels made in Japan would depict Godzilla as a sympathetic character who fights other monsters, which also appear to embody particular cultural and/or political concerns. These include the giant caterpillar/moth monster Mothra in Ishirô Honda's *Mosura* (Mothra) (1961), which can be seen as a rather explicit representation of socio-political transformations, particularly the signing of the Treaty of Mutual Cooperation and Security in 1960, which outlined the US–Japanese security relationship throughout the Cold War, and an improving economic situation, which had fallen sharply during World War II. Yet, just as Mothra's transformation from larva to butterfly/moth brings further destruction, the film is never entirely confident about the changes offered by US politicians. As Japanese perceptions of the US gradually changed from destructive enemy to defender and ally, portraits of Godzilla also changed. As Susan Napier puts it, 'Godzilla began as the ultimate alien who, as the series continued, became a friend to Japan, an insider, "one of us"'.[60] If Godzilla symbolised the 'sleeping giant' of the US awakened by war, later films conjured monsters to embody other superpowers and the threats they posed to Japan. The monster in *Ghidrah, the Three-Headed Monster* (*San daikaijû: Chikyû saidai no kessen*) (Ishirô Honda, 1964), for instance, can be seen to represent China which, after years of developing nuclear weapons, detonated its first atomic bomb in the year of the film's release. Rodan (in *Sora no daikaijû Radon* [*Rodan: The Flying Monster*, Ishirô Honda, 1956]) is largely believed to represent the Soviet Union, whilst re-emerging tensions between East and West are reflected in *King Kong vs. Godzilla* (*Kingu Kongu tai Gojira*) (Ishirô Honda, 1963).[61]

Of the *Godzilla* canon, Chon Noriega observes that the films persistently conclude with a sense of the monster's imminent return, an unequivocal narrative denouement for such a 'polysemous figure' who must return to resolve contradictions in cross-cultural meaning.[62] However, over the course of the *Godzilla* sequels, notions of return and continuation began to take on significantly different meanings. Light years away from the original representations of cross-cultural return and historical repetition in Honda's films, Roland Emmerich's Hollywood version, *Godzilla* (1998), is far more interested in returns and repetitions of the box-office kind. Godzilla's persistent employment as a representation of a catalogue of cross-cultural anxieties and relationships had, over the course of the twentieth century, started to crumble, until nothing but the representation of a representation remained. None the less, high hopes and much finance were banked on Emmerich's $130 million blockbuster. Although the film recouped $379 million at the international box office,[63] *Godzilla* was considered a massive critical failure. Fans of the series saw none of the monstrous potency, cultural heritage or comic lip-synching paraded in the previous films; instead, Emmerich opted for a version of the scaly, sabre-toothed stars of *Jurassic Park*, even cribbing Spielberg's famous close-up of the T-Rex's eye to advertise *Godzilla*, with elements of *Aliens* (James Cameron, 1986) and Emmerich's own film, *Independence Day* (1996), thrown in as aesthetic influence. The special effects that had wowed the world in *Jurassic Park* were on display in virtually every scene in Emmerich's film, but with none of their original impact. Critics felt the film was 'vacuous'[64] and 'one of the most idiotic blockbuster movies of all time'.[65] Plans for two sequels to the film were swiftly abandoned.

Geoff King puts *Godzilla*'s failure into perspective in his observation of the film's mediatisation of the monster, indicated by endless shots of characters risking their lives to get a photograph of the beast, and of news reporters being flattened by its giant foot, captured on video as the camera keeps rolling even after the death of its owner. Of Emmerich's investments in mediations, King reflects that

> the insertion of the act of representation within the narrative space can also function as the implicit form of disavowal. It naturalizes the production of spectacle, decreasing the distance between the spectator-as-consumer-of-spectacle and those depicted on screen.[66]

The spectacle of commercialism is the film's primary spectacle, and it is precisely this that disconnects the film from its serial heritage. Much like the textually plural sequels of the silent period discussed earlier in this chapter, Emmerich's blockbuster sought to commingle and continue too many texts, thereby blending the contextual and cultural specifics of the *Godzilla* franchise with texts that were utterly unrelated to the franchise and, in fact, operated only to display an ignorance and disavowal of its legacy and cross-cultural meaning.

Was Emmerich's *Godzilla* a consequence of excessive sequelisation, or of the excesses inherent in the structure of the sequel? Lianne McLarty's observations of the sequel as announcing no less than 'the end of originality', resulting in 'the triumph of surface over depth, spectacle over meaning and history'[67] resonate throughout Emmerich's film, which was produced in an era in which new media technologies and digital culture were claimed to mark such an end to both originality and historicity. But the sequel is a force here, too. Increasingly used to (re)package 'more' of the popular aspects of a production, the sequel is marked in Emmerich's *Godzilla* as a framework of excess, or as an important scenario by which the explosive, spectacular constituents of a blockbuster can be played out to their full extent. At another level, the sequel here clashes against its source, enlivening a concept of the past without any sense of the cross-cultural meanings by which that past continued in the critical consciousness. Evocative of its own specific temporal juncture, Emmerich's *Godzilla* failed to resurrect the character of Gojira as a prominent (and lucrative) feature of Western popular culture ultimately because the film's strident reflections of the contemporary moment were not sufficiently reconciled with the overtly historical portraits throughout the series.

SEQUELS IN THE BLOCKBUSTER ERA

Emmerich's film represents a model of filmmaking unique to a specific era of Hollywood history. 'Sensation' films were prevalent very early on in cinema's history, as evidenced by Gunning's phrase, the 'cinema of attractions', as well as the term for film serial in Germany, loosely translated as 'sensation-film'. It has also been argued that Griffith's massively budgeted epics throughout the 1910s were early blockbusters. Yet neither of these types of early effort quite matches the vertical integration of the Hollywood studios throughout the 1970s onwards; the latter encompasses all aspects of media entertainment, and accounts for the creation of a kind of film that exploited predictability and mass appeal, the commercial potential of which was further expanded by saturation booking, expensive marketing campaigns, special effects, star power, merchandising, and a carefully charted box-office 'life' that peaked at its opening weekend.[68] Beginning with the unprecedented box-office success (and subsequent spin-offs) of *Jaws* (Steven Spielberg, 1975), which was swiftly outdone by the $775 million box-office revenue taken by *Star Wars* (George Lucas, 1977), the 'blockbuster' is the most solid example of Hollywood's economic strategies and impact in the international market. Intended to appeal to audiences all over the world, blockbusters commonly bleach out cultural and political differences in favour of an altogether 'global' and spectacular film experience.

The sequel became prevalent in this environment primarily as a method of extending the life and commercial potential of a production. Commencing as part of the synergistic logic of high-concept movies, sequels initially operated in an industry that, having experienced a recession in the 1960s and 1970s, was particularly keen to keep revenue on the up. Far from making a clean break from earlier industrial practices, however, sequelisation and blockbuster production after the 1970s can be seen in terms of a repetition of the industry's inception. Similar to the film serial – which Singer notes as heralding industrial investments in advertising, publicity, literary tie-ins and the cult of the celebrity, often resulting in producers spending more on marketing than on the film's production[69] – the blockbuster remains defined by its economic imperatives.

In 1916, an article in *The New York Times* claims,

> The crying need of the movies is ideas. In their onward sweep they have devoured so many novels, short stories, and plays that the stock of available plots is about depleted and the more aggressive producers are casting about for stories for their pictures.[70]

By 1975 it seemed nothing had changed. In October of that year, Judy Klemesrud wrote in *The New York Times*, 'the way things are going, it won't be long before almost every new movie is a sequel to an old movie.'[71] Although blockbusters remain the focus of often derogatory attention (as *Godzilla* proved), they are almost always followed or preceded by a sequel, to the point that 'sequelitis',[72] not 'blockbuster syndrome', became perceived as the fatal flaw of the Hollywood industry and all international industries that utilised the sequel. In hundreds of articles from around 1975 to 2007 there is an overall tone of despair at sequel production that blights the cinematic aesthetic, and a general perception that sequels are a large part of the continued theme of unoriginality. Sequels, these articles claim, are 'more mechanical and more exploitative' and 'less responsible, less detailed, less personal, less serious and less fun' than the original[73] – a far cry from the claims of 'more' of everything offered by the sequel during the 1910s and 1920s. None the less, the sequel 'phenomenon' trundled on towards the new millennium, with studios throwing more and more megabucks at 'part twos' which, in turn, tended to bring home much more bacon than the original. In such a lucrative market, why did originality matter?

One person to whom originality apparently did matter was Francis Ford Coppola, a young writer/director/producer who won an Academy Award in 1971 for his screenplay for *Patton* (Franklin J. Schaffner, 1970), and a second Academy Award the following year for his film adaptation of Mario Puzo's novel *The Godfather* (1972), which had also enjoyed history-making box-office success. Before *The Godfather* was even released, Paramount had planned a sequel. Despite having clashed with the studio throughout the production of *The Godfather*, Coppola accepted the chance to direct its sequel – most likely because he was offered almost complete creative control and a virtually unlimited budget (including a pay cheque of $500,000 for writing, directing and producing the film, as well as 13% of the film's adjusted gross). The studio also offered to schedule the project around his existing contracted productions. The sequel, in short, was Coppola's blank canvas, with a decent wage to boot. As Coppola later put it, 'Charlie [Blühdorn, former owner of Paramount Pictures] let me name my own price . . . He said I could do anything I wanted with the sequel.'[74]

Coppola's reasons for directing the sequel appeared to be rooted firmly in authorial control. Having no desire to fall into the 'trap' commonly laid by sequels of covering old ground, Coppola's efforts to utilise the sequel format to champion creativity and narrativity are well documented. Whereas the first *Godfather* venture had been based on Puzo's novel, Coppola co-wrote the sequel with Puzo. Explaining that he wanted to ensure that the sequel looked as if 'it was essential that it be made, and that it wasn't an appendix that came after the first', Coppola later announced that *The Godfather Part II* would be 'a very unusual kind of film' which was 'being designed to fit with the first one so that the two of them may be played together'. When a distribution deal fell through to re-release the original alongside the second instalment as a complete six-hour movie, Coppola toyed with other methods of creating a visible narrative dialogue between the two films, opting at last for 'a movie that would work freely in time, that would go both forward and backward in time'.[75]

The Godfather Part II accomplishes this by devising a sequel in human form, Michael Corleone (Al Pacino), who is portrayed as following his father/predecessor, Vito Corleone (Robert De Niro) in his role as mafia 'godfather'. Whereas the first film focused on Vito's later years, *Part II* outlines Vito's entrance into America and his ascent from poverty row to a successful and well-respected mobster. Coppola cuts back and forth between the parallel narratives of a young Vito to Michael's journey from idealistic rejections of his mafia heritage to an almost inevitable assuming of his father's role. The structure of the sequel facilitates not only the continuation of the narrative, but also informs the characterisation of Michael, as well as the specific family and cultural ties that result in generations of mob activity. Michael's decision to forgo his initial reluctance and idealism in order to perform the role of Don Corleone in the event of his father's death is suggested as a result of the complexities of nostalgia and tradition. Unable to break free of his family ties and reach for his dreams of true-blue legitimacy, Michael is lulled by nostalgic incantations of Old Sicily to the point where he emigrates there and takes a Sicilian bride. The death of Michael's wife in a car bomb intended for him is suggestive of the dramatic explosion of his ideals. The Sicily to which he has returned is the Fatherland of those ideals, a concept which is also suggested by the Corleone name, taken not from his bloodline but from the town in which his family originated (Vito Corleone was originally named Vito Andolini, but took on the name of his home town upon coming to America – a symbolic act, of course, of embodying one's home). Michael's journey back to his Fatherland symbolises his return to and continuation of his father's legacy. Corleone's involvement in Mafia crime and the consequences of that involvement follow Michael wherever he chooses to reside – even in the past. Similarly, the parallel narratives of Michael and his father underline the patriarchal continuation of one generation's blood crimes in another. Kay (Diane Keaton)'s abortion – and Michael's jarring question, 'was it a boy?', upon hearing the news – is paralleled by Michael's order to execute his brother Fredo. The sequel facilitates the integration of both original narrative and its continuation, at the same time as it proves vital in interpreting the film's narrative framework and characterisation.

Although *The Godfather Part II* went on to win an Academy Award for Best Film – the first film sequel ever to do so – it was initially met with a great deal of skepticism. Coppola's efforts to employ the sequel as a method of characterisation and narrative integration did not cut it for the critics. Writes Vincent Canby of *The New York Times*,

> *'Part II'* . . . is not a sequel in any engaging way. It's not really much of anything that can be easily defined. It's a second movie made largely out of the bits and pieces of Mr. Puzo's novel that didn't fit into the first. It's a Frankenstein's monster stitched together from leftover parts. It talks. It moves in fits and starts but has no mind of its own.[76]

Other critics wrote of the film as 'one of a multitude of spin-offs headed your way in what may well go down . . . as the Year of the Sequel',[77] yet Canby's criticisms in particular indicate a general misrecognition of Coppola's sequel as nothing more than part of the outpouring of retreads which audiences had witnessed across the previous decade. Canby's suggestion of the film's 'Frankensteinian' structure betrays confusion over just how and what the sequel was doing on a deeper textual level. A later review of George Lucas's *Star Wars* sequel, *The Empire Strikes Back* (1980), is equally dismissive, as Canby complains the film 'has no beginning or end, being simply another chapter in a serial that appears to be continuing not onward and upward but sideways'.[78] The sequel as a critically engaging form was proving difficult for critics, but was a cause for success for studio bosses. Six Academy Awards and five Golden Globe Awards later, *The Godfather Part II* was eventually received as a Hollywood masterpiece; it went on to be ranked as the 'greatest movie of all time' in *TV Guide Magazine*'s '50 Best Movies of All Time', and as number seven on *Entertainment Weekly*'s list of the '100 Greatest Movies of All Time'.

Just as Coppola's sequel has since been celebrated as a Hollywood classic and – far more rare – 'better than the original', so does the film subscribe to and reflect the kinds of filmic 'revisionism' that became prominent at the dawn of the blockbuster, as this new commercially motivated vehicle called upon film history as a method of engaging audiences. The specific brand of nostalgia paraded in *The Godfather II* is not necessarily an allusive glance at films of the past (although *film noir* and the gangster film of the 1920s are a visible influence), the film's prioritisation of looking back, of flashbacks, and of juxtaposing past and present whilst calling upon the spectator to meditate upon the passage of time, evokes a visible investment in nostalgia. This investment does not seem to have been limited to Coppola's film; Andreas Huyssen notes that after the 1960s a shift occurred in 'memory discourses' in the West 'in the wake of decolonisation and the new social movements and their search for alternative and revisionist histories', and points to a 'culture of memory' from around the late 1970s.[79] Manifested across a throng of newly minted memorials and activities of remembrance, this culture of memory was also attended, he says, 'by multiple statements about endings: the end of history, the death of the subject, the end of the work of art, the end of metanarratives'.[80] Characteristic of postmodernity, the act of looking back at the past became a dominant part of Western society and was heightened by changes that reflected 'endings' of various kinds. A temporal juncture defined (if it is possible to define the deliberately undefinable) by afterwardness, or what 'has *just-now ceased to be*',[81] postmodernity witnessed the collapse of the 'new' that was celebrated by modernity and the rise of a reproduced and re-presented past. In *The Godfather Part II*, the 'new' generation collapses into the old, whilst the new beginning suggested by Kay's pregnancy (and Michael's insistence upon creating a new, wholesomely legitimate lifestyle) is presented as an ending. The spiralling repetition of history offered by the sequel here indicates that much more complex forces of retrospect than mere nostalgia are at work.

The significance of reproducibility and re-presentation, as apparent in the narrative structure of *The Godfather Part II*, is enforced by the numerous ways in which the film has been reproduced and represented across multimedia formats. An NBC TV series named *The Godfather Saga* (1977) realised Coppola's dream of cutting and running the two films chronologically. This production added scenes that were not included in the films, and toned down the films' depictions of sex and violence to achieve a rating of TV-14. A second film sequel, *The Godfather Part III* (Francis Ford Coppola, 1990), effectively trilogised the films, but failed to use the sequel structure as effectively as did *Part II*. *The Godfather DVD Collection* was released in 2001, including all three films and a morass of extra material, such as deleted scenes, interviews, deleted footage, a look inside the director's notes and a Corleone family tree. And in 2006, Electronic Arts released *The Godfather: The Game*, a video game based on the films and featuring the voices of most of the cast. The game encourages the player to have seen (and have a working knowledge of) *The Godfather* films and their previous incarnations, and also enables the player to interact with the original narrative and play an active role in its outcomes. Of note is the contribution made to this production by novelist Mark Winegardner, author of *The Godfather Returns*, which offered an alternative sequel to Mario Puzo's original novel and became a *New York Times* bestseller in 2004. Winegardner is credited as providing 'story editing and fiction insight' to *The Godfather* video game.[82] Coppola, however, plays no such authorial role, insisting that 'I did not give permission for the game, nor was I asked . . . I did not cooperate with its making in any way, nor do I like or approve of what I saw of the result.' In many ways a conflation of sequel, original, remake and video game, *The Godfather: The Game* offers a dense map of narrative and authorial crossovers and tensions.

In this regard, it is worth noting the rash of *Godfather* imitations and 'inspired' productions in India, amongst them *Dharmatma* (Feroz Khan, 1975), *Nayakan* (Mani Ratnam, 1987), *Zulm ki Hukumat* (Bharat Rangachary, 1992), *Aatank hi Aatank* (Dilip Shankar, 1995), *Mumbai Godfather* (Balraj Deepak Vij, 2005) *Sarkar* (Ram Gopal Varma, 2005), *Family* (Rajkumar Santoshi, 2005), and *Maqbool* (Vishal Bharadwaj, 2003) – this last film an interesting conflation of Shakespeare's *Macbeth* and Coppola's *The Godfather* – all of which re-articulate Coppola's films according to South Asian cultural values and cinematic codes. The journey of *The Godfather* across so many media and narrative formats – novel, film, sequel, serial, video game, cross-cultural remake – charts varying registers of reproduction, repetition, retrospectivity and indeed sequelisation across postmodernity. In each case the structure employed by Coppola's sequel is developed and continued both to reflect and to exploit emergent reception practices, media formats and technologies, industrial shifts and cultural transitions – all of which impact the meaning of the sequel.

This impact is visible in many productions leading up to the end of the twentieth century. One of many films of the era devoted to commercially inflected portraits of heroic masculinity, Reaganism and the Vietnam War, *Rambo: First Blood Part II* (George P. Cosmatos, 1985) sends Rambo (Sylvester Stallone) back into Vietnam to retrieve lost POWs, but not before the hero asks his Colonel, 'Do we get to win this time?' – referring, of course, to America's defeat during the Vietnam War. Here Rambo – the muscle-clad action figure to whom President Reagan repeatedly made reference during his speeches – vocalises the film's revisionist sentiments, or taps into what would appear to be a collective desire ('we') to win the war in retrospect. 'It's up to you!', Colonel

Trautman (Richard Crenna) assures him, but his response is directed at the spectator, not Rambo, in what appears to be a screen fantasy of re-enactment and return, or Vietnam: The Sequel.

Similar ideological imperatives appeared across a throng of sequels during the 1980s and 1990s. The sequel's historicity and circularity – or indeed the circularity of history – proved a compellingly successful framework for the presentation of time travel and historical interception in *Terminator 2: Judgment Day* (James Cameron, 1991). Notably, the stakes here are no less than the end of history – a particularly striking evocation of postmodern sentiment couched within the genre of action movie. Along with *Aliens* (James Cameron, 1986) and (to an extent) the *Back to the Future* series (Robert Zemeckis, 1985, 1989, 1990), *Terminator 2* also juxtaposed representations of heroic masculinity as portrayed across numerous sequels throughout the previous decades with heroic femininity. Yet distinctions between heroic masculinity and heroic femininity are made clear by the sequel as conceptualised in each production; where the male is depicted as a figure of return, the female in these sequels tends to function as a figure of prolepsis, functioning to 'bring forth' and signify subsequent narratives and prevent closure. Conversely, the male looks back to his progenitors and invokes an analeptic spectatorial engagement, looking to past (and related) narratives. In short, the female's 'heroism' is kept quite separate from that of the male's brave endeavours by the corresponding elements of return and progress offered by the sequel. Mediated according to gender roles, the sequel here accommodates gender equalities on the surface, whilst still retaining an overt prioritisation of masculine heroism as its ideological framework.

The blockbuster era – which has arguably morphed now into what could be called the franchise era – made the sequel's inherent excesses, or its latent suggestion of 'more', a box-office star. As a result, the sequel during the twentieth century's last decade became increasingly synonymous with spectacle and, as Fredric Jameson commented of postmodernism, a new 'depthlessness' and a weakening of historicity.[83] Particularly at home within the genres of sci-fi and action adventure, the 1990s version of sequelisation struck chords of similitude with its earlier relative, the serial, setting muscular heroes, not serial queens, out on similarly episodic adventures to fight bad guys. Despite its frequent appearances across a range of low-budget cult movies, the sequel drew further comparisons during this period with the move from plagiarism to improvement and attempts at 'newness' during the early era. The postmodern 'waning of effect', created by layers of self-reflexivity in most productions that seemed to tip the entire concept of sequelisation into an endless cycle of meaningless re-representation, slowly appears, as in *The Matrix* and its sequels (Larry and Andy Wachowski, 1999, 2003, 2003), to take the form of a consciously philosophical engagement with shifting notions of originality, reproduction, simulacra and re-presentation. This also occurs at a crucial historical moment – the end of the century and the brink of the new millennium – and at a time when, not unlike the dawn of modern life, emergent technologies and socio-political shifts made such a reconsideration of meaning in Western society absolutely critical. Likewise, reconsiderations of temporality as pervasive in the modern era appear here in the form of temporalities afforded by digital culture, particularly the creation of 'bullet time' in *The Matrix*, a computer-generated simulation of variable speed. 'Bullet time' effectively transcends both filmic time and real time to offer a digital expression of motion that operates as a third temporality, or – most appropriately – a conflation of 'real' and fictional temporalities. A compelling indication of the possibilities of digital technology, 'bullet time' also marks the point at which ideology, economics and aesthetics conjoin.

Central to the ideologies, philosophies and religious systems referenced in the *Matrix* films is Jean Baudrillard's notion of simulacra, or 'copies of a real without origin', which serves as a rather explicit textual source – indeed, Baudrillard's book *Simulacra and Simulation* serves in the film as a storage unit for illegal software – for the film's hypothesis of a false reality, a Baudrillardian 'desert of the real',[84] constructed by machines. This notion of originality is pitted against all the forms of copying generated across a century of cinema. This is apparent in the construction of parallel false/real realities, which are inhabited by characters that appear not strictly as copies or simulacra, but as 'sequels' to other characters. Thomas Anderson (Keanu Reeves), the film's protagonist, is a computer nerd in the 'false' world. In the real world, Neo is no less than a superhero of choice, a saviour of truth and a Messiah of the 'real'. Early scenes in the first film show a number of apparently minor characters from the world of Thomas Anderson, including Choi (Mark Gray), Dujour (Ada Nicodemou) and his grumpy boss (David Aston), who all find comparables later on in the form of characters from Neo's world, respectively Morpheus (Laurence Fishburne), Persephone (Monica Bellucci) and Agent Smith (Hugo Weaving). The comparisons between each of these characters are marked by the sequel's logic of 'more of', at the same time as the relationship between the 'real' world and the matrix is constructed according to continuation and repetition. Such are the confluences in the 'desert of the real' and the 'world' of Thomas Anderson's unconsciousness that one is never sure which is 'real', or where the original is to be found. The notion of 'without origin' appears to be taken up as a site of contesting concepts. The film suggests that it is simply not possible to talk about, or to prioritise, the idea of originality after a century of reproductive technologies, imitative practices, cultures of copying and virtual realities. Rather, the film suggests the deconstruction of originality by such practices and technologies as a much more important point of discussion. Within such a dense tapestry of critical concepts and ideological positions, the sequel functions as a starting point for the re-positioning of 'originality', re-production and repetition within their new, millennial contexts.

SEQUELS IN THE TWENTY-FIRST CENTURY

Writing in 2008, it seems futile to discuss the sequel over a period as brief as eight years, yet this has arguably been the sequel's most important stage of development. It is for this reason that much of the following book is devoted to sequel production during this era, though a brief outline is necessary here. I have argued previously that the sequel has re-emerged in recent years in much more experimental and progressive forms than has been witnessed in times past. More specifically, the sequel in its present stages can be seen across a number of productions to operate far beyond its prior manifestations of continuation and repetition to achieve cross-media interpretation and contextual negotiation of a far more sophisticated register. The significance of the sequel depends on its innovation and engagement with the times. Like Lang's *Das Testament der Dr Mabuse*, designed as 'a portrait of the times', the sequel offers a deft negotiation of the specific contexts within which films are now being consumed: on DVD, for instance, in undergraduate classes, at theme parks, in video games, as allusions, remakes and parodies in other films, on YouTube. As many of these methods of consumption involve activities of continuation in various ways, the sequel similarly takes on new meaning as a vehicle by which continuation is interactive and participatory. Amongst the scores of sequels produced in the last two years, many do not conform to such ideals of innovation, and many treat the sequel as if the last fifty years never happened. Yet there is also evidence of rigorous advancements in film sequelisation that indicate the form is a long way from its decline.

The sequel's long catalogue of historical interactions with the serial continues to grow in the twenty-first century, but arguably in ways that have not previously been realised. These interactions have shaped current practices of each format; broadly speaking, the serial now plays a significant part in TV production and consumption, not too far from its early uses as a method of episodic narration and mass entertainment. Amongst its own set of discrete functions and purposes, the serial is a form of consistency and coherency; things rarely change too much in the serial, and difference is eschewed for consistency and uniformity. The sequel's advancements are quite the opposite, however. The sequel's twenty-first century manifestations operate within the ever-expanding network of narrative developments and discursive boundaries of film production as both a method of continuation and a system of connection. Still rooted in its commercial contexts, the sequel none the less urges a reconsideration of the contexts of consumption, as well as the currency of connection, continuation and memory, in the age of digital culture.

NOTES

1. The sword is a persistent symbolic across Griffith's works, bringing together a number of personal and symbolic meanings. See Rogin, ' "The Sword Became a Flashing Vision" '.
2. Gunning, 'The Intertextuality of Early Cinema', 128.
3. Ibid., 129.
4. Gaines, 'Early Cinema's Heyday of Copying', 232.
5. Gunning, 'The Intertextuality of Early Cinema', 129.
6. Film serials began to decline in popularity around 1936; however, Republic Pictures continued to produce serials until 1955.
7. Crawford, *No Time to be Idle: The Serial Novel and Popular Imagination*.
8. Hunter, 'Serious Reflections on Farther Adventures', 289.
9. Hughes and Lund, *The Victorian Serial*.
10. Gunning, 'The Cinema of Attractions'.
11. Elsaesser, 'Fantasy Island', 145.
12. For an outline of the leisure time of US audiences during this period, see Jowett, 'The First Motion Picture Audiences'.
13. Singer, *Melodrama and Modernity*, 267.
14. See 'Now – The $10,000 Sequel to *The Diamond from the Sky*'.
15. Such strategies are fortified and informed by a visible emphasis in the early period on film budgets. Popular film serial *The Perils of Pauline* (Louis J. Gasnier *et al.*, 1914) and *The Sequel to The Diamond from the Sky* are both advertised respectively as *The Eclectic Film Company's Great $25,000 Prize Photo-Play* and *The $10,000 Sequel to The Diamond from the Sky*, whilst a host of reviews persistently report budgets and note serials as showing 'money well spent'.
16. Traill, *The New Fiction and Other Essays*, 1.
17. Iampolski, *The Memory of Tiresias*, 69.
18. Quoted in Ramsaye, *A Million and One Nights*, 397.
19. Note that an alternative title for this film is *La Jardinière et le petit espiègle*. As Jane Gaines points out, 'this was one of the unofficial titles used for the film until the publication of the Lumière company print sales catalogue in 1897.' See Gaines, 'Early Cinema's Heyday of Copying', 232.
20. Brown, 'Film and Postcards', 243.
21. John L. Fell also notes 1906 as a date that roughly marks out a period when 'consolidation with respect to organised, predelineated narrative design begins to assume consistent visibility'. See Fell, 'Motive, Mischief and Melodrama'.
22. Hansen, *Babel and Babylon*, 47.
23. Ibid., 1.
24. Musser, 'The Nickelodeon Era Begins', 257–8.
25. For more on copyright laws, see Decherney, 'Copyright Dupes'.
26. Leyda, 'A Note on Progress', 29.
27. 'Now – The $10,000 Sequel to The Diamond From the Sky'; Malaney, 'Excuse My Dust'.

28. Dyer, *Pastiche*, 35.

29. Elizabeth Ezra notes the killing of the moon people as subtly recollective of the imperialist conquests of Méliès's home country, implying the fight between astronomers and Selenites as colonial aggression and the moon's social infrastructure – with a throned king and his inferior subjects – as reminiscent of social hierarchies on earth. See Ezra, *Georges Méliès*, 120.

30. Schwartz, *Spectacular Realities*, 150, 151, 157.

31. Ibid., 176.

32. Quoted in Ramsaye, *A Million and One Nights*, 395–6.

33. For an excellent study on the significance of the train during the early twentieth century, see Schivelbusch, *The Railway Journey*.

34. Ezra, *Georges Méliès*, 128.

35. Abel, *The Ciné Goes to Town*, 72, 71.

36. Méliès, 'Letter of February 6, 1906', quoted in Hammond, *Marvellous Méliès*, 66.

37. Higgins, *Harnessing the Technicolor Rainbow*, 7.

38. Thanks to Joshua Yumibe for this point.

39. Abel, *The Ciné Goes to Town*, 78.

40. Quoted in Hammond, *Marvellous Méliès*, 119.

41. Frazer, *Artificially Arranged Scenes*, 148.

42. See Quinn, 'Distribution, the Transient Audience, and the Transition to the Feature Film', 40; Thompson, *Exporting Entertainment*.

43. See Fielding, 'Hale's Tours: Ultrarealism in the Pre-1910 Motion Picture'.

44. Popple and Kember, *Early Cinema from Factory Gate to Dream Factory* 109; lecturing, or *katsuben*, was a virtual phenomenon in Japan. Silent films were regularly shown there with a spoken narration accompaniment (*benshi*); this was also commonplace in Italy, Germany and France. In Japan though, at the peak of the *benshi* era there were more than 7,000 *benshi* in Japan, and they were active over a period of 30 or 40 years. Japan is the only place in the world where the *benshi* became such a big popular attraction. In the early days, the *benshi* were big stars in their own right, and were more of a box-office draw than the actors. *Benshi* tradition had phased out by 1937. By 1908, the lecturer had become 'a mere "describer" of the action onscreen'.

45. Singer, *Melodrama and Modernity*, 263.

46. See Cook, *A History of Narrative Film*, 49.

47. Gerow, 'Swarming Ants and Elusive Villains'.

48. See Singer, *Melodrama and Modernity*, 264.

49. See 'Special Service Section on Ruth Roland in *The Tiger's Tail*'.

50. Krebs, 'Fritz Lang, Film Director Noted for "*M*", Dead at 85'.

51. Manvell, '*Doktor Mabuse der Spieler; Das Testament des Dr. Mabuse*'.

52. Gunning, *The Films of Fritz Lang*, 141.

53. Ibid., 142.

54. Interview with Erwin Leiser, West German TV, 1964. Available on Disc Two of the Criterion *Testament*.

55. Nietzsche, *The Will To Power*, 3.

56. Freud, 'The Uncanny'.

57. Nugent, 'Consider the Sequel'.

58. Jennifer Cunico, Personal Communication, 10 August 2007.

59. Miller, 'Struggling With Godzilla'.

60. Napier, 'Panic Sites', 349.

61. Miller, 'Struggling With Godzilla'.

62. Noriega, 'Godzilla and the Japanese Nightmare', 75.
63. http://www.boxofficemojo.com/movies/?id=godzilla.htm
64. Ibid.
65. http://www.reelviews.net/movies/g/godzilla.html
66. King, *Spectacular Narratives*, 162–3.
67. McLarty, ' "I'll Be Back" ', 201.
68. For more on this see Maltby, *Hollywood Cinema*, 205–17.
69. Singer, 'Serials', 106.
70. See 'Notes Written on the Screen'.
71. Klemesrud, 'Film Notes'.
72. Hoberman, 'Ten Years that Shook the World', 58.
73. Greenspun, 'Something Happened on the Way to the Sequel', 47.
74. Lebo, *The Godfather Legacy*, 212–15.
75. Ibid., 215.
76. Canby, ' "*Godfather, Part II*" is Hard to Define'.
77. 'Here Come the Sons and Daughters'.
78. Canby, ' "*The Empire Strikes Back*" Strikes a Bland Note'.
79. Huyssen, *Present Pasts*, 12, 14.
80. Ibid., 14.
81. Toulmin, *The Return to Cosmology*, 254.
82. http://www.ea.com/official/godfather/godfather/us/features.jsp
83. Jameson, *Postmodernism, or, The Cultural Logic of Late Capitalism*.
84. Baudrillard, *Simulacra and Simulation*, 1.

CHAPTER 2

Screaming, Slashing, Sequelling: What the Sequel Did to the Horror Movie

'Let's face it, baby, these days you gotta have a sequel!'
Stu in Scream (Wes Craven, 1996)

'Is she dead?'
'I don't know. They always come back.'
Gale and Sidney in Scream 2 (Wes Craven, 1997)

There is much to suggest that the film sequel operates as a genre or, at the very least, as a sub-genre. As the previous chapter has shown, early formative exercises in film 'kinds' led to the western, slapstick comedy, *film noir*, and lately to a host of hybrid generic formulations to alert cinema-going audiences to what they might expect of any film that subscribed to genre codes. A number of theories describe the ways by which audiences are alerted, but central to the operation of genre is the address of expectation. In its repetitious re-organisation of familiar features, genre shares much in common with sequelisation. According to Steve Neale, genre involves 'repetition and variation', and according to Barry Keith Grant, 'genre movies are those commercial feature films which, through *repetition and variation*, tell familiar stories with familiar characters in familiar situations' (my emphasis).[1] Similarly, the sequel is described as 'repetition-with-variation' by Paul Budra and Betty A. Schellenberg.[2] How, then, to differentiate between the two?

The immediate connection between sequelisation and genre is found in processes of variation, or, more exactly, in intertextual strategies by which 'variation' marks the modulations between textual reproductions. Such 'variations' or differences are crucial to the establishment of reading/viewing positions. The forms of interaction between audiences and filmmakers that occur in the genre film perpetuate stabilisation; a comparable process informs the sequel. Genre films not only promise predictability, but they also define the viewing experience by offering methods of reconnecting with previous genre films and the intertexts with which those films engaged. Similarly, the sequel makes accessible the processes of reiteration and continuation of a source text.

This chapter examines the ways in which the sequel operates in conjunction with genre to facilitate discourse, institutional practices and spectatorial engagement – to heighten, in short, each others' aesthetic and industrial imperatives. In particular, the sequel seems to me to be a primary mechanism of stabilisation – so important to film genres – as it consistently renegotiates generic meanings and values across periods of time. The prioritisation of a source text in the case of sequels to genre films tends to lie within genre itself, as the sequel re-states and affirms genre 'fundamentals' at the same time as it identifies ways in which we can find pleasure in yet another generic instance. Yet this relationship is reciprocal; genre naturalises sequelisation as part of its own circular logic. Conversely, by engaging audiences within the stabilising framework of a sequel, the sequel effectively markets, interprets, substantiates and re-identifies generic cues, texts and origins, thereby promising a much more participatory spectatorial experience. In an environment where studio control is limited, the combination of genre and sequelisation plays a key role in managing consumption.

My aim here is not to imply the sequel as a genre; nor do I consider genre as a process of sequelisation. Rather, I wish to explore the ways in which the sequel operates in conjunction with genre to achieve common goals of exploitation, spectatorial interaction and expectation, and narrative formulas. The ways in which film genres have used the sequel format tell us much about the sequel's historical development and about the relationships the sequel has negotiated between cinema audiences and film producers. To a point, the relationship between genre and sequelisation also explains the sequel's denigration in popular culture as, for instance, a method of digging old plotlines up from their graves, or sucking the life-blood out of successful narrative formulas. Suggestive of a monster from a 1950s horror B-movie, such pejorative perceptions of the sequel can be traced to the prevalence of horror sequels in Hollywood from the 1940s to the 1970s that (to a point) brought an otherwise successful relationship to no-budget B-movie depths. The production or quality of film sequels is rarely a matter of the sequel's 'inherent' structural or semantic virtues; rather, it is a consequence of the contexts in which films are produced.

I want to argue that an increasingly popular horror sub-genre – the slasher movie – both exploits and contributes to the sequel's (perceived) function as a mode of cannabilising old stories, zombie-fying dead texts, and altogether 'slashing' traditional forms of originality. Considered 'the most disreputable form of the horror film',[3] the slasher movie tends to endorse consumerism and the pornographic display of carnage, always gesturing towards the position of the spectator as both 'victim' and producer of the display of blood and gore. A predominantly Hollywood product, the slasher movie normally figures sub-versions of American ideals – most prominently, the family unit – and suggests subversions as somewhat skewed 'sequels' to an impossibly perfect model. The slasher movie is also notable for the way in which it figures generic repetitions not only in terms of unkillable killers but in terms of repetitious viewing. Indeed, repetition is central to the generic framework of the slasher movie. In her assessment of the derivative and repetitious nature of the slasher film, for instance, Vera Dika draws attention to the slasher 'cycle' which, by repeating genre codes and conventions in the form of endless sequels and remakes, con-structs a kind of 'game play' in which the spectatorial experience is heightened by negotiating recurring scenarios in familiar settings.[4] More recently, Valerie Wee has argued that the 'teen slasher film' initiated 'the trend toward spin-offs, sequels, and imitators' within the horror genre, while Angela Ndalianis has highlighted the slasher genre's persistent hyperconsciousness of its own his-toricity, to the point where literal and discursive figurations of reflexivity and participation have materialised in slasher films.[5] With these critical offerings in mind, I argue that the slasher sub-genre operates as a textual commentary on the processes of reading and spectatorship in the horror genre as repetitive and 'sequelising' exercises. That is to say, sequelisation does not co-operate with the slasher movie simply at the level of continuous instalments, but is persistently couched within the slasher's structure and modes of response.

Wes Craven's *Scream* trilogy (1996, 1997, 2000) exposes generic conventions and prescribed reading strategies to suggest genre as a product of its own reception. In their depiction of the methods by which genre is produced, each of the *Scream* films is produced with specific horror sub-genres and texts in mind; the typical female heroine (or 'Final Girl', as Carol Clover puts it)[6] is Sidney Prescott (Neve Campbell), whose memories of her mother's recent murder and the media aftermath are stirred up by a series of murders in her hometown, Woodsboro. Figured at one point in *Scream 2* as Cassandra – who, Greek myth informs us, was cursed by the gods to repeatedly foresee the future – Sidney is, first and foremost, a spectator of the events that take place across the trilogy. Her characterisation is grounded in repetitious spectatorship of different versions of the past; at 'stake' is the threat of these copycat killings continuing into the future, claiming Sidney as their next victim. In various ways, the copycat murders in the *Scream* films emerge as products of Sidney's spectatorship, as if the activity of repeatedly watching generates mechanisms of repetition, to the point where the killers seek mediation, publicity, and inevitably to be copied.

Like Sidney, the *Scream* spectator is constructed as a producer of textual meaning, consumption and reproduction. Called upon not only to read the *Scream* films but to reread the horror genre (and a number of its texts), the spectator is continually asked to draw upon his or her foreknowledge of generic conventions and sequel rules – made blatant within the film and by its publicity – which are deemed necessary tools for viewer participation. Moreover, the act of reading in the film is implied as not an individual activity, but rather a communal exchange of identification, knowledge and pleasure. Portraits of cinema audiences, media reportage, film class discussions and communal viewings of old horror films abound throughout the trilogy, arguably in full recognition of the contemporary conditions of spectatorship and mediation which, informed by the hyper-interactive spaces offered by the internet, video games, mobile phones and reality TV shows, are increasingly reflexive, interactive and aware. The film's engagement with slasher codes works to identify genre as a construct of the movie-going and film-reading experience. Just as the horror film typically invokes communal spectatorship – with cries of 'Behind you!' and other forms of screen address underscoring an equally interactive spectatorship – so too does the film directly construct the horror film fan as a Cassandra figure, consistently witnessing genre 'rules' repeated and recycled across many individual film texts which, if not accessed via sequel logic, would arguably fail to bring the pleasures of recognition, identification and communal engagement. That is to say, it is through the framework of the sequel that genre conventions and imperatives are enabled.

BACK TO THE BEGINNING: SEQUELS AND THE EMERGENCE OF THE SLASHER FILM

The sequel has played a major role in the horror movie from cinema's inception.[7] Throughout the horror movie canon there is an implicit expectation that the sequel format will conceptualise generic portraits of death, resurrection and hauntings, or act as a space between the real and its representation in which the process of mutation between two states of existence can be reported. In many ways, the relationship between the horror genre and the sequel is triangulated by their connection to cinema's ontological investments in representation and reality. A strong case can be made for the link between the phantoms and devils that appeared on film at the end of the nineteenth century and cinema's ontology, hotly discussed at its beginnings as a mechanism in which, not death nor life, but a kind of 'half-life' existed. In fact, the horror object can be seen to appear before rather than after cinema's invention, as seventeenth- and eighteenth-century optical illusions and magic-lantern acts were regularly screened for public entertainment in 'dark rooms where spectres [rise] from the dead'.[8] As with the contemporary horror film, the 'spectre-show[s]' of early cinema and before suggest cinema's origins as invested in the phantasmagoric.

The relationship between the horror movie and cinema can be seen to develop across the twentieth century in terms of reception, spectatorship, and the boundary between the real and its representation. The first of these is created by economic restrictions. Commonly low-budget, horror films depend upon an explicitly formulaic structure to create a fan base in place of expensive stars, explosions or sets. Methods of (successfully) connecting with the public have tended to draw upon revamped urban legends and innovative advertising campaigns. James Wan's urban legend-flick *Saw* (2004), for instance, opened to $18 million during its first weekend in the US, despite featuring a cast of relative unknowns and costing just over $1 million to make. Or consider the sweeping success of *The Blair Witch Project* (Eduardo Sánchez and Daniel Myrick, 1999), whose pioneering, internet-based promotional strategy brought box-office revenue of proportions fit for the *Guinness Book of World Records*.

As evidenced by *Saw*, *The Blair Witch Project* and their sequels, the horror film defines a particularly engaging spectatorial activity because of the repeated concept of a masked villain who hides in order to claim unsuspecting victims. As a method of audience connection/interaction, the promotional activities external to the film's plot are internalised to establish a much more participatory spectatorship. Recent horrors have used this internalisation as a plot-line (that usually extends across several sequels and remakes), such as Hideo Nakata's Japanese horror, *Ringu* (1998), in which a video-tape is circulated and causes the deaths of its viewers; Sripal Morakhia's Bollywood horror *Naina* (2005), in which a corneal transplant brings about horrorific visions of a particularly cinematic kind; and Kimble Rendall's Australian slash-fest *Cut* (2000), in which a group of filmmakers decide to finish an original horror film (which stalled once the cast and crew were murdered), and find themselves being victimised by a serial killer. Horror's generic interest in spectatorship frequently positions its characters in terms of their gaze, additionally figuring the film's spectator as a double agent, both watching and watched.

From its origins, the horror movie has integrated the spectatorial experience into its generic formula, whilst consistently seeking new ways to create the discursive practices of group-viewing and committed fans. It is in this way that the relationship between the horror genre and the sequel has come into being. Although the appearance of spectral beings (particularly the devil) occupies much of Georges Méliès's work, for instance, it is not until the teens of the twentieth century that the horror genre developed as a vehicle for the ubiquitous undead protagonist who, 'doomed to repetition',[9] naturally became the subject of a range of successful sequels. Early horror sequels such as Paul Wegener's *Der Golem und die Tänzerin* (1917), the sequel to his *Der Golem* (1914), Fritz Lang's *Das Testament des Dr Mabuse*, (1933), the sequel to his *Dr Mabuse der Spieler* (1922), and *Dracula's Daughter* (Lambert Hillyer, 1936) each employ the sequel format in markedly different ways, though commonly to exploit an unkillable protagonist in various scenarios which demonstrate his or her ability to cheat death. Despite the success of the 'sequel-enduring'[10] horror object, Hollywood's sci-fi hybrids and shoddily produced B-movies of the 1940s and 1950s helped largely to diminish the genre's mainstream esteem, but also gave rise to an underground cult following. The appearance of a number of successful sub-genres during the 1960s and 1970s saw the horror genre consistently deployed as a commentary on cultural and political affairs (such as Vietnam in Wes Craven's *The Last House on the Left* [1972] and Tobe Hooper's *The Texas Chain Saw Massacre* [1974]). The ground-breaking box-office success of Steven Spielberg's *Jaws* (1975) also brought the concept of a monstrous killer lurking in the shadows (or in this case, the shallows) swiftly back into public favour.

In co-operation with the rise of blockbuster logic (to which *Jaws* played an enormous part), 'sequelling' became common practice to the horror genre and its sub-genres.[11] Carol J. Clover argues that the purported 'sequels' to popular horrors during the 1980s – which are usually little more than shoddy duplications – produced only 'slight variation[s]' of too-familiar narratives, so that 'by the end of the decade the form was largely drained'.[12] By the end of the twentieth century and beginning of the twenty-first century, horror sequelisation is not as simple as the production of 'part twos' to successful films, as it was some sixty or seventy years ago. Rather, horror 'sequelling' now involves a combination of some of the dominant (and often inseparable) constituents of generic conventions and sequelisation, particularly referential acknowledgement of the genre's fan base, as well as the genre's discursive parameters, the intertextual and extratextual relationships forged during the genre's development, and systems of diegetic repetition that specifically reference cultural forms of repetition and/or seriality, such as the construction of the serial killer in the slasher sub-genre.

It is to the slasher sub-genre that the sequel adds a vital interpretive element. Intrinsically preoccupied with the repetitive nature of serial killing, the slasher film reworks repetition, death and resurrection as mutual characteristics of real experience and the horror sub-genre. As noted previously, sequels were made of horror films as far back as the 1920s, yet the particular propensity for horror sequelisation during the 1970s and 1980s notably coincides with the escalation and subsequent identification of a type of homicide that was labelled 'serial murder' by FBI profiler Robert Ressler in 1976 after the murders committed by Ted Bundy and David Berkowitz, and later Jeffrey Dahmer, rocked America.[13] Ressler named this kind of homicide after the abundance of TV and cinema serials during the 1930s and 1940s (repeated throughout the 1970s and 1980s) that were charged with tension and repetition. As Ressler puts it:

Now that I look back on that naming event, I think that what was [. . .] in my mind were the serial adventures we used to see on Saturday [. . .] Each week you'd be lured back to see another episode, because at the end of each one there was a cliff-hanger. In dramatic terms, this wasn't a satisfactory ending, because it increased, not lessened, the tension. The same dissatisfaction occurs in the minds of serial killers.[14]

The sense of dissastisfaction that is experienced by the serial killer appears to be bound up with repetition and improvement. 'After a murder', Ressler says, 'the serial murderer thinks of how the crime could have been bettered.'[15] Each subsequent act of murder, then, is a recapitulatory improvement of the previous one – a sequel, in other words, that is filled with the 'lure' of serial logic.

Similar also to the psychological profiling of a type of murder was the reality/fantasy dialectic that, already a generic undercurrent, became increasingly foregrounded as a method of interpolating audiences. Take the advertisement for Wes Craven's *Last House on the Left* (1972), which featured the instruction, 'To avoid fainting, keep repeating, it's only a movie . . . only a movie . . . only a movie . . . only a movie . . . only a movie . . . only a movie . . . only a movie.'[16] Here the combined ingredients of repetition and distinction between reality and illusion centralise the generic tendency to break boundaries between film and reality, but also mark the film's proposed realism. By finding dialogues with killers, disasters and wars at large in the public sphere, the horror genre recites and signifies these contexts as part of its 'genre recognition'.[17]

SPECTATING THE SLASHER

Genre recognition is taken up a notch in Craven's 'postmodern horror film', *Scream*, which was followed less than a year later by a sequel, *Scream 2*, and finally by *Scream 3*, with talk of a fourth instalment.[18] One of the most successful horror franchises of all time, the *Scream* trilogy self-consciously generates discursive practices which situate all texts, dialogues, genre conventions and spectatorship within the film's diegetic boundaries. Continually likening everything to the movies, *Scream*'s reality/illusion dialectic becomes much more expansive, to the point that 'it's all just one great big movie.' The *Scream* trilogy as a whole operates according to such ideological positioning arguably to comment and trade upon generic preoccupations with representation, but also to foreground the inherent dynamic between serial killing and the creation of a media spectacle. As Mark Seltzer tells us, '[i]nteractions between the serial killer and public media [. . .] have formed the profile of serial murder [. . .] for serial murder is bound up through and through with a drive to make sex and violence visible in public.'[19]

Accordingly, the *Scream* serial killers merge killing with theatricality, filmmaking and media reportage, of which more later.

Perhaps more important, however, is the discursive activity that is shown in the *Scream* trilogy to trigger serial killing. Although the murderers in each *Scream* instalment are killed at the end, each film features a renewed, copycat killer who adopts the same ghostly mask and is named until identified as 'Ghostface'. Despite his repeated incarnation by a variety of serial killers, Ghostface's motives, actions and victims are uniform. In fact, each of the murders across the trilogy is continually linked to a single murder conducted by the original Ghostface – that of Sidney's mother, Maureen Prescott (Lynn McRee) – which is copied, re-enacted, re-presented, and re-visited through multiple killings until the original event comes full circle. The murders that follow Maureen Prescott's death are implied as the mediation of the original murder, and as part of the repetitious, mediated discourse that is attributed to serial killing.

It is in this regard that the sequel plays an important part in the organisation, shaping, and consumption of the *Scream* films. Firstly, knowledge of how the sequel operates in contemporary film (and its history throughout the horror canon) is necessary to understand the mechanisms of circularity that are presumably inherent to the horror genre, and to expose and endorse the artificiality of genre conventions. Conscious of the double barriers posed by the low cultural status of the horror genre and sequels, Craven took advantage of the sequel's 'homicidal parallel, copycat killers' in order to take on the genre's pejorative cultural status like a 'bull by the horns'.[20] By continually staging the horror genre and then subverting it, Craven successfully ducks and dodges the genre's worn-out imperatives whilst calling attention to the forms of discursive activity by which it is sustained.

The plot of *Scream 2*, for instance, does not return an unkillable killer, but instead offers us a serial killer who has 'taken their love of sequels too far'. A scene from the film takes place during a college film class in which students discuss the latest murder as a 'real-life sequel'. Calling attention to the increasing number of claims that films – horrors in particular – have influenced murders, the scene eschews any kind of resolution to this social debate (that is, of course, continuing) but instead offers a contextualising ideology through which the modes of repetition and continuation exploited throughout the trilogy may be appreciated: life imitates art imitating life. The textual dialogues that occur in the event of the sequel between a source text and its continuation underscore the (implicitly inevitable) interaction between cinema and society that is to be understood as a form of imitation until the boundary between the real and its representation is destroyed.

Although 'the movies' are shown to be complicit in this boundary destruction, it is explicitly the horror genre that is cited in *Scream* as a mechanism of 'rereading'. Rereading is to be understood in the *Scream* films as not simply slotting interpretations within the context of lived experience, but actually living out the meaning of what one has read. Consider, for example, the opening scene of *Scream*, in which a teenage girl is killed (or, as a character later reflects, 'splatter-movie killed') after failing Ghostface's telephone horror film quiz (the right answer to which informs the endings of both *Scream* and *Scream* 2).[21] Preparing to watch 'some scary movie', Casey (Drew Barrymore) receives a phonecall and, soon after, is asked 'what's your favourite scary movie?' What follows is a self-conscious iteration of fan dialogue – 'is that the one where the guy had knives for fingers?' – and the parallel staging/subversion of horror 'rules': the death of a lone blonde female at the hands of a masked male killer, the picket-fence home in the middle of nowhere, the masked predator at the back door instead of the front, and, to keep audiences on their toes, the unconventional death of a film star in the first ten minutes. An otherwise artificial event that announces its own artificiality is presented as the 'real' event which is restaged word for word, scene by scene as a film called *Stab* in *Scream 2*, which is 'based on a true story', or a remake of the events of *Scream*. As I go on to show, the film-within-a-film plot operates to heighten rereading practices, particularly by destabilising temporal boundaries between the text and its reading. Roland Barthes famously described *re*-reading as follows: 'Rereading draws the text out of its internal chronology ("this happens before or after that") and recaptures a mythic time (without before or after)'.[22] The reading of this text, *Scream* posits, takes place before the text is produced: in fact, it is the method by which the text is produced.

Scream 2 figures both rereading and 'mythic' time as specific effects of cinema-going, fandom and film production. As a continuation, or extension, of *Scream*'s opening scene, *Scream 2*'s opening scene shows two characters, Maureen (Jada Pinkett Smith) and Phil (Omar Epps), going to see *Stab* on its opening night at a local cinema. After some self-reflexive dialogue about genre typicalities – 'the horror genre is historical for excluding the African-American element' – the scene goes on to show both (African-American) characters' deaths at the hands of Ghostface in parallel with the cinema screening of *Stab*. In addition, the scene cuts continually to *Stab* on-screen, which features a well-known blonde actress (Heather Graham) playing a horror movie version of Casey (replete with shower scene). As the *Stab* character is stabbed to death *à la* Casey's death at the beginning of *Scream*, Maureen is stabbed while watching *Stab* by Ghostface, who she believes to be her boyfriend, Phil, wearing the Ghostface mask. Because the Ghostface mask has become a souvenir for film fans – and is worn by almost every member of the *Stab* audience, along with glow-in-the-dark fake knives which they 'stab' into the air while watching the movie – the 'real' Ghostface killer is able to move, and kill, freely. Maureen struggles, dying, up the stage steps in front of the screen and, as the *Stab* Casey dies, cries out to the *Stab* audience, who do nothing because they believe her 'death' to be part of the film.

Maureen's death is presented as a consequence of rereading. Her vocal responses during the *Stab* screening – 'No, no, no, don't do that!' – and increasing engagement with the film form a significant textual prelude to her murder, which is offered as a symbolic connotation of the levels of involvement and interactivity inherent not just in film viewing, but in generic participation. The three temporalities present in this scene – namely, the temporality of *Stab*, the temporality of *Scream 2*, and the temporality of the *Scream 2* spectator – equally signal the 'mythic time' of rereading as a generic ingredient; that is, the codes, conventions and participatory cues of the genre invoke processes of remaking, sequelling, alluding and cross-referencing to the extent that a linear narrative temporality is impossible. The notion of a 'real-life sequel' is not limited to the interactions of the copycat Ghostface with Sidney's past; rather, it is a concept that underscores the ways in which audiences participate with the horror genre, by repeat viewings, buying/wearing souvenirs, film discussions, and so on. Such discursive activity, the film suggests, effectively breaks the boundaries between reality and artifice.

It is significant in this regard that Ghostface's 'discursive activity' is conducted not only with a 9-inch blade, but through a telephone mouthpiece and voice-transmitter that, in *Scream 3*, imitates the voices of other people, suggesting Ghostface as never just one being, but many: a community of killers behind the insignia of the mask. Continually plaguing his victims with questions and film rhetoric, Ghostface is much more than a mask; s/he is an identity construed of multiple appropriations and by a distinct methodology of appropriation. Based on Edvard Munch's 1893 painting, *The Scream*, Ghostface is charged with the existential angst attributed to this artwork and, in addition, to the forms of imitation that surrounded its creation. Existing in several original versions and repeated across a welter of pop culture forms, *The Scream* has persistently seeped through the boundaries of its original contextualisation to find new modes of expression throughout its multiple replications. The original expression of Munch's painting adds another (culturally freighted) textual reference to the film's discussion of life imitating art. The circularity of repetitive forms deconstructs the authenticity of reality or, more exactly, is employed as a framework within which to consider the deconstruction of authenticity by technologies, genres of repetition and media intertextuality as an agent of artifice.

The repeated visualisation of *The Scream* in a reproductive context announces the duplicity of the Ghostface character, which is exploited as a signifier of the prevalence of reproduction and consumerism at the core of the horror genre. As the film's dominant source of 'inter-textual relay',[23] Ghostface embodies the notion of rereading a host of images, texts and genres, as well as their own networks of signifiers and discourses. In *Scream 2* s/he appears in the form of merchandise and on the promotional material for *Stab*; in *Scream 3* Ghostface is a massive film studio logo, and a studio room is shown to be filled with Ghostface costumes in which the 'real' Ghostface hides to claim another victim. Hiding here within his/her own iconography, Ghostface seemingly enacts the idea of the 'original' present with its own replications, remakes and sequels – except the Ghostface in *Scream 3* is in fact the fifth mask-wearer, yet another copycat killer who couches his own motives, moves and, above all, meaning within the discursive territory that Ghostface has come to represent.

That Ghostface is repeatedly appropriated by serial killers who clearly link their motives and meaning to 'the movies' suggests Ghostface as a specific method of spectatorial participation, or of acting out characters and plots from previous films as 'sequels' to a filmed source. *Scream 3* makes this connection crystal clear by figuring Ghostface as a 'real-life' movie director who is not only directing a remake of the events in *Scream 2* (titled, this time, *Stab 3: Return to Woodsboro*) but is also bent on creating a 'real-life rewrite' of the script by killing off the actors playing *Scream* characters. But, like *Scream 2*, this rewrite is shown to be a sequelised version of the script (which is, of course, a remake of 'real-life' events), as the targeted victims are secondary imitations of purportedly 'original' characters. Perhaps more significant is the construction of the spectator who, as a participant in the film's 'game', is now armed with an arsenal of genre codes and ordered (along with the surviving characters of *Scream* and their *Stab* performers) to learn the rudiments of a final chapter of a trilogy in order to figure out the trilogy's outcome and its generic organisation.

Yet the spectator's participation is not simply premised upon puzzle-solving; rather it is continuously reiterated as a necessary instalment in a much larger community of knowledge and discussion. Fuelled by such necessity, spectatorship is intensified as an integral part of the text's production, as a primary method by which its discourses are re-circulated, and – apparently – as a means by which representation is integrated with reality. It is this last involvement that seemingly implicates the spectator in a (massive) cultural debate of moral responsibility that is rooted in the contentious issue of the impact of films on social violence. This influence is underscored by a copycat tendency that – somewhat too conveniently – yokes a number of killing sprees to Hollywood. Notably, the original plot of *Scream 3* involved the killings of a new group of high school students, but when two teenagers went on a shooting spree at Columbine High School in Colorado in April 1999, resulting in fifteen deaths, the film-within-a-film plot was swiftly conjured as a replacement.

Sadly, Columbine was not an isolated incident. Between 1996 and 1999, thirteen shooting incidents had occurred in high schools throughout the US alone.

Following Columbine, seventeen further high school shootings occurred in the US between 2000 and 2005, and, as I write in April 2007, a 23-year-old student named Cho Seung-Hui has killed himself and thirty-two students at Virginia Polytechnic Institute and State University on yet another copycat shooting spree: so far, the worst act of gun violence in American history. Citing the Columbine killers as 'martyrs', Seung-Hui sent a 'multimedia manifesto' to the National Broadcasting Corporation (NBC) in between shootings, including video footage, a letter, and photographs of himself in various poses holding guns – all of which were released online and via news media within two days of the event. Having planned his own suicide all along, Seung-Hui intended the media manifesto as a post-mortem extension of his 'message'. Seung-Hui wanted his crime to be read and reread, shooting and splicing his video six days before the event as the 'lens' by which we gaze upon it.

And the media has bought into it. In a startling contradiction to the outcry in Columbine's aftermath against movie violence – such as then-President Bill Clinton's threat to introduce tougher restrictions on movie content, and George W. Bush's suggestion that cinema was responsible for 'pollut[ing] our children's minds' – media coverage of the Virginia Tech massacre has circulated Seung-Hui's video footage and photos for mass consumption.[24] Although the images are neither graphic nor gory – and definitely not Hollywood-produced – their content is definitively violent, with the express purpose of defining the massacre as a link in the chain of a larger terroristic discourse. In an attempt to connect the tragedy to Hollywood's horror output, an article in the *Daily Mail* bears the headline, 'Killer Made his own Horror Film for the YouTube Generation,'[25] and features images from Seung-Hui's NBC package alongside stills from Chan-wook Park's violent revenge-flick, *Oldboy* (2003) – all making the incredulous and opportunistic suggestion that, by holding a gun to his head and an axe in the air, Seung-Hui was acting out scenes from a horror movie. Two Hollywood productions – a film based 'on a true story', titled *Dark Matter* (Shi-Zheng Chen, 2007) and starring Meryl Streep, and a documentary, again 'based on a true story', titled *The Killer Within* (Macky Alston, 2007) – have been temporarily shelved because of their 'eerie' connection to the tragedy, just as the release of numerous films with resemblances to the events at Columbine was delayed in its wake. In all of these connections, both Columbine and Virginia Tech have been presented in the media as a muddled blend of reality and fantasy. This is due to the video footage directed by each of the shooters in relation to the crime they planned to commit and the media spectacle that erupted both times, along with what I would call 'communities of catharsis', such as massive web blogs and globally broadcasted video diaries of reaction and responses to the tragedies. There is no longer 'the event itself', but rather the discourses by which it is circulated and, regrettably, copied.

REMEDIATING GENRE

Wes Craven has described the discussion in *Scream 2* of the 'real-life sequel' as a reminder 'that before we start to be so heartily amused by some of these things, we should remember that, in a sense, we're talking about the suffering of real people'[26]: more out of respect, then, than moral responsibility – yet, as Craven goes on to observe, the responsibility does not fall entirely into Hollywood's hands. What the media furore surrounding Virginia Tech informs us of, however, is that this kind of interactive mediation effectively collapses the real and its representation, and is complicit with the perpetuation of discursive activity of a highly dangerous nature. By sending his filmed manifesto to the NBC, Seung-Hui directed the image or representation of the event, much like the murderers throughout the *Scream* trilogy who are shown to be 'actively involved in the reportorial representation of the events that they have set in motion'.[27] The experiential spectatorship constructed here is additionally a method by which the representation overturns the real. Gazing directly into the camera lens and telling the viewer that 'you raped my soul,' Seung-Hui's address is targeted not at any specific individual, but rather at the masses. Interestingly, one of the reasons behind the 1984 video recordings act which banned many horror films in Britain was that 'such films force the viewer to identify with the killer through subjective camerawork.'[28] Giving detailed access to Seung-Hui's motives, beliefs and intents, what else does his manifesto do but 'force the viewer to identify with the killer through subjective camerawork'?

In part a rereading of an earlier school shooting, Seung-Hui's manifesto – in tandem with the event itself – purposefully engulfs the 'real' in its representation and spectacle. The real is subsumed as spectacle, its representation simply its effect. As Slavoj Žižek tells it,

> [t]he authentic twentieth-century passion for penetrating the Real Thing (ultimately, the destructive Void) through the cobweb of semblances which constitute our reality thus culminates in the thrill of the Real as the ultimate 'effect', sought after from digitalised special effects, through reality TV and amateur photography, up to snuff movies.[29]

The power of the image in this case is such that it invades both public and private spaces of interpretation and spectatorial engagement, rendering the viewer complicit with the values and discourses it seeks to transmit. Inherent in Craven's depictions of a reality/fantasy dialectic and generic intertextuality is an address of 'real-life' tragedies of the sort played out by the Ghostface killers that, in turn, are not simply influenced by the movies, but which draw upon the relationship between screen and spectator, and particularly the dynamics of communal viewing, in order to achieve a goal or satisfy desire. The somewhat generic organisation of these real-life tragedies – that is, patterned after a specific list of codes, characters and outcomes – fuses the event with meaning, significance and 'effect', but not entirely in terms of accurate reportage; in its scramble to mediate, the media has turned the event into 'one great big movie'.

By touching upon the real-life implications of movie 'influence' and copycat discourses, *Scream*'s circularity of exchanges between art – or, in this case, the horror genre – and reality is offered as a form of sequelisation. The skewed and conflated temporalities presented in the opening scene of *Scream 2*, for instance, stage the discombobulated temporalities of the real and representation, which are comparable to the processes of remediation and revision inherent in sequelisation. Like Lev Manovich's description of 'the new media culture' as 'an infinite flat surface where individual texts are placed in no particular order',[30] the methods and technologies of 'the new media culture' presented in the *Scream* films and throughout the reportage of Columbine and Virginia Tech effectively sequelise discourse as a continuation, and not just a mediation, of the 'real'. When the 'rules' of the sequel are rehearsed in *Scream 2* as an apparent method of survival, or more exactly as a way to figure out who the killer intends to kill, what is actually being described is a discursive 'lens' by which to comprehend the 'real' world of the *Scream* characters, and by which to predict the future. The connection between these 'rules' and the media spectacle generated by and provided for the school shooters is that this framework is composed of fore-knowledge, identification of similar and repeated elements, and statistics that call attention to the unfortunate 'more'-ness of dominant generic features. This 'real', it seems, is just another re-presentation of a previous event.

Likewise, genre and sequelisation break down the idea of a source text's unequivocal originality, positing instead the notion that all texts exist in a spiralling chain of repeated discourse, iconography and interactivity. Whereas sequelisation is the process of circulation and repetition, genre is the discourse that is repeated and circulated. The difference between the two is made clear by the end of *Scream 3*, in which the link between the Ghostface killers is registered through reconsiderations of Maureen Prescott's murder. Operating as a connective undercurrent throughout the first two films, Maureen Prescott's murder is now foregrounded as a major part of the third film's plot. Fulfilling the same role as instructional-film-geek, Randy (Jamie Kennedy) (despite his death in *Scream 2*) makes an appearance in *Scream 3* via video footage filmed as an educational tool in the case of his death to tell us that, in the sequel to a sequel, or the final chapter of a trilogy, the original sequel rules do not apply. Instead, there are three new rules to follow: firstly, the killer is 'super human'; secondly, anyone including the main character can die; and, thirdly, as he puts it, 'whatever you think you know about the past, forget it. The past is not at rest.'

Sidney's mother functions in *Scream 3* as the tie that binds all three new rules and all three films together. Despite making only a single appearance across the trilogy as a ghostly figure of Sidney's nightmares, the late Maureen Prescott is resurrected as a contextualising figure in terms of the particularly familiar impact of the *Scream* murders on Sidney – reprising, as they do, her mother's death and Sidney's subsequent trauma – as well as the reason for Sidney's boyfriend's (Billy Loomis, played by Skeet Ulrich) descent into serial killing (cited as 'maternal abandonment', caused by his father's affair with Sidney's mother, for which he murdered her). In *Scream 2*, Loomis's mother (Laurie Metcalf) returns to seek vengeance for her son's death – and she does it by acting out the role of 'mother' to a surrogate, serial-killing son, Mickey (Timothy Olyphant). In the final chapter, Sidney's mother serves as context once more as it emerges that she slept with a director in a bid to become a film star (of horror movies, of course). As a result, Sidney's half-brother (Roman, played by Scott Foley) was born, who also happens to be the director of *Stab 3: Return to Woodsboro*. Shunned by Maureen (because she said he was the son of her screen persona, Rena Reynolds, not the 'real' Maureen Prescott), Roman seeks vengeance on the child that Maureen accepted (Sidney).

By the end of the trilogy, Maureen is presented as a figure of both sequeli-sation and genrification in the forms outlined above, in so far as she is able to 'reproduce' in the form of recurrent memories and nightmares, personas and serial-killing offspring. Having literally given birth to both Ghostface and his primary target, Sidney, Maureen sets up the repeated genre typicalities of the rejected abject subject and his intended victim. Because Maureen is not around to receive her punishment, Ghostface's revenge is transferred to her daughter – her sequel – Sidney. Originally figured as an innocent victim of murder, Maureen is 'rewritten' in *Scream 3* as a wildly promiscuous adulteress, whose excessive sexuality has resulted in excessive forms of reproduction that lead to not only the sequelisation of her memory but also the circumstances of her death. Killed by the 'original' Ghostface for her promiscuity, Maureen is figured as a procreational genre author who propagated the 'great big movie' in which Sidney finds herself.[31] This works on a number of levels. Citing the figuration of maternity in horror films of the past – Norman Bates's appropri-ation of his mother's identity in *Psycho* (Alfred Hitchcock, 1960); the repre-sentation of single mothers as 'catalysts for horror'[32]; abject maternity in *Aliens* (Ridley Scott, 1986)[33] – as well as their theorisation in college settings not unlike that of *Scream 2*, the film constructs Maureen as a genre characterisa-tion, an agent of intertextuality, and a subject of critical debate.

By announcing its own signification of a larger network of textual dis-course, the film further suggests each of these figurations of maternity as interconnected within the Maureen figure. In subversion of the horror movie rule of 'sex equals death' (cited by Randy in *Scream*, just as Sidney is losing her virginity), Maureen's sexuality is highlighted across all three films as subversive to idealised notions of maternity and as an almost axiomatic motive for her murder. The intertexual references and gestures to other horror portraits (the original Ghostface killer, Billy Loomis, is named after characters in *Psycho* and *Halloween*) suggest Maureen as a 'sequel' of sorts to each of these references which, fuelled by Randy's suggestion that the sequel promises 'more' of everything, construct her as a heightened figuration of monstrous maternity. By consciously depicting theoretical investigations of the abject horror mother, the film further flirts with Freudian notions of Maureen as a representation of 'primal scene phantasies' – Ghostface's phallic knife, for instance, as both a weapon of castration and a symbol of the origin of sexual desire; the recurrent memories and nightmares of Sidney's mother as a form of 'repetition-compulsion' by which the serial killings are triggered; Randy's suggestion that the only way to kill the killer is by decapitation is linked to castration, which, according to Freud, is 'linked to the sight of something'.[34]

The organisation of the film's presentations of maternity – or rather, its employment of generic discourses of maternity – suggests maternity in the horror movie as a source of the processes of genrification, sequelisation and film viewing which, through this common foundation, are shown to be interrelated. The idea that the various intertextual, generic and particularly theoretical strands of Maureen's figuration are 'linked to the sight of something' brings the spectator to the discursive table, implying that the act of spectatorship is involved in the figuration and operation of maternity. In particular, the mother's embodiment of genre conventions not only spells out the rules of the horror movie, but also uncovers the meaning and, purportedly, the function of genre. In her comparison of the etymological resemblances of the words 'genre' and 'gender', Mary Gerhart notes 'the categorical and the productive' roots of each, which pertain respectively to 'the meaning "of a kind or sort" ' and 'to the act of rooting, begetting, bearing, producing'.[35] As a figure attributed with the 'begetting' of the original Ghostface killer, his victim, and the re-enactment of her own murder across throngs of copycat killings, Maureen sources the root of the film's generic ties, which in turn is identified as a mode of sequelisation. The link between the two organises the *Scream* trilogy's operation within generic boundaries, at the same time as it makes clear the trilogy's reflexive engagement with those boundaries and its intention to perpetuate the discursive activity by which they are continually redrawn.

To this extent, the film's much-noted self-reflexivity operates as its own discourse, its own paratexuality. The ways in which Maureen facilitates discursive activity in the film – memories (Sidney's), imitative responses (copycat killings) and revision (discovering her alter ego and past life) – are reflective of the ways in which the film assembles its own methods of engagement. Gérard Genette's notion of paratextuality as textual marginalia (for example, movie posters, trailers, DVD extras) is apparent in *Scream*'s numerous instances of promotional material; citations of the rules of the horror movie, the sequel and the trilogy; movie trivia; the film-within-a-film plotline and its own paratextual activities; and a contest created by MTV and Miramax for an MTV viewer to win a part in *Scream 2*.[36] Furnishing the source text with a 'setting and sometimes a commentary', the paratext also moves the source text further and further away from its artificiality or, as Linda Hutcheon puts it, is 'the central material mode of textually certifying fact'.[37] *Stab*, for example, is purported to be 'based on a true story', thereby certifying *Scream* as fact. Despite the various forms of reportage internalised in the *Scream* trilogy – such as news footage, taped interviews, hidden cameras, photographs, and filmed legacies – our attention is drawn not to the persistent remediation of a fictional narrative but to the increasing presentation of fiction against what becomes, by way of comparison, fact.

Perhaps the most solid method by which processes of rereading come into play, the invention of paratextual associations across the trilogy is both a conformity to and announcement of generic paratextuality. As discussed earlier, examples of paratexts as promotion gimmicks or marketing material abound in the horror genre, such as *The Blair Witch Project*'s internet-based promotional campaign and 'mockumentary', aired by the Sci-Fi Channel, which featured fabricated interviews with friends and relatives of the missing students, paranormal experts and local historians; Craven's poster for *The Last House on the Left*; and *Scream*'s spin-off spoof franchise, *Scary Movie* (Keenen Ivory Wayans, 2000), which spawned a genre-spoof sub-genre, culminating in a long list of films such as *Date Movie* (Aaron Seltzer, 2006), *Epic Movie* (Jason Friedberg and Aaron Seltzer, 2007) and *Not Another Teen Movie* (Joel Gallen, 2002). But whether we identify such ancillary texts as paratexts, intertexts, or as what Umberto Eco calls 'extratextual quotations',[38] the relationship between a text and its surrounding texts is marked by the particularly discursive functions of the latter in both confirming and disseminating the factuality of the former.

By factuality, connotations of naturalism and knowledge also come to the fore. Genre acquires all three meanings through its relationships with associated texts. Defined by Robert Scholes as a 'network of codes that can be inferred from a related set of texts',[39] genre is not only inferred in *Scream* through its related paratexts but is identified as a mechanism by which fiction can become 'fact', or part of 'real-life' experience. Continually drawing attention to its generic artificiality and likening everything to the movies, *Scream* reworks the tragedies of real life – that, as I have shown, have contentiously and repeatedly been likened to horror films – as texts to which films like *Scream* operate as paratexts. This, the trilogy suggests, is part of the reason why the line between fact and fiction is so often disturbed, because 'fact' is being discussed and distorted through the codes and generic reconstructions of fiction. Condemned by the media as implicit in the perpetuation of these tragedies, the horror genre is reworked in *Scream* as an important artefact in the discursive activity surrounding real-life events. The horror movie is noted as a product of its own reception or, as the *Scream* trilogy indicates, is shown to be consistently redeveloped, rewritten and reread by the conditions of spectatorship. As the media spectacle surrounding the Virginia Tech massacre regrettably proves, these conditions are impacted upon not only by the various genre texts at the local cinema but by the 'real-life' texts on our TV screens of events that are mediated as horror movies.

Far beyond any other genre, the horror movie is continually invoked as a framework by which to understand real-life tragedies, as well as their causes. Despite Sidney's wish for her life to be 'a Meg Ryan movie', the generic framework of 'a Meg Ryan movie' (presumably a romantic comedy) is rarely cited as a cause or connection to lived experience. The horror movie, however, is cited and constructed as a means by which we can interpret the mediation of traumatic events. Writing in 1999, Rick Altman stresses that it is imperative that we 'recognise the extent to which genres appear to be initiated, stabilised and protected by a series of institutions essential to the very existence of genres'.[40] After 9/11 – the most mediatised tragedy in history – and the persistent imbrication of increasingly mediatised tragedies with the movies, it is fair to say that one of the major 'institutions' by which the horror genre has been 'stabilised and protected' is the mass media.

As I have suggested above, the ways in which media representations intersect with 'real life' can be understood as a process of sequelisation, in so far as these representations structure our engagement with the 'real' not simply as transferring knowledge, but in ways that underscore repetitious spectatorship and processes of rereading as integral elements of mediating and discussing real life. Although the relationship between genre and sequelisation has altered radically across cinema history, it would appear that this relationship is marked in recent years by explorations of spectatorship as a form of discursive activity. The specifically communal spectatorship that has become a generic element of the horror film relates to the 'communities of catharsis' created in the wake of real traumas, and more generally to growing online communities which – as evidenced by websites such as YouTube and MySpace – is a source of generative interactivity and consumption. Heightened by both repetition and interactivity, sequelisation is a vital part of the horror genre not only in terms of the scores of sequels that are continually produced to successful (and unsuccessful) horror productions, but by the forms of communal reception and spectatorial engagement that, in turn, operate to 'stabilise and protect' this genre.

CONCLUSIONS

I have deliberately focused my attention here on the horror genre in order to examine the ways in which the relationship between genre and sequelisation is played out and employed to serve specific ideological and industrial imperatives. Of course, the sequel has played and continues to play a variety of roles across each of the current film genres, as well as operating in broader generic contexts with similar and markedly different results, all of which calls for further analysis to that presented here. Common to all genres, however, is what James Naremore describes as 'a loose evolving system of arguments and readings, helping to shape commercial strategies and aesthetic ideologies'.[41] Whereas the recycling and development of this system is argued to be enabled by film parody[42] and likened to pastiche, both of these forms are similarly impacted upon by generic stabilisation and 'commercial strategies'. Neither, however, match the sequel's prioritisation of 'repetition and variation' as a primary method for genre development. That is to say, although parody and pastiche perceivably sustain and stabilise generic codes and conventions – and whilst genre itself, like the remake, is concerned with returning to and perpetuating an originating framework as a structure of origination – the sequel is the process by which 'return' can co-exist with continuation. In addition, sequelisation marks the process by which repetition – a generic dominant – is synthesised with variation, in so far as 'variations' of key generic elements are connected to genre's originating framework. Such variations are persistently read against previous generic instances as 'continuations' of genre codes and conventions, at the same time as they serve to repeat and stabilise generic imperatives through the logic of sequelisation. In short, the spectator of the genre film comprehends the co-existence of repetition and variation as well as the necessity of these as vital parts of the spectatorial experience by engaging, first and foremost, with the re-connective, interactive and remembering activities that underline the sequel.

NOTES

1. Neale, 'Questions of Genre', 56; Grant, 'Introduction', ix.
2. Budra and Schellenberg, 'Introduction', 17.
3. Pinedo, *Recreational Terror*, 71.
4. Dika, *Games of Terror*, 22.
5. Wee, 'Resurrecting and Updating the Teen Slasher', 52; Ndalianis, ' "Evil Will Walk Once More" '.
6. Clover, 'Her Body, Himself', 294.
7. See also Tudor, 'From Paranoia to Postmodernism? The Horror Movies in Late Modern Society'.

8. Quoted in Castle, 'Phantasmagoria and Modern Reverie', 30.
9. Kawin, *Telling It Again and Again*, 65.
10. Budra, 'Recurring Monsters', 190.
11. 'Sequelling' is Andrew Tudor's term. See Tudor, 'From Paranoia to Postmodernism?'.
12. Clover, *Men, Women, and Chainsaws*, 23.
13. Ressler, *Whoever Fights Monsters*, 45–7; see also Tithecott, *Of Men and Monsters*.
14. Ressler, *Whoever Fights Monsters*, 46; see also Jenkins, 'Catch Me Before I Kill More', 15.
15. Ressler, *Whoever Fights Monsters*, 46.
16. This caption formed part of the film's citation of the explicit realism of the violence depicted, which additionally sought to find ties with the violence and public trauma caused by Vietnam. For more on this, see Lowenstein, *Shocking Representation*, 111–143.
17. Andrew Tudor suggests 'the act of genre-recognition' as 'part of the process of making sense of the social world, a source of shared frameworks through which we come to understand, among other things, what is fearful and what it is to be frightened'. See Tudor, 'Why Horror? The Peculiar Pleasures of a Popular Genre', 48.
18. Budra, 'Recurring Monsters', 190; Sciretta, 'Craven Talks *Scream 4*'.
19. Seltzer, 'The Serial Killer as a Type of Person', 97.
20. Applebaum, 'Scare Stories'.
21. This goes as follows: Ghostface asks Casey who the original killer was in *Friday the 13th* (Sean S. Cunningham, 1980) and she answers Jason. Ghostface informs her that the original killer was Jason's mother, Mrs Voorhees, and that Jason didn't 'show up until the sequel'. Conversely, Ghostface's mother is one of the killers in *Scream 2*.
22. Barthes, *S/Z*, 16.
23. Lukow and Ricci, 'The "Audience" goes "Public"'.
24. http://news.bbc.co.uk/1/hi/world/americas/921219.stm
25. Harris, 'Killer Made his own Horror Film for the YouTube Generation'.
26. Applebaum, 'Scare Stories'.
27. Tietchen, 'Samples and Copycats'.
28. Whitehead, *Slasher Movies*, 9.
29. Žižek, *Welcome to the Desert of the Real*, 12.
30. Manovich, *The Language of New Media*, 77.
31. The phrase 'procreational genre author' is a paraphrase of Lucy Fischer's comment that 'if the genre audience is childlike, the genre author is procreative.' See Fischer, *Cinematernity*, 9.
32. See Lewis, '"*Mother Oh God Mother . . .*"'.
33. See Creed, *The Monstrous Feminine*.
34. See Freud, 'Medusa's Head', 273; see also Creed, *The Monstrous Feminine*, 110–11.
35. Gerhart, *Genre Choices*, 98.
36. Shapiro, 'On MTV, Studios Find No Such Thing as a Free Plug'.
37. Hutcheon, 'Postmodern Paratextuality and History', 304.
38. Eco, 'Innovation and Repetition', 23.
39. Scholes, *Textual Power*, 2.
40. Altman, *Film/Genre*, 85.
41. Naremore, 'American Film Noir: The History of an Idea', 14.
42. See also Harries, 'Film Parody and the Resuscitation of Genre', 281–93.

CHAPTER 3

'It's All Up To You!': Sequelisation and User-Generated Content

'Every year network TV loses more of its audience to hundreds of niche cable channels. Males age eighteen to thirty-four [are] shifting more and more of their screen time to the Internet and video games . . . the number one [TV] show today wouldn't have made the top ten in 1970.'

Chris Anderson, *The Long Tail*, 2

'The problem is choice.'

Neo in *Matrix Reloaded* (Larry and Andy Wachowski, 2003)

It is 20 July 2007. The last and, as its author promises, final book in the Harry Potter *series is due to hit bookstores at one minute past midnight tonight. A tsunami of 'Harry mania' is sweeping across the globe. It's unusual for me to read a novel, but I've read five of the* Harry Potter *books. I own DVD copies of the first four films and, just last week, was 'really lucky' to get the last two seats for a screening of the fifth film,* Harry Potter and the Order of the Phoenix *(David Yates, 2007). Supermarkets are overflowing with* Harry Potter *merchandise in the form of toys, clothes, games, collectibles and food. An MSNBC webpage titled '7 signs you're infected with* Harry Potter *fever' displays photos of one fan's limb-sized* Harry Potter *tattoos,[1] whilst online news videos gush about the forthcoming* Harry Potter *theme park – actually a theme park within a theme park – which is due to appear within Universal's* Islands of Adventure *theme park in 2009: the first completely immersive* Harry Potter*-themed environment. If immersion is to be understood in terms of impact, no need for the theme park.* Harry Potter *has saturated the planet, and unless I want to feel cut off from my friends and family for months to come, I'd best be in the queue at midnight tonight.*

This chapter looks at sequelisation as a method by which audiences are able to continue, interact with and re-experience a film. 'User-generated content' is now a chief mode of consumer activity, or the defining characteristic of technology's most prominent 'sequel', Web 2.0. As consumer choice expands, along with the gamut of interactive technologies, immersive environments, media crossovers, hypernarrative formats and consumer products, the sequel has begun to register the reception practices, paratexts and marketing strategies by which a film is continued, or rather exploded across multiple media platforms and consumer contexts. The idea of an 'original' commonly adheres to linear progression between texts. But in the digital era, or what could be called the age of connectivity, linearity is replaced by what Henry Jenkins has called 'spreadability', or a media text's ability to be circulated by fans throughout fan communities.[2] Says Jenkins: 'if it doesn't spread, it's dead.' Hollywood has picked up on this idea by producing a swathe of merchandise, endorsements, media intertexts, cultural events, gaming tie-ins, related websites, themed activities and cross-media marketing strategies surrounding contemporary Hollywood and international film productions. Many of these methods have been in existence for decades. From the creation of a serial comic tie-in to anticipate and accompany the release of Disney's *Snow White* in 1937 to the creation of a $100 million Bollywood theme park in 2008, cinema's history is marked by escalating developments in media convergence. The global, technological and cultural contexts within which film production increasingly operates have impacted the reception process to dramatic effect, and thus also the marketing, promotion and production processes. These processes stretch the film experience far into the distant horizon – or at least until the next film instalment. As Steve McBeth, vice-president of consumer products for Disney, puts it of Disney's McHappy Meal fluffy toy tie-ins: 'it's a way of letting the fun of the movie continue.'[3] But how exactly does the movie continue? What does continuation mean here, and why is it important?

Equally assigned with the task of deferring the end of a film, or at least deferring the end of the film experience, tie-ins and paratextual commodities essentially 'spread' content across a number of media contexts. In the case of *Harry Potter*, if film-going is not your thing, you can still cast spells on Harry Potter's enemies by playing the massively-multiplayer online role-playing game found at www.hogwartslive.com, or contact Harry Potter at his MySpace profile, or jump on the Knight Bus as it tours through various locations across the US.[4] And, of course, none of these media contexts simply repeats the original *Harry Potter* narrative. Their appeal lies directly in the creation of an access point into a story 'world', and in the construction of continuations of a narrative concept. But, perhaps more importantly, such transmedia storytelling efforts have generated unprecedented revenue and fan interest specifically because continuation is being given over to fan communities as a method of participation and interpretation. Although transnational media corporations still provide the context, consumers hold sway in the generation of content. Continuation is important because it supposedly empowers the consumer.

I have argued earlier in this book that a major source of complaint against film sequels is grounded in the interpretive imposition created by a 'part two' which extends, and usually ends, an 'original' narrative in a manner contrary to a fan's preferred ending/extension. Here I would like to consider this theory in a little more detail. A recent article describes this sense of dissatisfaction as 'a sequel too far', [5] indicating the narrative obscurities and 'unnecessary' endings that film sequels commonly propagate, whilst *MSN Movies* gives some helpful hints to filmmakers wishing to participate in a 'part 2-to-infinity tent-pole film', including ways to enrich the previous film with nuances, consistencies and improvements, and, again, a warning to know when (and how) to grind the whole thing to a halt. [6] The 'sense of an ending', as Harold Bloom put it, is clearly problematic in the concept of sequelisation. This is precisely due to the inherent relationship between the film sequel and the reception process. As social networking websites and methods of getting audiences to interact with both a film's multimedia outputs and each other continue on the up and up, the sequel's relationship with reception activity is becoming more and more defined by connectivity and user-generated content, to the extent that some broadband serials now include an invitation for fans to vote on the ending of each 'webisode'. More on that later.

Put briefly, twenty-first-century reception activity is collaborative and participatory in nature. As my comment above about feeling cut off from friends and family is designed to suggest, much of the motivation behind participating in a film or any of its related events or texts is shifting away from *critical* response to *connective* response. Any number of dedicated web blogs will attest that the film/concept in question serves as a point of discussion, interpretation and collaboration; it generates a community of continuation, its own force of viral marketing. Consider in this regard David R. Ellis's film *Snakes on a Plane* (2006), which achieved a substantial cult following well before its release date,[7] resulting in a welter of fan-generated paraphernalia, from websites and blogs to poems and songs. In response to these songs, the film's production company, New Line, joined forces with popular social networking website TagWorld.com to launch an online contest for fans to have their song included in the film's soundtrack.[8] A five-day re-shoot is also said to have been triggered by calls to include dialogue scripted by fans specifically for the film's star, Samuel L. Jackson.[9] Despite all its hype, however, *Snakes on a Plane* bombed at the box office. This suggests that, to communities of continuation, the 'original' is insignificant; in the age of connectivity, the mechanisms of collaboration and participation facilitated by any text, event or commodity are of utmost importance.

There are a number of reasons for this. 'Web 2.0' – a term made popular by IT guru Tom O'Reilly in 2004 – commonly refers to a form of second generation internet usage in which collaboration, social networking and blogging are the chief modes. A number of websites trade upon and contribute to this kind of web usage. In February 2005, YouTube was launched as a free-to-use 'premier destination to watch and share original videos worldwide through a Web experience',[10] and was one of the fastest growing websites by June 2005. The site now attracts upwards of 72 million individual visitors each month. Although YouTube has been joined by a growing number of social networking, broadcasting and photo/video-sharing sites, such as Facebook, Bebo, MySpace, Flickr and Revver, the collaborative and participatory activ-ities per-formed across such platforms are less about these specific technologies/'utili-ties' than they are about the larger transmedia experiences of which these sites form a part. Throughout a number of texts devoted to the study of such trans-media experiences prevails an overriding assumption that video games differ from other kinds of media in their provision of interactivity and agency. However, recent practices in film production and cross-media franchising indi-cate methods of engagement with film and other media as defined by exactly the sort of interactivity and agency that such texts identify within video gaming. In short, it is impossible and generally nonsensical to separate film pro-duction and consumption from the systems of convergence and electronic media that have consistently re-imagined the role of the consumer; hence my consideration of some productions in this chapter that are not films, but which otherwise engage the cinematic experience at an intermedial and spectatorial level.

My argument is that the methods by which continuation is celebrated and facilitated across multiple media platforms can be described as a form of sequelisation. This is specifically due to the spectatorial renegotiation of nar-rative spaces and trajectories made necessary by new industrial categories. Take media franchises, for instance – Tom Apperley observes these as enabling spectators 'to experience a sense that each product is a part of a wider medi-ated universe that is largely constructed in the minds of the audience through the process of assemblage of the disparate media'.[11] The concept of sequeli-sation seems to be invoked here in terms of the process of creating multime-dia narrative 'worlds' that both repeat and extend an 'original' concept in the formation of an immersive, transmedia narrative space. In exploration of this idea, I take as my case studies a variety of franchises and narrative 'worlds', including the first online video blog serial, YouTube's *lonelygirl15*, and its 'sequel', Bebo's *KateModern*, both hailed as bringing to the world 'a new (and quantifiably compelling) format for narrative motion pictures online'.[12] Throughout these video blogs, or 'vlogs', each of which is serialised online over a period of years, it is possible to witness the construction of exactly the kinds of narrative space or 'world' outlined above, but more important are the ways by which these are constructed. In his study of cross-media productions, Espen Aarseth discusses content transfer, or content migrations, from one medium to another, as dependent on certain factors, such as 'spectacle making' and a malleable narrative structure, and is most successful 'between forms that are alike'.[13] These factors, I argue, are to do with emergent developments in spectatorial activity and narrative continuation, and shed new light on sequeli-sation in its new media enterprises.

HYPERTEXTUALITY AND THE READER–TEXT DYNAMIC

The marketing events and merchandising activities by which fan communities are galvanised operate as extensions of the narrative concept, rendering every consumer activity as one that grants access to the narrative 'world'. Of the mid-night bookstore queues for *Harry Potter and the Deathly Hallows*, Frank Cottrell Boyce says that the books 'function like multiplex culture', insinuating that the integration of films into the production and consumption of the novels means that 'people [will] queue on the opening weekend, hunt for rumours, make up theories,'[14] and generally invest in the recontextualisation of movie marketing as a narrative technique. In other words, camping out at one's local bookstore for two nights to buy the latest literary instalment of a successful franchise can be seen as correspondent to an immersive transmedia storytelling experience.

With such intimacy being generated between film narratology, intermedial-ity and consumerism, it is perceivable that contemporary understandings of each must assume the presence of one in the other. A primary impact of the immersive and narrative nature of movie marketing strategies is the integra-tion with marketing and merchandising within the film narrative: like the merchandise-themed sequel *Toy Story 2* (John Lasseter *et al.*, 1999), in which most of the characters are movie merchandise, or, famously, *Jurassic Park* (Steven Spielberg, 1993), in which the corporate space of Hollywood market-ing – and, in a self-reflexive gesture, the film's own merchandise – is stalked by man-eating dinosaurs. In each case, the co-existence of movie merchandising and the film's narrative form a vital part of the overall experience.

Likewise, the storytelling mechanisms of marketing and merchandise are increasingly integrated with the formal structure of many films. Take, for instance, the website for Lacuna Inc. (www.lacunainc.com), the fictional memory-erasing company featured in *Eternal Sunshine of the Spotless Mind* (Michel Gondry, 2004). Released a year before the film and incorporated into the film's cinema trailer, the website stages the Lacuna company as a 'real' entity with which the film's spectators can engage and – like the film's charac-ters – erase unwanted memories. As memories are presented in the film as nar-ratives of the past, what Lacuna commodifies is a new personal narrative without the bad bits. Concomitant with the dilemma presented in *Eternal*

Sunshine of the Spotless Mind between what is 'real' and what is remembered, the website operates according to paratextuality's fact/fiction dichotomy, as explored in Chapter 2. By including photographs of fictional satisfied Lacuna customers, testimonials, sound-bites ('"I got my confidence back!" [Edward from New York]'), several polls, an online contact page, a commercial, cut-out coupons, register-for-updates links, and a 'friendly postcard' one can send to friends and family to advertise the company, the website is a send-up of other websites such as WeightWatchers.com and Slimfast.com, which sell personal 'narratives' to consumers, promising the close of one life chapter and the beginning of 'a new slimmer you'.

The range of links included in the Lacuna website is a fitting context through which to approach the film's narrative structure, which is composed of a network of narratives, and predominantly two narrative threads that inter-twine: the remembered past and memories that are re-enacted in the present. Both the structure of *Eternal Sunshine of the Spotless Mind* and that of the website are presented as essentially hypertextual, narratological and collabora-tive. The film's protagonist re-enacts the past as his 'erased' memories are con-jured up by a chance encounter with the ex-love he previously erased; so too is the film's spectator invited to participate in a collaborative remembering/ forgetting scenario, in which their recounted 'stories' as potential Lacuna cus-tomers are invited. George Landow describes hypertextuality as a 'decentred' reading experience wherein any text acts as an origin from which a textual network may be accessed, and by which the reader 'transforms any document that has more than one link into a transient center'.[15] Like memory, then, *Eternal Sunshine of the Spotless Mind* presents the idea that any memory can act as an access point to the mnemonic 'network'. The hypertextuality of both website and film is thus congruent with the hypertextual nature of memory. But in each case, consumerism is the context in which hypertextuality is played out and understood. The same storytelling techniques which underline memory, Lacunainc.com and indeed the film are employed to 'sell' the film's concept throughout the website. Containing concealed links to various promo-tional paraphernalia for the film (such as a link to 'experience the procedure', which takes the viewer to another browser with links to purchase the DVD), the website acts as a hypertextual 'link' in a larger hypertextual framework within which the otherwise separate entites of film narrative, marketing and memory are conjoined to form an immersive narrative experience.

In *Eternal Sunshine of the Spotless Mind*, as well as immersive environments such as Disneyland that offer the physical 'experience' of the film, 'reading' becomes a form of participation, whilst the 'text', or narrative concept, is made available as a fluid and collaborative entity. The hypertextual structure of the internet is a ready example. Here users can contribute prolifically and without substantiation, creating links ad infinitum to any piece of online text. Naturally, a variety of new storytelling mechanisms have been generated online. For example, Rob Wittig's online serial novel *Blue Company* (2001–2) delivered instalments to subscribing readers via email. Of note is the impact of subscribers' emails on the direction and style of the novel. One of Wittig's subscribers, Scott Rettburg, created a sequel in the form of *Kind of Blue* (2002), and in turn admits to drawing upon emails from subscribers:

> The writing style of one character . . . was informed by the style of Larry McCaffery's emails. In particular messages, I may have been trying to amuse Nick or William, or have imagined how Shelley might respond to a certain kind of note.[16]

With strong overtones of the Barthesian concept of 'author-as-destination', or indeed Landow's notion of the 'reader-author',[17] the audience/reader plays an important part in the text's direction and composition.

Other texts are not simply influenced by their readers, but incorporate the reading experience (and the readers themselves) actively into the narrative. *OnlineCaroline.com*, Rob Bevan and Tim Wright's award-winning twenty-four-part online serial drama, features a fictional twenty-something protagonist named Caroline with her own weight issues and romance dramas, but the narrative centralises the relationship that is generated between Caroline and her readers/subscribers, who receive the narrative in email instalments, watch Caroline's webcam and read her online diary. Subscribers must fill in personal details and answer questions, all of which are stored in a database and used to generate an 'online friendship' with Caroline. This personalised reading experience seems not only to integrate the reader into the narrative, but also to turn the tables on the reader/text dynamic until the 'real' narrative appears to be the actual lived experiences of the reader. Cataloguing the subscriber's activities within the website, Caroline's responses betray an almost voyeuristic interest in the individual reader. Having clicked randomly on a button marked 'Unlucky' on the website beneath a header 'What kind of person are you?', I later received an email from Caroline with the comment, 'You said you were an unlucky person. Sounds intriguing.' This was followed by a couple of postscripts with similar comments on my browsing activities:

> p.s. What?! No pressies from [the] 'Send Me Things' [link]?
> p.p.s. Glad you didn't hit the 'Dump Me' button straight away. Nice to know it's there, though, huh? A couple of clicks and I'm out of your life forever. If only it was always that simple.

What these comments indicate is that the reader becomes read by the 'text'. It is by this method that the text never ends, but is transferred into the realm of lived experience, into the reader's experience. Continuation is a result of the shift of dynamics that occurs between text and reader. The reader no longer simply reads, nor provides the content; he or she instead becomes the content within the context of the narrative.

Each of these notions – hypertextuality and the deconstruction of the reader-text relationship – are present in contemporary conceptualisations of the film sequel. Within the ever-expanding interactive environments offered by the internet, 'pervasive play'[18] arenas and fan communities, sequelisation no longer refers solely to film production but also to a methodology of fan consumption, or of turning the fan and all fan activities into a 'text' that is 'read' by the narrative concept to which fans respond. By expanding the notion of narrative into a concept that spills across various media contexts and reception practices, sequelisation can be understood as the mode of transition from one platform to another, or the specific method by which a spectator gains access to the network of narrative generated by a multimedia concept, and, more importantly, plays a part in the continuation and expansion of that network. The consumer thus understands and engages with the media crossovers of any given narrative concept in terms of the sequel's mechanisms of response, memory and repetition. Sequelisation is the key by which 'reading' becomes a much more responsive, interactive and empowering activity.

LONELY GIRLS AND CONSUMER INTERACTIVITY

This conceptualisation of the sequel is the organising principle of *lonelygirl15* and its sequel, *KateModern*. *KateModern*'s status as 'sequel' is understood in this regard as another narratological access point or platform by which the 'world' created by *lonelygirl15* can be entered. More importantly, both ventures are driven by the forces of sequelisation in terms of their use of audience response. Departing from both the success and the general plotline of *lonelygirl15*, *KateModern* tapped into the (as yet unrealised)[19] lucrative potential of its predecessor through the channels of product placement, and to an extent the series functions as one long advertisement for a number of consumer products. Yet, as I go on to show, the marketing logic of *KateModern* is composed as a necessary part of the series' interpretation, participation and overall narrative structure. In both cases, the concept of 'original' is never far from the notion of the sequel, leading to a little confusion. What is the 'text' or the original narrative: *lonelygirl15* or the commentaries surrounding it? Are both *KateModern* and *lonelygirl15* sequels to their own discourse? What does this indicate for the way film sequels are produced and consumed in the interactive multiverse?

Starring a 16-year-old girl named Bree from an unknown location in the US, *lonelygirl15* commenced on 24 May 2006 with a 41-second video titled

'Paytotheorderofofof vs. Dinosaur', an animation of dinosaurs stomping on and eating a house, including text inserts, a music track ('Mad World' by Gary Jules from the *Donnie Darko* [Richard Kelly, 2002] soundtrack), and shout-outs to popular YouTubers (such as 'thewinekone', 'disappearance', 'utubeterrorist', 'filthywhore', 'kaiserro11', 'brookers' and 'screamo'). The instant popularity of *lonelygirl15* was due to its self-reflexive continuation of a previous vlog series by *paytotheorderofofof*, a popular teenage YouTuber who had tired of the negative attention focused on her by other users, and who had signed off from her last vlog with a comment about dinosaurs eating her house. *lonelygirl15* tapped into the fanbase and cult status of *paytotheorderofofof* by offering a 'sequel' to this vlog series – which notably returned much later in sequel form as *paytotheorderofofof2* – and by a number of carefully crafted intertextual links to many 'texts' at large in the popular consciousness, all of which generated meaning by pulling together a number of genres and context-specific references. For example, the 'Mad World' track, massively popular in its own right and a cover version of an original track by the band Tears for Fears, has been described by its co-writer as 'a voyeur's song . . . looking out at a mad world from the eyes of a teenager'.[20] Considered *Donnie Darko*'s theme tune, 'Mad World' fittingly translated the 'madness' depicted in the film, which portrays a teenage boy suffering from delusions about the end of the world, and ultimately his own death: a fitting reference point for what was to become, throughout *lonelygirl15*'s lifespan, a portrait of teenage angst within the greater territory of religious ceremonies, cult killings and Bree's eventual death.

Three months after the launch of 'Paytotheorderofofof vs. Dinosaur' and some several million views later, suspicious fans 'outed' 'Bree' as a fictional character created by two independent filmmakers, Miles Beckett and Ramesh Flinders, and performed by 19-year-old Jessica Rose, an actress from New Zealand. This discovery did not stop the success of *lonelygirl15* in its tracks, as its creators feared. Rather, the show gained worldwide publicity. Bree appeared on the Jay Leno show and on the cover of *Wired* magazine, and a gamut of new fans tapped into the YouTube serials, apparently prepared to participate in a virtual reality scenario that some had believed would only work if actually 'real'. Not so. As of August 2007, 'Bree' still receives some 500 emails a day.

Whereas Hollywood executives typically budget around $100 million to market a film, the creators of *lonelygirl15* tapped into the structure of the sequel, in so far as the series departed from and re-interpreted a previous work, is structured according to progressive episodes, and both draws upon and incorporates reception activity into its framework. The result? An audience and fan-following that would translate into hundreds of millions of dollars at the Hollywood box office. What *lonelygirl15* has in fact translated into is a number of user-generated sequels that depart from the particular hypertextual method of storytelling popularised by *lonelygirl15* (and, no doubt, from the popularity of their predecessor) to compose a narrative that is essentially driven and defined by interactivity.

Thus *lonelygirl15* continued its reflexive portraits of online voyeurism as championed by YouTube and increased its popularity by finding new ways of continuing and referencing previous online 'texts'. Notably, this tendency for referencing was a tactic from the beginning when Bree's fictionality was still secret – mostly because she had not yet been cast, and would not appear until the third video instalment. The second 'webisode' of *lonelygirl15*, titled 'YouTubers Secret Language', is composed completely of clips from popular YouTube vlogs with textual commentaries at the bottom of the frame, beginning with the question 'Do YouTubers have a secret language?' and ending with 'Or maybe they were saying something else? What do you think?' The invitation for feedback proved successful – YouTubers posted responses to which *lonelygirl15* carefully responded, with comments like 'Wow, you're developing a YouTube philosophy. Ambitious! Can we call it Tubeism? :)' and 'I have a new video, hope you all like it.:)'.[21]

This comments-response mechanism built up intense fan anticipation and, when Bree made her first appearance with 'First Blog/Dorkiness Prevails' on 16 June 2006, ratings increased rapidly. A flurry of responses ensued, including several video responses, such as 'Crazy Girl' by a user named *jesmo*, which used the same soundtrack ('More than Words' by Frankie J) and featured a teenage girl trying out the same face-pulling exercises performed by Bree at the end of the previous vlog.[22] Viewed over 4,000 times, *jesmo*'s response was part of a growing network of responses and fan discussion circulating around *lonelygirl15*. Like the first webisode, Bree's first vlog referenced a vlog by popular YouTuber thewinekone, titled 'Hotness Prevails/ Worst Video Ever'. Bombarded by questions and responses, *lonelygirl15*'s third vlog (and fifth webisode), 'School Work in Summer . . . BLECHH!!!', saw Bree laying flat the 'facts': namely, that she was homeschooled, that her parents were religious, and that a guy called Daniel edited her vlogs. These three snippets of information tantalised Bree's audience (the next instalment begins 'A lot of you have been asking me who Daniel is . . .') and laid the foundation for the major strands of the *lonelygirl15* narrative.

Still continuing and increasing in popularity despite Bree's 'death' in August 2007 – Bree was voted No. 1 'Web celeb' of the year by *Forbes* magazine and won VH1's 'Big Web Hit of the Year' – *lonelygirl15* has yet to make any money. Thus, its creators brokered a deal with UK-based social networking website Bebo for what media reports referred to as a 'sequel', 'sister series' and 'spinoff', *KateModern*: another vlog series about a British teenage girl who is linked to and continues the 'world' of *lonelygirl15* via her connection to an ominous cult, the 'Hymn of One'. As *lonelygirl15* developed, the apparently innocuous world inhabited by Bree was revealed to be that of a secret order. Carefully structured plot points – such as Bree's secret 'ceremony' – and elements of the *mise-en-scène* – such as the plaster on Bree's arm in episode thirty-three, suggesting a blood test – reappear in *KateModern*, as Kate (Alexandra Weaver) is shown to have a rare blood type for which ominous members of the Hymn of One, who purportedly killed Bree, also appear to be hunting her.

Unlike *lonelygirl15*, *KateModern* received financial backing from a catalogue of corporations such as Orange, MSN and Paramount Pictures, who paid around £250,000 each for product placements that would be used, as far as possible, to support and generate the narrative. Tampax®, a tampon company, is featured and used to support the plot of episode forty-seven, in which Charlie (Tara Rushton) reveals her relationship with Gavin (Ralf Little) and admits to having had a pregnancy scare, gesturing to a box of Tampax in relief. In its promotion of the Paramount film *Disturbia* (D. J. Caruso, 2007), the series featured an episode showing Gavin winning tickets to see the film on its opening night, Kate, Charlie, Tariq (Tai Rajani) and Gavin going to see and coming out of the screening ('That film was amazing!'), and an episode (forty-nine) in which Kate discovers she is being watched in a manner similar to the narrative of *Disturbia*:

> Kate: 'You know when you let a really good movie get into your head? Well, *Disturbia* scared the hell out of me. It was a really cool movie, but I think I let a little bit too much of it get into my head'.

A teenage cover version of *Rear Window* (Alfred Hitchcock, 1954), *Disturbia* is about a teenage boy who spends his time spying on his neighbours, witnesses a murder, and finds himself the subject of voyeuristic scrutiny by a serial killer. He also appears as a friend on Kate's Bebo profile under his character name 'Kale Brecht'. Far from informing several *KateModern* episodes by way of mere product placement, *Disturbia* operates as a highly suggestive intertextual relative in more ways than one. Whilst the narrative of *Disturbia* resonates with the voyeuristic overtones of *KateModern*, the list of pop culture references that are paraded throughout *Disturbia*, amongst them *The Shining* (Stanley Kubrick, 1980), *Full Metal Jacket* (Stanley Kubrick, 1987), *The Shawshank Redemption* (Frank Darabont, 1994), and video games such as *Underground 2* and *Ghost Recon Advanced Warfighter* – both sequels, is at once suggestive of the film's generic hybridity (thriller-slash-teen-flick) and the technological and demographic contexts within which it seeks to correspond. *Disturbia* acknowledges the fact that it is speaking directly to the Web 2.0 generation, whose understanding of voyeuristic activity stretches far beyond that of a man with a pair of binoculars. Simply put, *Disturbia* does not just feature in *KateModern* as another product placement. Rather, *KateModern* features in *Disturbia* as another reference point for the emerging activities, lifestyles and reception practices brought about by technological and cultural changes in the twenty-first century.

THE CELEBRITY FAN

The forms of participation and reception practices exploited by both *lonelygirl15* and *KateModern* have been claimed by its creators as 'the birth of a new art form', or more exactly a type of 'storytelling where the line between "fan" and "star" has been removed'.[23] The removal of such a 'line', the creators suggest, is not so much about diminishing celebrity, but about celebritising the fan; the fan's experience, participation, ideas and opinions are now the 'star'. The ways in which the fan can become the 'star' are outlined on the *lonelygirl15* message forum. Here viewers are called upon by the creators to 'join us in the continuing story of *lonelygirl15*' by creating their own story, by making parodies or videos in response, by using the online forum to chat to other fans about characters and leave comments for the characters at the character interaction section of the forum, and by '[creating] your own characters and storylines within the Breeniverse'.[24] Consistently appealing to its audience to become fans of *KateModern* and active participants in the narrative, Kate's Bebo profile provides content for users to 'play' with, comment on and add to, such as a photo album bearing the description 'Please decode this!', 'Who IS this?' and 'Help Kate!'[25] The profile is maintained by 'super-fan' Sophie, who repeatedly informs viewers 'we've got to help Kate!', and who organised an offline fan activity based on one of the photo albums, during which fans were told to meet up at a specific location in London to solve the 'riddle' of several pictures left on Kate's mobile phone, which was subsequently filmed as episode thirty-one, and which generated another piece of the narrative puzzle – a clear attempt at turning the *KateModern* narrative into a kind of online game.

By offering the fan experience as involving much more writing of the text than reading it, the creators went on to suggest the (questionable, and as yet unrealised) lucrative possibilities of this kind of fandom: 'We hope that you will . . . help us usher in an era of interactive storytelling where . . . dedicated fans like yourselves are paid for their efforts.'[26] Wishful thinking. But fandom is clearly marked as achieving a variety of consumer desires and, more importantly, as enabling the circulation, expansion and continuation of the 'original' narrative concept. A primary example of the value of fandom is demonstrated by the 'stars' of both *lonelygirl15* and *KateModern* – Bree and Kate – who are defined across each series as fans. This includes, for instance, Bree's admiration for *paytotheorderofofof* and other YouTubers; Charlie's fan moment when she bumps into Jamie Bell, the star of *Hallam Foe* (David Mackenzie, 2007); Kate's 'shout-out' to *lonelygirl15* fan LaurinB in episode 2 in response to Laurin's comments on the first episode; and of course the cast of *KateModern*'s awestruck turnout at the London première of *Disturbia*. In both cases the deconstruction of 'fan' and 'star' is an important narrative device, in that the entire narrative framework is reconceived as organised by 'fans', who are also re-identified most intimately as 'friends'. In episode seventeen, for example, Kate asks rhetorically, 'Are my parents right? Should we avoid speaking to strangers or are they just friends we haven't met yet?'[27] At the end of episode ten, she tells the viewer(s) 'thank you for being my friends', before kissing the screen and signing off. The 'poaching' activity of fans previously outlined by Jenkins is not only championed here, but commodified.

The line that has been removed between 'fan' and 'star' can be rethought in terms of a line removal between reading and writing a text, in so far as the fan becomes the star of a narrative 'world'. A concept home to hypertext theory, one thinks here of Gunnar Liestøl's comment (of hypertext fiction) that 'the reader not only recreates narratives but creates and invents new ones not even conceived of by the primary author.'[28] A host of platforms, texts and environments beyond those listed previously mirror this idea. Consider this statement found at *ItsAllInYourHands.com*, an online video channel for series such as the Emmy award-winning thriller *Satacracy 88* and *[blankslate]*:

> At *ItsAllInYourHands.com* we are vigorously pushing at the boundaries of internet story-telling. In the future, we will continue to find and invent new kinds of interactivity and offer our audience even more ways to control the direction of their favorite shows. Your opinion powers this machine and builds the stories and ideas of tomorrow. It's for you. It's from you. It's all in your hands.[29]

ItsAllInYourHands.com offers audience control in the form of end-of-episode votes that are used to generate the direction of the series. But where *ItsAllInYourHands.com* differs from *lonelygirl15* and *KateModern* is in the specific methods by which fans are invited to participate; at *ItsAllInYourHands.com*, the narrative trajectory is decided by fan consensus. In *lonelygirl15* and *KateModern*, collaboration, not consensus, is key. The reader/fan also taps into the celebrity/broadcasting culture championed by YouTube – and demonstrated by the *lonelygirl15* phenomena – thereby turning the fan into a celebrity, whether by writing a comment on Kate's Bebo profile (which creates a link to the fan's Bebo profile which Bebo users anywhere in the world can visit, unless the user restricts his/her visibility to friends), by submitting a video response to *lonelygirl15*, by getting a 'shout-out' from either Kate or Bree, or by participating in online forums.

Why should either series seek to make stars out of its audiences? Surely this would diminish the importance of its own stars and, perhaps, the authority, legitimacy or 'reality' of the series? On the contrary; by encouraging and facilitating almost unprecedented audience involvement, *lonelygirl15* and *KateModern* achieve exactly the kinds of continuation and circulation noted earlier in this chapter that, as the sequel proves, are most lucrative and important to the success of media production. Unlike *ItsAllInYourHands.com*, neither *lonelygirl15* nor *KateModern* operates as hypertext, though both operate within hypertextual environments. Rather, they are analogous to what Matt Hills describes as a 'hyperdiegesis', a 'vast and detailed narrative space' in which 'only a fraction . . . is ever directly seen or encountered' within a given text, 'but which nevertheless appears to operate according to principles of internal logic and extension'.[30] In both cases, every space within which the series operates or to which it refers is transformed by an 'internal logic' as part of its own larger diegetic framework. Content is crucial to its 'extension' and expansion, but this content is always recontextualised within the hyperdiegesis. Thus the 'new' narratives referred to in Liestøl's comment about hypertext fiction are apparent, but they always function within carefully prescribed parameters. Like the 'content' or information that I provided as part of my subscription to OnlineCaroline.com, it does not change a thing about the story, but rather is used to expand the 'world' of the hyperdiegesis.

The process by which the 'reader' becomes the 'text' – and is therefore 'read' by the larger textual network in which s/he participates – is a process of sequelisation. This is, first and foremost, due to the commerical mechanisms put into play by which the text responds to and continues its own reception. Always looking back at both the 'original' work and its reception – whether this reception is measured in box-office units, gags that got the most laughs, characters most audiences preferred, or otherwise – the sequel is essentially a performance of response. That is not to say that it follows the narrative continuation or pathway that every audience member desires or finds satisfactory, but rather it performs the acts of remembering, rereading and reinterpreting a previous text, showing how these acts can and do produce what can be argued to be 'new' narratives. The sequel expands and extends the diegesis of the previous text by generating new content, but is essentially a site of interactivity and participation between the text and its reception.

The sequel is, as Thomas Elsaesser puts it, 'not an end in itself, but rather the transitional form, the temporary state whereby a whole series of socio-economic processes and textual practices are put in motion'.[31] Viewed another way, sequelisation is about transition, or transmission, rather than any kind of ending. It suggests a continually expanding hyperdiegesis with which consumers or spectators can engage as many times in as many ways as possible. The range of merchandise, marketing strategies and reception practices gestured to above is also sold on the express basis of their 'sequelising' properties. A similar logic applies to multimedia platforms and film tie-ins. Note the language used to market *The Official Harry Potter Website*, which, it tells us, 'offers content, games and activities which seamlessly *extend the magical world of Harry Potter* beyond the big screen' (my emphasis).[32] *The Matrix Online* offers 'a continuation of *The Matrix* stories. When the third movie comes to an end, *The Matrix*

Online literally picks it up from that moment and goes forward with it.'[33] Continuation is prioritised here in tandem with the notion of creating or participating in a narrative 'world' within which one may interact with, as the *Pirates of the Caribbean* Massively-Multiplayer Mobile Game states, 'thousands of other players.'[34] The complicity of continuation with collaboration is a prerequisite for the creation of narrative 'worlds'.

But it is at this point that the empowerment or agency of the consumer is challenged. Marie-Laure Ryan claims that 'one of the properties that contribute to the intrinsic *tellability* of a story . . . is the diversification of possible worlds in the narrative universe' (her emphasis).[35] This 'diversification' is a primary principle of immersive arenas; within immersive arenas the consumer does have plenty of choice, but this choice is always carefully controlled and defined by distinct boundaries. The main method by which choice is controlled lies in the repetitious circularity of narrative 'worlds', which circulate and recycle a narrative across multiple plot possibilities, characters/avatars, intertexts and discourses. Fan activity within these environments is therefore always repetitious and geared towards re-circulating the 'original'. Interactivity, already disputed by many media theorists,[36] can be seen to occur between fans far more dynamically than it occurs between fans and the 'original'. In this regard, Jane McGonigal's studies of 'pervasive play' and 'immersive gaming' reveal much about the kinds of fan activity prescribed by media entertainment producers. McGonigal's study makes two points that prove relevant here: that both forms of game play operate to extend the gaming experience, and that they do this precisely by pervading all areas of reality, revealing 'game patterns in non-game places' and thus continual 'opportunities for interaction and intervention'.[37] This kind of pervasion occurs in the creation and continuation of narrative 'worlds'. Fans create and continue narrative discourse across formats and modalities that are not always already prescribed. Just as Hills observes that 'fans are always already consumers,'[38] so too is it important to remember that sequelisation as a form of fan activity is not disengaged from its industrial contexts. This is not to claim passivity as a dominant component of consumption, but rather to make aware the starkly and deliberately 'pervasive' reading, rewriting and continuing practices that are generated by commercial bodies.

Connective response is not entirely about the amalgamation of reading, writing and continuing an 'original' text; nor is it strictly about the ways in which a 'fan' may be translated as a 'star' or part of a narrative environment. Rather, it is about the means by which a narrative provides a means of community building and collaboration, and it is for this reason that continuation is important. I have mentioned that, of course, continuation empowers the consumer, and is therefore an important element of any business model for successful film production. But in terms of the kinds of sequelisation that take place in the form of reception activities, whether as family discussions about the ending of the latest *Harry Potter* book or 'what the Matrix is', or in the form of dressing up as Captain Jack Sparrow from *Pirates of the Caribbean* (Gore Verbinski, 2003) for a themed party, there occurs a narrative discourse that is, as the sequel suggests, repetitious and continuing in nature, and which empowers the consumer precisely because the interpretive imposition traditionally created by film sequels is given over, in part, to fans. And although I have demonstrated that the 'writing' activities of fans rarely impact the narrative to any extent greater than simply adding another potential trajectory to the narrative network, it is the narrational capabilities offered by multimedia platforms and immersive environments that can be perceived as a source of fan empowerment, and as a facilitator of endless consumer agency. As agents of narration, fans are able to create narrative entry points, cues for participation, and methods of deferring and preventing any sense of an ending from ever occuring.

CONCLUSIONS

With talk of more *lonelygirl15* and *KateModern* sequels on the horizon,[39] it appears that further inroads have been made by such emergent forms of sequelisation on the independent film market. While sequels have certainly occupied this market in the past – most prominently, Peter Jackson's *Lord of the Rings* trilogy (2001, 2002, 2003) – the specific uses of sequelisation across the productions explored throughout this chapter, as well as the possibilities offered to independent filmmakers by emergent technologies such as the webcam and mobile phone-cam, perceivably redefine the sequel as a much more interactive and experimental format to filmmakers than ever before. Quite a far cry from their original intentions to get a break in filmmaking, the *lonelygirl15* and *KateModern* creators are now 'pushing at the boundaries' of online filmmaking and 'networked storytelling', and have contributed to an escalating debate over controversial copyright issues surrounding 'fanfic'.[40] Situated within the larger media environment of user-generated content contests for TV pilots and,[41] as the recent agreement by British rock band Radiohead heralds, fans deciding how much they want to pay for a music album,[42] the emphasis on and developments of user-generated content mark the sequel as territory for vigorous collaboration and participation with all aspects of transmedia culture, and suggest emergent modes of narration and spectatorship. It is quite possible – though it remains to be seen – that the employment of the sequel in these contexts will re-imagine the commercial imperatives of sequelisation as liberating, rather than narrowing, the creative, personal, and interactive elements of film production.

NOTES

1. http://www.msnbc.msn.com/id/19838658/
2. http://www.henryjenkins.org/2007/04/slash_me_mash_me_but_please_sp.html
3. Twitchell, *Carnival Culture*, 142.
4. www.myspace.com/harrypotter; http://www.scholastic.com/harrypotter/events/tour.htm
5. http://www.brightlightsfilm.com/52/sequel.htm
6. http://movies.msn.com/movies/article.aspx?news=153381&mpc=2
7. The reasons for this are up for debate. There is an argument that the film's no-nonsense, clear-as-crystal title posted on the New Line Cinema website triggered some early responses, whilst Henry Jenkins has devoted a blog entry to speculating why the film gained such hype. Amongst his reasons Jenkins lists 'grassroots intermediaries', 'niche consumption', and a film company that closely monitored fan response See Jenkins, 'The *Snakes on a Plane* Phenomenon'.
8. 'Online Fan Sites, Songs Inspire *Snakes on a Plane* Reshoots'.
9. http://defamer.com/hollywood/snakes-on-a-plane/snakes-on-a-plane-the-reshoots-162510.php
10. http://www.youtube.com/t/about
11. Apperley, 'Getting Stuck on Level One'.
12. West, 'Lonelygirl15 Creators Announce Spinoff'.
13. Aarseth, 'The Culture and Business of Cross-Media Productions', 210.
14. http://arts.independent.co.uk/books/reviews/article2806620.ece
15. Landow, *Hypertext*, 11–13.
16. http://tracearchive.ntu.ac.uk/frame/index.cfm?article=77
17. Landow, *Hypertext*, 117.
18. McGonigal, 'A Real Little Game'.
19. *Lonelygirl15* was funded from the outset by its creators; a business model did not exist to generate income. However, before the end of season 1 the creators came up with the idea of a sponsored character, Spencer Gilman, a new friend for the *lonelygirl15* characters, who was sponsored by Neutrogena; his character was a scientist who worked for the company.
20. Edgers, 'Out of the Realm of Imagination'.
21. http://www.youtube.com/watch?v=51hodDsxxMc&watch_response
22. http://www.youtube.com/watch?v=sAeF5JRrc4M
23. http://www.lonelygirl15.com/forum/viewtopic.php?t=36
24. http://www.lg15.com/lgpedia/index.php?title=LG15_Spin-offs
25. http://www.bebo.com/PhotoAlbumBig.jsp?MemberId=4267180392&PhotoNbr=1&PhotoAlbumId=5493523934
26. http://www.lonelygirl15.com/forum/viewtopic.php?t=36
27. http://www.BeboTM.com/Profile.jsp?MemberId=4267180392
28. Liestøl, 'Wittgenstein, Genette, and the Reader's Narrative in Hypertext', 98.
29. http://www.itsallinyourhands.com/about/
30. Hills, *Fan Cultures*, 137.
31. Elsaesser, 'Fantasy Island', 157.
32. http://www2.warnerbros.com/orderofthephoenix/
33. http://www.thematrix101.com/games/matrixonline.php
34. http://disney.go.com/disneymobile/mdisney/pirates/about.html
35. Ryan, *Narrative as Virtual Reality*, 33.

36. Espen Aarseth argues that 'the term *interactive fiction* implies an equality between the reader and author beyond that found in other literary texts . . . Interactive narrative might imply some sort of user-directed story generator . . . A better term might be *heterarchic*, a structure of subverted hierarchies' (his emphasis). See Aarseth, *Cybertext*, 89.
37. McGonigal, 'A Real Little Game'.
38. Hills, *Fan Cultures*, 27.
39. http://www.nma.co.uk/Articles/34560/MySpace+begins+talent+search+for+UGC+movie.html
40. http://bits.blogs.nytimes.com/2007/07/30/a-soap-opera-embedded-into-a-social-network/
41. http://www.convergenceculture.org/weblog/2007/04/xbox_live_originals_contest_lo.php
42. http://news.bbc.co.uk/2/hi/entertainment/7021743.stm

CHAPTER 4

Adventures in Indiewood: Sequels in the Independent Film Marketplace

A t the end of his comprehensive study of American independent film, Yannis Tzioumakis notes that, in contradistinction to earlier moments in cinema history, twenty-first-century independent film is increasingly being replaced by such terms as 'niche' and 'speciality' 'to accommodate recent developments'.[1] Tzioumakis does not elaborate on these developments, but notes 'independent film' as an increasingly overburdened term. Now freighted with industrial agendas and institutional struggles, 'independent film' is used to signal both low-budget productions like *lonelygirl15* and $270 million projects like *The Lord of the Rings* trilogy (Peter Jackson, 2001, 2002, 2003).[2] Common to both ends of independent film's spectrum, however, are notions of uniqueness, transgression, authorial vision and independence from the major Hollywood studios: namely, Disney, Fox, MGM/UA, Paramount, Sony, Columbia/Tristar, Universal and Warner Bros. With this in mind, independent cinema seems an unlikely place in which to encounter the sequel. Yet the sequel shows up frequently in the 'indie' marketplace, from *L'Âge d'or* (1930), Luis Buñuel's surrealist sequel to his *Un Chien andalou* (1929), to Lars von Trier's politically charged *Manderlay* (2005), the sequel to his Brechtian USA commentary, *Dogville* (2003). If independent film across all its guises and contexts is designed to counter the commercial and ideological imperatives of the mainstream, what purposes does the sequel serve?

This chapter takes up some of the issues of independent film to explore the practice of sequelisation, and subsequently its meaning and currency, within the chief contexts of the independent film industry. Some of the questions framing this analysis are as follows: what exactly is 'independent' film in the twenty-first century? How does it differ from the throng of similar monikers use to define counter-Hollywood cinemas? Is an 'indie' film financially, aesthetically, culturally or politically antithetical to Hollywood? How can we begin to think about independent film sequels? How distinct is the independent film sequel from its Hollywood counterpart?

Several recent discussions of counter-Hollywood productions and genres appear identical to the assumed attributes of an independent picture. Amongst these are Murray Smith's definition of the avant-garde as an 'artisanal' or 'personal' mode of filmmaking, 'made by individuals or very small groups of collaborators', and funded 'either by the film-makers alone or in combination with private patronage and grants from arts and institutions'.[3] Such a definition not only fits a number of so-called independent productions that declare absolutely no investment in avant-gardism, such as *The Blair Witch Project* (Daniel Myrick and Eduardo Sánchez, 1999), *Clerks* (Kevin Smith, 1994), *Napolean Dynamite* (Jared Hess, 2004), *Garden State* (Zach Braff, 2004) and *Nacho Libre* (Jared Hess, 2006), but also trespasses on the definitional territory mapped in Nicholas Rombes's book on what he calls 'New Punk Cinema'. In his introduction, Rombes claims this kind of cinema to originate during the mid-1990s when 'a series of films from around the world began to emerge that challenged, or at least radically revised, many of the narrative and aesthetic codes that governed mainstream Hollywood fare'.[4] How does this differ from Smith's definition, or Jesse Fox Mayshark's description of 'post-pop cinema' as a trend of 'ironic self-consciousness' in American indies from the 1990s?[5] How does each of these definitions deviate from Peter Biskind's description of independent film as 'struggling young filmmakers maxing out their credit cards to pay their actors and crews . . . because they believe in what they're doing'?[6] Most helpful in challenging the polarity of 'mainstream' and 'independent', such critical vocabularies none the less seem to be applying a new name to the same mode of filmmaking.

What these 'new' names appear to share, however, is not just a similarity with the blanket term 'independent film', but more an identification of the increasing similarities between Hollywood and what has come to be known as 'indiewood'. Indiewood is a term given to the contemporary independent film industry – predominantly that in America, although increasingly prevalent in independent industries around the world – that is becoming more and more defined by its commercial tendencies and practices. A number of factors have contributed to this. The upswing of niche markets indicated in Chapter 3 of this book has arguably increased the value of those productions that are constructed not so much according to their box-office target than as being individual expressions of socio-political, historical or environmental issues. Certainly, the success of many low-budget productions in recent years has resulted in greater studio interest in smaller, quirkier productions, or, more generally, in an alignment of studio output with whatever is proving popular. Identifying the 'institutionalisation' of indies from the 1990s, Emanuel Levy further calls attention to the impact of independent successes such as *sex, lies and videotape* (Steve Soderbergh, 1992) and *The Blair Witch Project*, to the extent that, [whereas] indies have typically been seen as 'brassy innovators,' and the studios as the 'fortresses of corporate mediocrity,' a role reversal is now taking place. The major studios are willing to invest in 'edgy little films,' allowing creative control to the filmmaker, whereas indies are becoming more concerned with 'each and every detail'.[7]

In other words, independent filmmakers are now taking pains to ensure their production emulates the success of their competitors. And a competitive marketplace is exactly what independents now inhabit.

A glance at just some of the major film festivals proves this. The humble beginnings of the Sundance Film Festival – flopping in its first year, showing just six films and incurring a $40,000 deficit – have happily culminated in current successes that not even Robert Redford could have predicted, having taken over the ailing festival in 1985 with a vision to 'sponsor a category called independent film and fill it up with new voices and new talent that were being denied by the mainstream'.[8] As of 2007, the festival plays to audiences of 20,000 upwards, hosts stars, and screens films that regularly go on to win Academy Awards and/or big bucks at the box office. It is no surprise, then, that Sundance receives thousands of film submissions every year. Redford identifies Sundance's rapidly escalating 'market' tendency as a consequence of industrial shifts on the other side; the mainstream, he says, has pumped out 'product for younger audiences' in the form of 'blockbusters, animation, generally more cartoon-like stuff', meaning that actors have increasingly sought opportunities in independent films.[9] This is apparent in the number of established actors popping up in independents, from John Travolta's career-resuscitating role in *Pulp Fiction* (Quentin Tarantino, 1994) to Academy Award winner Christopher Walken's appearance in low-budget *Macbeth* spoof, *Scotland, PA* (Billy Morrissette, 2001). For actors, the creative process of the independent production is ostensibly much more satisfying. Says A-list actor Bruce Willis, 'every once in a while, I've got to satisfy myself. I can count on one hand . . . the number of films in the last couple of years that I looked forward to going to work every day.'[10] For studios, however, the bankability of indies is much more ensured by the bankability of their stars.

Critics have recently pointed not only to the competitiveness of Sundance, but also to its flagrant commercialisation. Of the 2006 Sundance Film Festival, Andy Goldberg reported 'corporate hospitality suites that shower[ed] stars with bags of swag while leaving struggling artists out in the cold – literally and figuratively'.[11] Andrew O'Hehir is much more scathing: '[Sundance] has become an ambiguous brand name, basically a pretty winter stopover on the ceaseless gravy train of celebrity and publicity.'[12] Sundance's celebrity status has created a gap in the market for other independent venues; this gap has been filled by a large number of alternative festivals, such as Slamdance, TriBeCa, the Toronto International Film Festival, and South by Southwest at Austin, Texas. Yet a prevailing competitiveness similar to Sundance has emerged throughout these festivals, each of which typically has between fifty and one hundred available screening slot. Slamdance received 4,700 film submissions for its 2006 festival;[13] TriBeCa received over 4,000 submissions in the same year;[14] the Toronto International Film Festival received 3,193 submissions as far back as 2003;[15] and South by Southwest, which apparently has 'more outsider cred' than either Sundance or Cannes, none the less predicts submissions of around 3,000 for its 2008 festival.[16]

The competitiveness and commerciality of the major venues for independent cinema, in tandem with the impact of indie hits noted above, suggest a rethinking of the current relationship between independent film and Hollywood in terms of an interdependency, and this is the stance the present chapter takes when considering the economies that govern Indiewood. Hollywood has historically absorbed and institutionalised many of the attributes of independent cinema, every bit as much as independent film is increasingly headed the way of the blockbuster. However, it is important not to ignore the realities of film production, whether independent or otherwise. Independent film is and always has been a marketplace, as it is dependent on the processes of distribution and exhibition if it is to achieve its purpose. With this in mind, I go on to examine the ways in which the sequel is redefined by its employment throughout the contemporary independent film scene. More specifically, I identify the ways in which the sequel functions in a marketplace that is underlined by tensions between commerciality and creativity. The stakes here are that the sequel may well serve to compromise the artisanal registers of independent film production, or in fact to reflect the independent industry's mainstream inclinations, but on the other hand may translate as something much more polemical, transgressive or 'original' in this context.

THE ECONOMIES OF INTERDEPENDENCY

As with studio-financed fare, the factors determining contemporary independent film production are production, distribution and exhibition. Any critical registers, personal visions or aesthetic goals are most often dictated to by these realities. A number of tactics are available to the ambitious indie filmmaker to overcome these barriers, or even work to his/her advantage.[17] These include:

1. controversy – Miramax is a major example here, having built up a considerable list of successes by foregrounding and marketing explicit content (such as the sexual twist in *The Crying Game* [Neil Jordan, 1992] instead of the film's political context as a marketing strategy); Mitchell Lichtenstein's

Sundance award-winning *Teeth* (2007) also courted controversy, and subsequently popularity, by taking on *vagina dentate* as comic subject.

2. new media technology – DV, webcams, mobile phone-cams and video sharing websites have resulted in the production and distribution of no-budget films, while *The Blair Witch Project* famously generated a massive following due to its website which, integrated with $20 million worth of 'traditional' marketing methods (such as trailers, posters and TV advertisements), generated $250 million at the worldwide box office.

3. getting a star on board – Bob Hoskins agreed to star in Shane Meadow's low-budget *Twenty Four Seven* (1997) for 'next to nothing'.[18]

4. tackling an issue at large in the popular consciousness, such as McDonald's and the consequences of fast food in *Super Size Me* (Morgan Spurlock, 2004), or US gun violence and the Columbine massacre in *Bowling for Columbine* (Michael Moore, 2002) and *Elephant* (Gus Van Sant, 2003).

To this list can be added the range of forms usually employed by the major Hollywood studios – recycling, remaking, pastiche, parody – as a method by which political and personal issues can be addressed. These forms also render a film identifiable and familiar according to its re-contextualisation and critiquing of previous films and/or the mainstream. An example of this is found in what Scott Macdonald identifies as 'recycled cinema'. Whereas filmic recycling is usually attributed to Hollywood fare, Macdonald notes its value to some independent filmmakers who 'have found a remarkably wide range of approaches . . . distinguished by their choices of film to recycle and particular recycling procedures', or in other words by its usefulness in criticising contemporary issues by reinterpreting symbols and images.[19] Critical filmmaker Matthias Müller puts the value of recycling in perspective:

> The process of accumulating borrowed images, as well as one's own, produces alternating currents. Films oppose each other, look at each other, interact with each other. Simply placing the appropriated images next to my own images recodes them.[20]

Müller's assessment of the currency of films that 'look at each other' has resulted in a body of work devoted to an engagement with the old through the 'lens' of the new. In particular, the meanings attributed to older, marginalised films are exposed and explored throughout Müller's work in an attempt to challenge methods of homogenisation and normalisation at work in contemporary culture. Despondent at the 'mainstreaming' and 'patterned models of identity' prevalent in contemporary gay culture that are perpetuated by the gay film industry, Müller resurrected and referenced films like Kenneth Anger's *Fireworks* (1947), Jean Genet's *Un Chant d'amour* (1950) and Tom Chomont's

Jabbok (1967) as notable influences and points of reference in his *Sleepy Haven* (1993). Although these films are from cinema's distant past, Müller uses them to articulate a past-bound ideology of the contemporary moment, or to draw attention to the lack of 'subversive energy . . . in today's gay cinema'.[21] A similar technique prevails in Clive Holden's *Trains of Winnipeg: 14 Film Poems* (2004). Here Holden examines the meanings of his past – and additionally the impacts of immigration, travel and home – by compiling new footage of trains in Winnipeg with old Super-8mm footage of his childhood, his schizophrenic brother and the settling place of his Irish immigrant parents. In each case, recycling, or the juxtaposition of the old with the new, proves a critical device in articulating personal and transgressive social issues.

In the case of the independent film sequel, a similar kind of juxtaposition often takes place, but with slightly different results. The sequel provides a way in which an independent filmmaker can overcome the barriers posed by lack of studio finance and publicity, at the same time as it enables a number of creative goals to be achieved. The independent arena has historically struggled between commerce and creativity. Jonas Mekas, one of the founders of the Filmmakers' Cooperative, states the conflicts facing filmmakers during the 1960s and 1970s, or what became known as the New American Wave, using methods very similar to those noted above:

> In order to get into the commercial theaters and succeed there, we had to use the same competitive, shark techniques as were used by the commercial distributors. The values of films had to be blown out of all proportion: the theaters stressed the secondary, often very marginal, aspects of the content, such as erotic references.[22]

Significantly, Mekas goes on to note that giving way to commercial practices afforded a means of achieving particular creative goals: 'we see it today as the only way of continuing our work on our own terms, not on the terms dictated by producers and distributors.'[23]

In the twenty-first century, the independent film sequel operates in similar ways. The specific commercial strategies inherent in the indie sequel – for instance, as a way of drawing attention to a director's previous work and showcasing authorial style – cooperate with a variety of artistic and personal aims as explored throughout the following examples. The sequel is therefore never disengaged from its mainstream imperatives in independent cinema, but is used to achieve a number of political, personal and aesthetic aims, all of which recast the sequel as a critical form. The sequel is contracted, expanded and virtually uprooted here from its Hollywood functions, to the extent that many critical registers are achieved within the context of a commercially familiar scenario.

A number of recent productions extend the sequel's configuration of narrative difference as a critical framework through which a variety of issues can be explored in terms of difference and change. This is apparent in James Benning's *One-Way Boogie Woogie/27 Years Later* (2005), which revisits and sequelises his 1977 film *One-Way Boogie Woogie* to portray landscape changes and urban decay in Milwaukee over a period of twenty-seven years. Iranian actress/filmmaker Mania Akbari's *10 + 4* (2006) continues her role in Abbas Kiarostami's docu-drama *Ten Conversations about Everything* (2003) (commonly known as *Ten*), in which she played herself as a divorced taxi driver who chats with her passengers about life and death. In *10 + 4*, such conversations are re-contextualised by Akbari's representation of her real-life experience with cancer. Here the sequel serves as a particularly striking illustration of the changes imposed by a sudden illness. As its title suggests, *10 + 4* signals a link between Kiarostami's *Ten* and the period of time (four years) separating Kiarostami's production and Akbari's sequel. *10 + 4* is therefore an exploration of change and temporal progression – or rather the changes brought about by temporal progression – within the framework of a narrative progression. The (potentially) terminal nature of Akbari's illness puts notions of change and temporal progression into sharp focus. It is entirely this kind of change and temporality that governs the film's temporality and the process of its production. A synopsis for the film on Akbari's website mentions that she is 'directed by her cancer in the process of making the film'.[24] The play on words here – the director 'directed by' her cancer – indicates the film's imaginative use of the sequel as distinct from its commercial practices, particularly in terms of the suggestion that Akbari is not in control of the film's direction; nor is the narrative pre-determined by a set of studio requirements. Rather, it is a force of the 'real' that governs the film's direction and outcome – Akbari's camera, like that of Kiarostami in *Ten*, sets out to capture these unknown factors.

Throughout such films, a number of contrasts emerge between independent cinema and the mainstream in terms of their treatment of the sequel. Firstly, the independent film sequel most often corresponds closely with a single previous text composed by the same director, and most often contends with the same issue that has previously been explored by its filmic predecessor. Secondly, the 'original' is commonly inserted inside the sequel in the form of clips and images, rather than existing outside or prior to the sequel. This internalisation of a previous text is key to the configuration of the sequel in these films. Quite distinct from the mainstream logic of an original/sequel hierarchy, the independent sequel typically operates according to an interdependency of meaning that is shared across more than one text. Finally, the narratological structure of the sequel operates as a reflexive, rather than simply continuative, format by which the politics of narration and representation are thrown into

question, and by which the contexts within which independent film is produced and consumed can be more critically assessed.

The first of these contrasts is demonstrated by Judith Helfand and Daniel
B. Gold's *Blue Vinyl* (2002), a documentary of the dangers posed by vinyl manufacturing and a 'sequel of sorts' to Helfand's earlier Sundance venture *A
Healthy Baby Girl* (1997), which documented her own struggles with cancer as
a result of her mother's ingestion of a prescribed synthetic oestrogen during
her pregnancy.[25] Here Helfand and Gold draw upon the genre, style, political
aims and personal narrative recounted in *A Healthy Baby Girl* to interpret
those of *Blue Vinyl*. Just as *A Healthy Baby Girl* aimed to set a private tragedy
in dialogue with the public consequences of the prescription drug (diethyl-
stilbestrol [DES], prescribed to millions of pregnant women in the US between
1947 and 1971), so *Blue Vinyl* returns to the boundaries of that private
tragedy – particularly in terms of Helfand's relationship with her parents – to
explore the social ramifications of vinyl panelling, which begins when her
parents decide to panel the side of their house with the stuff. Soon discovering
an alarming number of former polyvinyl chloride (PVC) workers suffering
from cancer, the filmmakers end up in Venice where several vinyl producers are
on trial for manslaughter due to the effects of PVC on their former staff.
Although *Blue Vinyl* takes a much different social subject as its focus, Helfand's
personal experiences with cancer as portrayed in *A Healthy Baby Girl* cast a
critical spotlight upon the sequel as a method by which to approach and interpret the issues that are raised. In particular, Helfand's experiences are highlighted as the motivating forces behind her initial decision to explore the
potential dangers lurking in PVC, with a similar aim to provoke corporate
responsibility and action. The personal and public are consistently negotiated
throughout and across both films, and it is precisely the structure of the sequel
that creates and heightens this connection.

Helfand and Gold's latest work, *Everything's Cool* (2007), demonstrates the
second point of contrast between mainstream and independent cinema by its
identification of a predecessor that was not produced by Helfand and Gold, and
by sequelising its source by inserting it into its own diegetic framework. The
source in this case is Al Gore's *An Inconvenient Truth* (2006), an Academy
Award-winning documentary on global warming. Without clarification,
Everything's Cool is pitched as 'both a prequel and a sequel' to Gore's documentary.[26] The sequel pitch is more convincing. This is because *Everything's
Cool* highlights the central issue of *An Inconvenient Truth* as one that is ongoing
and in need of further action and dialogue, and is not neatly resolved by the
narrative resolution of its predecessor. In parallel with its repetition of the issue
raised in *An Inconvenient Truth*, *Everything's Cool* also creates a point of distinction between its aims and those of its predecessor; whereas *An Inconvenient
Truth* created an awareness of the scale of the global warming crisis,

Everything's Cool – its title quoting George W. Bush – sets out to demonstrate the political element of the issue of global warming. More importantly, it aims to show what could be 'done at the local and federal level to deal with the problem'.[27] By inserting clips from *An Inconvenient Truth* into the narrative of *Everything's Cool*, Helfand and Gold reflexively highlight the major previous media representation of the issue with which most of their audience will already be familiar in acknowledgement of its impact and the necessity for further consideration. The structure of the sequel is presented here not simply as a continuation of a previous work, but instead to draw attention to the specifically continuous conversation and action that is needed to address global warming.

The sequel appears in a number of other productions to situate lived experience within the boundaries of fictionality, and vice versa. Similar to the insertion of a previous text as in *Everything's Cool*, the sequel in this case negotiates between factuality and fictionality, primarily to present the meaning one casts upon the other. Where one production presents a fictional narrative, its sequel contends with a personal, 'real' experience specifically by recalling the fictional structures that it follows, as if to understand the representational strategies by which the 'real' is mediated and understood, and by which the fictional is re-enacted. Take Garth Jennings's Sundance hit *Son of Rambow* (2007), for instance. Jennings's film pivots on the fictional concept of a young boy who makes his own *Rambo*-inspired home movie, nicknaming himself the 'son' of his idealised persona of masculinity and freedom, and marking his own entry into pubescence (and away from restrictions imposed by his family) by sequelising this character. The boy's misspelling of Rambo ('Rambow') marks this process as a return to and continuation of something quite different from the 'real' Rambo – it also helpfully negotiates copyright issues – at the same time as it invokes the discourses surrounding this fictional text (particularly those of heroic masculinity) to present real experiences and fantasies of male pre-pubescence. The use of 'son of' in the title also recalls a number of sequels from cinema's earlier period (for example, *Son of Kong* [Ernest B. Schoedsack, 1933], *Dracula's Daughter* [Lambert Hillyer, 1936], *The Son of the Sheik* [George Fitzmaurice, 1926]) that recapitulated the dominant traits and adventures of a previous character in their offspring. Through this intertextual association, the title of Jennings's film registers the conceit immediately.

More important, however, is the use of the sequel in articulating the relationship between *Rambo: First Blood* (Ted Kotcheff, 1982) and *Son of Rambow*, as well as the relationship between *Rambo* and the characters of *Son of Rambow*. Two diegetic levels are at work here. *Son of Rambow* plays out the responses of two young boys to a film; meanwhile, the audience is called upon to reconsider their own encounters with *Rambo* and its discursive and/or representational aftermaths throughout popular culture (Ronald Reagan's invocations of Rambo in his presidential speeches, for example). The notion of a film-within-a-film here re-imagines the tendency to insert a previous text into its sequel, as noted above, but the fictional internalisation of *Rambo* is employed specifically to achieve the kind of nostalgic recreation of a childhood experience as experienced by the filmmakers. Says the film's producer, Nick Goldsmith, *Rambo* is invoked not entirely because of the popular currency of Rambo as a figure of parody and symbol of masculinity, but because 'it inspired us as kids to want to make traps in the forest and pretend.'[28] The notions of nostalgia and re-enactment in *Son of Rambow* are intensified by their presentation within a sequel context.

Throughout all of the examples and kinds of independent sequel noted above, the sequel is used to convey an interdependency of meaning and viewing positions. The sequel is configured as reflexively relational to a previous work rather than strictly continuative; it responds to a previous work in terms of its personal and political aftermaths and the structures by which that work has been sustained in the popular imagination. On the other hand, however, the various uses of the sequel can equally be seen to offer a commercial legitimacy and pop culture heritage that are crucial in carving a niche in a competitive marketplace. For instance, although *Rambo* certainly lends *Son of Rambow* a host of cultural meanings pertinent to the film's portrait of coming-of-age, the commercial value of *Rambo* – and particularly the value this lends *Son of Rambow* – cannot be ignored. Similarly, *Everything's Cool* clearly trades upon the success, and not just the message, of *An Inconvenient Truth*.

Yet to perceive the economic and artisanal attributes of independent films as dichotomous is, for the most part, entirely misleading. Mekas's comment noted above indicates the historical dependence of independent cinema upon the same structures of commerce as mainstream production; what is usually separate, though, are the political and personal frameworks through which the independent is conceived and executed. As suggested earlier, however, there is much evidence to suggest that the boundaries that have traditionally separated independent film from the mainstream are fast becoming blurred in an environment of new technologies and crossover audiences. A number of critics have pointed to this phenomenon, evidenced by audiences going to see big blockbusters such as *Twister* (Jan de Bont, 1996) one night and to a screening of an independent like *Dead Man Walking* (Tim Robbins, 1995) the next.[29] However, the industrial mechanisms underpinning such audience crossovers indicate how far the roots of industrial interdependency lie; the mega-successes of independents such as *sex, lies and videotape* and *Super Size Me* have notably inspired studios to invest significant amounts of finance in festival favourites, and indeed to produce smaller films for growing niche markets.[30] Rather than generate merchandising to support their independent acquisitions, the majors cover the financial 'risk' of independents by marketing indie acquisitions as quality, intellectual and differentiated product. There are technological factors at work here, too. Patricia Zimmerman points out the impact of digital culture on the interdependency of Hollywood and Indiewood, suggesting that 'new technologies, distribution platform, political communities, and fluidity between formerly distinct sectors have erased [the] binaries' between the independent film scene and Hollywood, precisely because 'all media productions – even independent film – repurpose and remediate themselves across a range of formats, interfaces, and forms of various niche market segments across multi-platformed media environments.'[31] That is to say, studio projects such as *Star Wars: Episode III – Revenge of the Sith* (George Lucas, 2005) employ the same digital technologies as lower-budget productions whilst making use of the same low-cost distribution platforms as do contemporary independent films. As Chapter 3 showed, the internet has furnished independent film with a rich source of free marketing and distribution; the major studios have also made much use of this resource in markedly similar ways.

Each of these forms of interdependency makes it crucial to rethink independent film throughout the range of contexts within which it now operates. Although Zimmerman and others have rightly observed the increasing fluidity of practices across independent film and the mainstream, it is hard to ignore the perpetuation of many economic barriers which independents still have to cross in order to achieve success, not least the increasing competitiveness of the major independent film festivals as noted earlier. Despite the doors opened by digital technologies, a major barrier still exists in terms of the importance of brand identity. Zimmerman gestures towards this in her observation that despite 'the proliferation of DV, the large media transnationals still control the retail end of the business in all sectors, making it difficult for any kind of independent filmmaker to penetrate'.[32] The 'retail end' is made up of the marketing, merchandising and paratextual activities of the major studios across a range of multimedia ventures with which any independent will find it difficult to compete. An indie artist can certainly upload his/her production on YouTube, but may not have the means to produce a Massively-Multiplayer Online Role-Playing online game like *Pirates of the Caribbean*, or carve out an identifiable brand image amidst a sea of logos and corporate images. Yet there is arguably one method by which a brand identity can be forged without conjuring up gimmicky games or fluffy McHappy Meal tie-ins: the film trilogy.

THE RISE OF THE INDIE TRILOGY

A massive number of independent trilogies around the globe indicate that the term 'trilogy' is becoming increasingly synonymous with the up-and-coming independent filmmaker. There is, however, very little reason given as to why this should be the case. Indian-American filmmaker Shalini Kantayya recently commented that her 'ultimate goal is to do a trilogy of feature films about the environment and to create a mythology for our generation that makes it cool to be a change maker . . . And so that's the target of my films, to reach youth.'[33] Says Malayalam film director Murali Nair of his plans to follow his film *Unni* (2006) with two further parts, 'I felt I could not tell the whole story in one film. Hence the decision to do the trilogy.'[34] The indie trilogy has a considerable history. Indie pioneer John Cassavetes used the trilogy format to explore relationships in his so-called 'marriage trilogy' (1968–70), whilst Roman Polanski's *Chinatown* (1974) and *The Two Jakes* (1990) were originally intended to form a trilogy composed of 'elemental' themes.[35] Maverick blaxploitation filmmaker Melvin Van Peebles's *Sweet Sweetback's Baadasssss Song* (1971) is part of an as-yet-unrealised trilogy.[36] Sundance-winning director Kevin Smith still applies the term to his group of films devoted to the adventures of characters Jay and Silent Bob, despite his 'New Jersey Trilogy' being presently composed of five, not three, films. Historically, the trilogy has been fairly consistently treated as a set of three works related in subject matter and theme, as consistent in its employment in Euripides' Trojan trilogy circa 415 B.C. as it is in J. R. Tolkien's literary trilogy *The Lord of the Rings* (1937–49). Yet the term 'trilogy' is used very differently throughout a vast range of independent films, and the sheer scale of indie trilogies being produced suggests its importance in this realm. Why is the trilogy so important to these filmmakers? What discursive and industrial functions does it perform? How does it translate from its traditional commercial practices into independent practices?

In answering these questions, it is important to note briefly the trilogy's heritage in cinema. Successful three-part films such as Coppola's *The Godfather* trilogy, the (first) *Star Wars* trilogy (1977–83), directed by George Lucas, Irvin Kershner and Richard Marquand, Satyajit Ray's *Apu* trilogy (1955–9) and Sergio Leone's *Dollars* trilogy (1964–6) tended to set three narrative instalments in a beginning-middle-end structure, expanding the traditional Aristotelian format to convey the progression of a larger narratological unit. With so many characters and plotlines interweaving throughout these films, the trilogy served as an effective way to explore most of the possible outcomes and characterisations within the plot. The commercial success, generic paradigms and discursive aftermaths of such trilogies furnished later productions with a rich source of intertextual matter. The trilogy's inherited intertextual investments have gradually loosened the term from its original narrative connections to link up a range of somewhat more tangential and signifying properties and texts. Also, the trilogy's traditional presentations of a kind of repetitive, circular history have been recently reconfigured to furnish a three-part production with its own historicity, heritage and authenticity. Its narratological similarities to the sequel are founded in its presentation of progression and history. Says

Claire Perkins, 'the trilogy is an area in which sequelization [sic] is thought in more interpretive terms, and in which the conditions of remaking that ground all sequels are made explicit.'[37] But, as with the sequel, the modes of interpretation informing the independent trilogy, and particularly those conditions upon which remaking and continuing are predicated, are governed by a range of factors quite separate from the film trilogy in its mainstream forms.

For the most part, Hollywood trilogies (such as *The Bourne Ultimatum* [Paul Greengrass and Doug Liman, 2002, 2004, 2007], *Rush Hour* [Brett Ratner, 1998, 2001, 2007], *Shrek* [Andrew Adamson *et al.*, 2001, 2004, 2007], *Batman* [Tim Burton *et al.*, 1989–] and *X-Men* [Bryan Singer, 2000, 2003, 2006]) adhere to conventional notions of the trilogy by indicating narrative progression across three productions. The independent trilogy, however, rarely connects a series of narrative instalments. Instead, the independent trilogy acts as a unifying structure by which to articulate and associate a series of themes, styles and political issues. The indie trilogy rarely bothers setting its instalments up in a progressive part one-two-three format – indeed, Lucas Belvaux's metafictional trilogy, titled *Trilogy* (2002), deliberately confuses the conventional chronological trajectory, preferring instead to use the trilogy as a circular artistic construct that is perpetually in dialogue and without resolution.[38] Narrative is incidental; the trilogy is instead a narrational mode through which particular issues are rendered correspondent.

An example of this is found in Lars Von Trier's *Europe* trilogy, consisting of *The Element of Crime* (1984), *Epidemic* (1988) and *Europa* (1991), each of which serves to identify different aspects of European trauma and corruption. Paul D'Agostino's trilogy, *Trois fois par rien* (2005), is composed of three short experimental films (*Pas encore*, *La Défense* and *Le Contexte*), set in Paris. The impetus behind the project was to make cinematic narratives out of footage shot for no specific reason, but which are none the less linked thematically and visually. Godfrey Reggio's avant-garde Qatsi trilogy, so named after the Hopi Indian word meaning 'life out of balance', provides an incisive glance at the impact of globalisation, modernisation and war on contemporary life. Each of the three films plays a key role in exploring and unifying these impacts, and each film is constituted of a series of images instead of a discernible narrative. The first film, *Koyaanisqatsi* (1983), is at once 'an apocalyptic vision of the collision of two different worlds – urban life and technology versus the environment', whilst *Powaqqatsi* (1988) looks to the Third World to consider 'diversity and transformation, of cultures dying and prospering'. Most recently, *Naqoyqatsi* (2002) portrays the 'new world', or 'the transition from the natural milieu, old nature, to the "new" nature, the technological milieu'.[39] Says Reggio, '[t]he purpose of the trilogy was, in a very limited way, to hold up a mirror to life as it exists in the fast lane.'[40] Reggio's intentions for the trilogy are clearly far removed from the mainstream contexts of this term. Indeed, the film's message, as well as its minimalist soundtrack (composed by Philip Glass, performed by cellist and UN peace ambassador Yo-Yo Ma), indicate the film's political, rather than popular, foundations. Yet the trilogy operates here to fortify those foundations, and to present the statement at hand as part of a continuing discourse, rather than a single narrative unit.

The term 'trilogy' appears in other productions to perform similar methods of coherence in alternative contexts. Chan-Wook Park's South Korean cult film *Oldboy* (2003) is part of a trilogy dubbed 'Vengeance', composed of two other films, *Boksuneun naui geot* (*Sympathy for Mr Vengeance*) (2002) and *Chinjeolhan geumjassi* (*Sympathy for Lady Vengeance*) (2005). Krzysztof Kieslowski's *Three Colours* trilogy (1993–4) imagines the three colours of the French flag across three narrative contexts devoted to explorations of nationalism and cultural values, at the same time as the use of colour in each film achieves specific symbolic attributes that resonate throughout the trilogy. Australian director Baz Luhrmann's 'Red Curtain Trilogy', made up of his films *Strictly Ballroom* (1992), *William Shakespeare's 'Romeo + Juliet'* (1996) and *Moulin Rouge!* (2001), is so named and designed to articulate Luhrmann's artistic investments in theatricality. Notably, Luhrmann uses the trilogy to coin both a specific personal style and a set of new cinematographic terms, such as 'Super Macro Slam Zoom', 'Lightning Cut', 'Whip Pan' and 'Chopper POV'.[41] Played out in terms of a distinctive authorial aesthetic, Luhrmann's use of the term 'trilogy' serves, first and foremost, to announce the particular style that operates across his body of films.

Each of these operations of the trilogy in independent cinema is underlined by a common effort: to present an artistic and political concept or framework as a marker of commercial viability and distinctiveness. Loaded with economic appeal beyond its traditional, semantic functions – the linking of three works in an ultimately conclusive format – the trilogy functions in independent film to re-package a series of productions as paratextual promotions and articulations of directorial virtuosity and originality. A number of trilogies have worked to suspend the conclusivity of the trilogy by linking it to the continuous conceit of the sequel. This method redefines the form of the trilogy in terms of what it signifies in mainstream cinema, as the examples noted above demonstrate: as an intertextual, intermedial, authentic product with a particular history, originality and authorial voice.

In this light, a major difference between the sequel and the trilogy emerges. The trilogy has tended not to be criticised in the same pejorative terms as has the sequel. Although both share similar commercial advantages, the trilogy has largely retained its association with creativity and originality. Free of the animus surrounding sequel production, the trilogy therefore allows a filmmaker to tap into a number of important commercial avenues at the same time as his/her work is invested with notions of originality and significance.

The trilogy suggests that the narrative or concept being presented is of such cultural value that it requires three (or more) films to explore all its possibilities and outcomes. The tendency to create a title for the trilogy as well as each of the films under its banner announces the trilogy as a conceptual, organising framework with a specific set of values, like a genre or series. It offers a particular viewing position with a set of expectations. The productions under the banner of the trilogy's title are organised by clearly identifiable parameters, and as contributions to a greater conceptual whole. The viewing experience is intensified by this 'whole' and its components as continuous and participatory. In addition, the issue with which the trilogy contends (for example, Europe in von Trier's *Europe*, the US and the Bush administration in his 'America' trilogy) is textualised and treated as a marker of importance and commerciality. Similar to Thomas Elsaesser's identification of what he calls a 'paradigm of autonomy',[42] or the way in which European cinema categorically distinguishes itself from Hollywood, the trilogy operates in the independent marketplace as a mode of difference and distinction from Hollywood. It also performs commercial functions. Where the logo of a major studio is not possible, the naming of a trilogy after an issue of particular importance in popular culture, or indeed a genre, distinctive style, experimental form or geographical location, serves equally well to mark a body of work as distinctive amidst fierce competition.

The above is not intended to be cynical or suggestive of compromises within the independent film scene; rather it is intended to identify the trilogy as a framework within which the commercial and creative are currently synergised. In particular, the ways in which this synergy occurs furthers understanding of the economies of interdependency between the independent scene and the mainstream. Although independent film series and sequels have been in practice for some time, it is significant that the trilogy is re-fashioned in contemporary indie productions as a kind of brand identity with a host of economic and political imperatives attached to its meaning.

The trilogy's significance in the indie scene is further suggested by the tendency of audiences and critics to impose a trilogy title upon a body of works as an interpretive lens. Indie filmmaker Wes Anderson[43] has never declared the themes, characters and styles of his work to operate as a trilogy or series, yet critics have assigned him several: Anderson's films *Rushmore* (1998), *The Royal Tenenbaums* (2001) and *The Life Aquatic with Steve Zissou* (2004) have been called a 'juvenile lit meets *The New Yorker*' trilogy and a 'Great-Search-for-a-Father-Figure Trilogy', whilst another critic sees *The Royal Tenenbaums*, *The Life Aquatic* and *The Darjeeling Limited* (2007) as forming Anderson's 'Daddy trilogy'.[44] Certainly, the issue of fatherhood is explored frequently in Anderson's films. Each of *The Royal Tenenbaums*, *The Life Aquatic* and *The Darjeeling Limited* plays out this issue across portraits of reluctant fatherhood, the conception of a son and the death of a son. The notion of literariness high-lighted by the trilogy title 'juvenile lit meets *The New Yorker*' is apparent in his films in terms of the organisation of *The Royal Tenenbaums* as chapters, nar-rated from the pages of a novel, and the play upon the idea of metafictionality in *The Darjeeling Limited*. One critic notes the value of the interpretive struc-ture provided by the trilogy:

> [V]iewed in the context of a trilogy, each thematically depending upon the films it is linked to, the literal progression of age may be seen. Simply put, the three films trace the growth of an ambitious child to a cynical adult.[45]

Where the term 'trilogy' is assigned to a body of works by audiences or critics, an access point, or a method of interpretation and participation, is created by which to navigate a film's intertextual or thematic relationships. The trilogy here situates a work in context. It also enables the boundaries of this context to be carefully defined according to a director's style, voice and recurrent themes.

A number of important overlaps between the trilogy and the sequel are to be found at this point. Both the sequel and the trilogy seek to continue narrative instalments; both seek to connect these in terms of a number of recurrent or repetitive features. The trilogy does not, however, seek to highlight differences between the plot points, themes, characters or styles being carried from one instalment to the next. Conversely, the sequel is all about difference. This important narratological characteristic of the sequel therefore shows up in the hybrid trilogy format at work in contemporary independent cinema as an industrial tool, mapping out the difference between an indie film and a Hollywood production, between a body of work and its competitors, between one personal vision and the millions of personal visions on display at film fes-tivals across the world. The sequel can therefore be seen as an important niche mechanism, informing the continuous transformation of the trilogy and heightening its currency.

THE ECONOMIES OF INTERMEDIALITY

The sequel as a niche mechanism is not always couched within the currently in vogue trilogy format. For instance, despite the attempts to label his productions under the trilogy banner, Wes Anderson released his own self-described 'prequel' to *The Darjeeling Limited* a couple of months before the film's release in the form of a 13-minute film, *Hotel Chevalier* (2007), as a free download on Apple Inc.'s iTunes website. Was *Hotel Chevalier* promotional bait or narrato-logical necessity? Says Anderson,

> I don't know if it's a wildly commercial idea, and it is probably a little con-
> fusing to people who are thinking, 'Why is this separate from the movie?'
> But [you] have to see the short [film, *Hotel Chevalier*] in order to get
> everything that's in *Darjeeling*.[46]

Like the indie trilogy, Anderson's conceptualisation of the prequel here
reworks its traditional imperatives. Later presented in cinemas before the
screening of *Darjeeling*, *Hotel Chevalier* essentially carves out some back story
for the main feature in the form of an encounter between one of *Darjeeling*'s
main characters (Jack, played by Jason Schwartzman) and his ex-girlfriend
(played by Natalie Portman, literally credited as 'Jack's X-girlfriend') in a hotel
room in Paris before he sets off on the journey portrayed in *Darjeeling*. At the
very end of *Darjeeling*, Jack pulls out a notepad and reads to his brothers an
excerpt from a fictional short story he has been writing. A number of previous
scenes focus on Jack's inability to write fictional stories, or at least his inability
to perceive the difference between fiction and autobiography. Once more, the
story he recounts at the film's end to his brothers is, verbatim, an account of
the events portrayed in *Hotel Chevalier*.

Hotel Chevalier adheres strictly to the prequel's investments in 'beforeness',
at least in terms of presenting a narrative segment that chronologically precedes another. The concept of 'back story', however, is tangential. Anderson's
'prequel' serves not entirely as a historical context or narrative prologue to
Darjeeling, but rather as a play upon the metafictional and intertextual structures comprising this film, particularly Anderson's self-conscious return to
father-son relationships, and, in a kind of remake of a scene from *The Life
Aquatic*, a markedly similar portrait of a surrogate father carrying the bloodied
dead body of a drowned son from water. There is also the well-documented
influence of Ray's *Apu* trilogy. Symbolically, the fictional world of *Darjeeling*
seems to bleed into the real, and vice versa. But there are other factors at work
here, too. Note the number of downloads for *Hotel Chevalier* – 500,000 from
one website in one month – not to mention the attention drawn to what was
actress Natalie Portman's first nude scene. If Anderson's 'prequel' fails to
inform *Darjeeling* beyond a brief signification of metafictionality, it has certainly succeeded as marketing tactic.

More important, however, is the intermedial connection drawn here
between the prequel and Anderson's feature. Shot for free over two days and
edited on Anderson's laptop, *Hotel Chevalier* demonstrates the multimedia
platforms available to the low-budget filmmaker for independent exhibition
and distribution. Of note is the use of the term 'prequel' in creating a stir about
Darjeeling – indeed, few blockbuster trailers can claim a download rate as
impressive as *Hotel Chevalier* – as what was clearly on offer at the iTune's
website was at once a free short film by an acclaimed indie director and a

paratextual commodity that trades upon the YouTube/iPod environment. Put another way, the novelty of a downloadable 'teaser' film capitalises entirely upon the methods of interaction, word of mouth and intermediality which form the infrastructure of online culture.

Both Anderson's prequel and the use of the trilogy in independent cinema can be thought of in terms of the increasing significance of intermediality within the indie scene. Prevalent throughout developing technologies, online communities, and what Zimmerman observes as a 'more variegated independent film political economy' throughout the last decade,[47] intermediality denotes new relationships between all sectors of the media industry in terms of the fusion and transformation of media forms. Refashioned and transformed across a range of productions in a variety of contexts, both the sequel and trilogy have served as methods by which to achieve creative and commercial objectives, but additionally have been transformed by their operations throughout these contexts. New methods of engagement and spectatorship facilitated by online spaces circulate such forms as 'sequel' and 'trilogy' amidst emergent terms and multimedia practices, creating myriad connections across texts, spaces, cultures and media formats. It is in a similar manner that the definition(s) of 'independent film' must be contested. The commercial and 'institutionalising' economies of interdependency between the indie scene and the mainstream must be rethought in terms of the numerous issues arising from intermedial dynamics, such as issues of access and transmission as facilitated online, hand-held viewing platforms, user-generated content, the impact of fan communities and video websites, and digital exhibition. Far from operating within their traditional intertextual modes, the forms of 'sequel' and 'trilogy' can be seen as taking on entirely new guises and contexts within the intermedial environment.

CONCLUSIONS

These forms in their new guises cast new light on 'Indiewood' and its relationship to Hollywood. The 'interdependency' between both industries may better be thought of as a fluidity between industrial networks. Less helpful in defining multimillion-dollar projects that somehow qualify for the category 'independent film', this term may instead be used to mark a kind of filmmaking in which personal, critical and political objectives are prioritised. Note the selection criteria for the Independent Spirit Awards – 'original, provocative subject matter'[48] – and one is hard pressed to find any mention of finance. Similarly, the independent film sequel appears unfixed from its mainstream operations to signify and contextualise a wealth of critical issues. More important, however, is the reinvention of this term by its participations with and performances throughout alternative media platforms as a much more complex category of difference and contextualisation. Enabling the transition between media to be understood within its (narratological) context of continuation, the sequel is redefined by these connections by the dynamics of the various media platforms across which it appears, to the extent that it stretches to accommodate the paratextual, interactive and commercial operations noted above.

Writing as I am in December 2007 amidst the writers' strike in Hollywood, the impact of such industrial action upon the independent film scene is palpable. Now operating as a 'seller's market',[49] the indie marketplace is apparently taking giant strides towards redefining its creative boundaries against the industrial impositions created by Hollywood. There are, however, a number of commercial imperatives that continue to govern the independent film industry, and these too have a significant impact upon the ways we think about the film sequel. Like the film trilogy – which has been identified as serving a range of commercial and creative purposes – the sequel can be thought of as a kind of rebranding, or as a method by which an independent filmmaker marks his or her authorial approach as creatively distinct and commercially attractive. It provides an access point to a filmmaker's body of work, suggesting a production as part of a larger, and much more personal, cinematic canon. The independent film sequel conveys a sense of authorial progression or development, at the same time as it enables a filmmaker to re-explore the same theme or critical issue throughout a range of different scenarios. It is important therefore to identify the film sequel not only as a format that serves both commercial and creative agendas, but also as a category that successfully articulates many of the critical registers that pervade independent film.

NOTES

1. Tzioumakis, *American Independent Cinema*, 283.
2. Ibid., 2.
3. Smith, 'Modernism and the Avant-Gardes', 395.
4. Rombes, 'Introduction', 2.
5. Mayshark, *Post-Pop Cinema*, 2.
6. Biskind, *Down and Dirty Pictures*, 1.
7. Levy, *Cinema of Outsiders*, 504.
8. http://www.filmfestivaltoday.com/dailies_item.asp?ID=792; quoted in Anderson, 'We Called it a Festival, but it Became a Market'.
9. http://film.guardian.co.uk/features/featurepages/0,,1993650,00.html
10. Quoted in Levy, *Cinema of Outsiders*, 503.
11. Goldberg, 'Snow, Swag, Sparkle Challenge Sundance's Indie Spirit'.
12. O'Hehir, 'Beyond the Multiplex'.
13. http://www.dailybruin.ucla.edu/news/2006/jan/19/unraveling-sundance/
14. http://manhattan.about.com/od/artsandculture/a/tribecafilm2006.htm
15. http://www.tiffg.ca/content/divisions/tiff.asp

16. http://2007.sxsw.com/film/press/ffaq/
17. See also King, *American Independent Cinema*, 32.
18. Null, 'An Interview with Shane Meadows'.
19. Macdonald, *A Critical Cinema 5*, 281.
20. Ibid., 287.
21. Ibid., 288.
22. Mekas, 'Independence for Independents' , 32.
23. Ibid., 31.
24. http://www.mania-akbari.com/10plus4movie.htm
25. http://www.nextwavefilms.com/bluevinyl/sundance.html
26. Plasse, '*Everything's Cool* at Sundance'.
27. Ibid.
28. Goldsmith, Personal Communication, 29 November 2007.
29. Levy, *Cinema of Outsiders*, 513.
30. Ibid., 513.
31. Zimmerman, 'Digital Deployment(s)', 220.
32. Ibid.
33. http://www.blogher.com/using-film-change-world-interview-shalini-kantayya
34. http://www.rediff.com/movies/2007/mar/26murali.htm
35. Jack Nicholson, the star of both films, makes this claim: 'We wanted it all to be tied into elemental things. *Chinatown* is obviously water. *The Two Jakes* is fire and energy. And the third film was meant to be about Gittes' divorce and relate to air.' Quoted in Horowitz, 'Jack Nicholson Talks!'
36. http://www.electricsheepmagazine.co.uk/features/2007/05/29/interview-with-melvin-and-mario-van-peebles/
37. Perkins, 'Remaking and the Film Trilogy'.
38. http://www.kamera.co.uk/interviews/a_quick_chat_with_lucas_belvaux.php
39. http://www.koyaanisqatsi.org/films/film.php
40. http://www.indiewire.com/people/int_Reggio_GOD_021018.html
41. Pearce and Luhrmann, *William Shakespeare's 'Romeo and Juliet'*, 9, 152, 154.
42. Elsaesser, *European Cinema Face to Face With Hollywood*, 23.
43. Anderson offers another instance in which the boundaries between independent and mainstream filmmaking are rather blurred. Although his first film, *Bottle Rocket* (1994), was independently financed, Disney came up with the $50 million budget for *The Life Aquatic*. Despite moving towards higher budgets, Anderson is still regarded as an 'indie' filmmaker.
44. http://www.mamapop.com/mamapop/2007/02/a_fun_music_lis.html; Tucker, 'The Life Examined with Wes Anderson'. For more on the theme of paternal conflict in Anderson's films, see Gooch, 'Making a Go of It', 26–48.
45. http://www.notcoming.com/features/tragiccomedy/
46. Quoted in Sanders, 'Coming Soon'.
47. Zimmerman, 'Digital Depbyment(s)', 227.
48. Holmlund, 'Introduction', 4.
49. http://www.nytimes.com/2008/01/17/movies/17sund.html?_r=1&oref=slogin

CHAPTER 5

Signifying Hollywood:
Sequels in the Global Economy

At the 2007 Federation of Indian Chambers of Commerce and Industry Convention (known as FICCI-Frames), a discussion between representatives of international film industries marked a significant change of attitude towards the film sequel. Italian director Adriano de Micheli remarked that sequels and prequels 'target audiences with two different [kinds of] movies – and why not!', whilst Indian film director and scriptwriter Sudhir Mishra noted the benefits of sequelisation in recasting old stories and characters in a new light: 'what we add to the older scripts is our personal experience in today's reality.' Some delegates spoke of the sequel as a way to indulge in the 'sheer passion of filmmaking'; others saw further advantages in the sequel as a way of 'making yourself perform better than your previous best'.[1] Quite distinct from rumblings in the West about the sequel as creative bankruptcy and industrial faux pas, these discussions pinpointed the film sequel as a structure that holds great potential for the growth of film markets around the world.

Established in 1927, FICCI states its main objective as 'to integrate the Indian economy with the global mainstream',[2] and to this end the Mumbai meeting brings together over 2,500 figures from film industries all over the world each year at what is Asia's biggest global entertainment industry convention. In the context of FICCI's aim to globalise Bollywood cinema, as well as a number of recent developments in Bollywood and beyond that I go on to explore here, the sequels discussion at FICCI-Frames seems indicative of more burgeoning issues of globalisation and the expansion of domestic film markets. Bollywood – the name given to the Hindi film industry based mainly in Mumbai – is the largest film industry in the world. Attracting anywhere between 13 million and 26 million cinema-goers every single day,[3] Bollywood also pumps out around 1,000 films across fifty-two languages per year; Hollywood produces around 250 films per year.[4] Until quite recently, sequels were hardly to be found amongst Bollywood's massive film output, which has tended instead to adhere to a strict set of cultural values and plot formulas. In the twenty-first century, however, sequels are a hot new trend in Bollywood, facilitating a range of generic, cultural and industrial connections with Hollywood. With such a committed home audience – Indian cinema-goers see a film up to fifteen times[5] – it seems strange that Bollywood filmmakers are re-introducing a Western format that has previously alienated home audiences.

The FICCI-Frames discussion suggests that it is not the domestic market that is being targeted by the Bollywood sequel, but rather the rest of the world. On the other hand, however, recent research shows that a desire for all things Hollywood has been on the upswing since the introduction of international TV channels to South Asia. As filmmaker Gurinder Chadha puts it, 'The world's coming in on Indian TV, so people are rejecting movies that are cliché-ridden.'[6] However, recent Bollywood sequels have in fact fared extremely well at the box office, indicating a shift in attitudes amongst both Bollywood filmmakers and audiences. Both at home and abroad, the Bollywood sequel is designed to tap the lucrative marketplace of Hollywood which, despite producing much less than half the films that Bollywood produces per annum, dwarfs Bollywood in terms of its economic stature. Whereas Hollywood's highest-paid actor commands around $60 million per picture, Bollywood's highest-paid star receives a comparatively paltry $3 million per film.[7] By creating new audiences around the globe, Bollywood apparently hopes to bring some of Hollywood's revenue to South Asian shores. What is at stake, however, is the transposition of specific cultural principles and identities. The questions this chapter poses are therefore as follows: how do the cultural resonances of the film sequel translate in Bollywood, and in what ways does this format address the social and political values of Bollywood cinema? To what extent does the Bollywood sequel act as an imperialistic category? Is it treated differently by Bollywood filmmakers? In what ways does the circulation of the Bollywood sequel across Western boundaries impact current notions of sequelisation?

Before going on to consider these issues, it is important to map briefly the resurgence of the sequel in the global film economy. In Russia, Timur Bekmambetov's *Day Watch* (*Dnevnoy dozor*) (2006), the sequel to his massively successful 'blockbuster' *Night Watch* (*Nochnoj dozor*) (2004), produced for just £1 million, made history by taking over $20 million at the domestic box office in just nine days. Paris, France, formerly the home of *auteur* filmmaking, has recently increased its sequel output, with Brahim Chioua, Managing Director of Studio Canal, commenting that 'sequels are linked to the success of French cinema at the moment.'[8] In Germany, several new sequels were recently supported by Bavaria's regional fund (FFF Bayern) to the tune of 6.6 million euros, whilst in Portugal, ninety-six-year-old filmmaker Manoel de Oliveira marked his final directorial effort by producing a sequel to Luis Buñuel's surreal classic, *Belle de jour* (1967), in the form of *Belle toujours* (2007). Further afield, South Korean cinema has recently been blitzed by domestic comedy sequels, such as Yong-ki Jeong's *Gamun-ui buhwal: Gamunui yeonggwang 3* (*Marrying the Mafia 3*) (2006), which sold 1.25 million tickets in its first weekend, generating a massive return of $8.4 million, and Dong-won Kim's *Twosabu ilchae* (*My Boss, My Student*) (2006), which now holds the record for a Korean comedy with over six million cinema admissions and an income of $41.1 million. The Hong Kong-based *Infernal Affairs* sequels (*Mou gaan dou II* [2002] and *Mou gaan dou III: Jung gik mou gaan* [2003], directed by Wai-keung Lau and Siu Fai Mak) broke box-office records at home, whilst the first *Infernal Affairs* film was picked up by Hollywood and remade in the form of Martin Scorsese's *The Departed* (2006), which went on to win four Academy Awards. In Japan, Shusuke Kaneko's sequel *Desu nôto: The last name* (*Death Note 2: The Last Name*) (2006) garnered $41.2 million at the Japanese box office with more than 4 million admissions. In Tibet, director Wanmacaidan marked the success of the first ever Tibetan language feature film, *Silent Holy Stone* (静静的嘛呢石) (2007), by announcing two forthcoming sequels.[9]

It is Bollywood, however, that holds my attention here for a number of reasons. I propose that sequelisation operates in Bollywood cinema in the two major contexts that preoccupy this book. As indicated above, sequelisation forms an increasingly large part of industrial practice in Bollywood. As a theoretical paradigm, sequelisation further enables the relationship between Hollywood and Bollywood to be examined successfully throughout the contexts of repetition and difference by which it operates. This relationship has previously been considered in terms of remaking, particularly given the rather large number of Bollywood re-hashes of Hollywood from the 1970s to the current moment. A comment by Indian filmmaker Mahesh Bhatt proves the currency of the remake in Bollywood filmmaking:

> I remember once when I was struggling to put an 'original' script together, I. S. Johar, the renowned comedian and Bollywood's first intellectual, laughingly advised me, 'son, why don't you ask your rich producer to buy you a ticket to London, see an American flick, and come back and remake it with Indian actors. It is cheaper, less bothersome and guarantees success'. At the time, I was horrified. Little did I know that in later years, I would take that advice of his too seriously.[10]

By 'too seriously', Bhatt is referring to the catalogue of Hollywood copies he has produced, from his scene-by-scene copy of *It Happened One Night* (Frank Capra, 1934) in the form of *Dil Hai Ki Manta Nahin* (1991) to his remake of *Double Indemnity* (Billy Wilder, 1944) in the form of *Murder* (2004).[11] Bhatt defends such plagiaristic practices as necessary in an increasingly commercial environment, but figures indicate that audiences are bored with the same old

Bollywood formulas, whether they remake a Hollywood film or not. Domestic fare has tended to outdo Hollywood productions at the Bollywood box office, yet several Hindi-dubbed Hollywood films (including *Spider-Man* [Sam Raimi, 2002] and *The Mummy* [Stephen Sommers, 1999]) have topped domestic films at the Bollywood box office. In 2003, 124 out of 132 films shot in Mumbai crashed and burned at the domestic box office.[12]

If such 'remaking' of Hollywood has been intended to commercialise Bollywood, it has resulted in other repetitions and juxtapositions of a much more cross-cultural register. In particular, the issue of Bollywood remaking has recently been challenged in terms of the representation of Indian identity. In 2003, the Film Federation of India (FFI) rejected six potential Academy Award entrants on the basis that they were 'too Westernised and did not reflect Indian culture'.[13] FFI Chairman Harmesh Malhotra noted that the films seemed like 'remakes of English films', and that the selection criteria required films that 'sound and look Indian'. Yet the notion of what constitutes 'Indian-ness' in Bollywood is clearly up for contest; comprising a multitude of languages and cultural identities, Bollywood signifies an Indian identity that is coded according to cinematic conventions and the trends of popular culture. As Priya Jaikumar puts it,

> [Bollywood] does not signify all Indian cinema, but a certain form of Indian cinema . . . that has gained visibility in the global market through wide international distribution . . . Bollywood is not really a term by which Indian films are referred to within India as frequently as they are abroad. In general the term erases historicity and heterogeneity, but raises Indian cinema's profile as a commodity abroad.[14]

The formal structures and categories by which Bollywood signifies Indian cinema and also, arguably, a kind of national identity are explored here in relation to a global pattern of signification that relates much more explicitly to sequelisation. Bollywood's repetition of Hollywood productions can be thought of as a form of signification that achieves both transnational and national imperatives, as the genres, aesthetics and narratives that are pilfered from a range of successful Hollywood films – notably, *The Godfather* (Francis Ford Coppola, 1972), as explored in Chapter 1 – and remade according to a distinct Bollywood formula of song, dance, costumes, religious ideologies, gender roles, and cultural standards, each of which essentially signifies, rather than remakes, an 'original' text. In so doing, Hollywood is signified according to Bollywood's cultural values, industrial practices and textual categories. The creation of a signified text, and additionally a signified Hollywood, motivates my consideration of Bollywood's 'remaking' of Hollywood as much more akin to the processes of sequelisation.

Sequelisation is therefore removed here from its predominantly Hollywood meanings and practices to refer to issues of nationality, ethnicity and homogenisation. The forms of repetition that appear to pervade most, if not all, elements of Bollywood cinema – from the tendency to remake Hollywood to repetitive audience behaviour, manifested across a number of activities such as re-enacting scenes, repeating dialogue and, of course, viewing a film 10–15 times – suggest that certain cultural rituals, traditions and ideologies are foremost in the kind of 'Indian' identity that is constructed on-screen. In brief, previous notions of remaking, repetition and sequelisation are insufficient to contend with the globalising imperatives and cross-cultural conversations that are clearly at work throughout these forms beyond Hollywood. Others have argued that cinema's role in constituting notions of nationhood and citizenship in India's culturally diverse economy is also the driving force behind Bollywood remakes of Hollywood films, and that this tendency is not as simple as copying for commercial gain, but is evocative of the 'inter-animation between the global and the local'.[15] Aditi Menon-Broker puts it succinctly when she observes that 'the Hindi commercial cinema's tendency to recycle and repeat familiar plots problematises the conventional notion of a "remake" as a theoretically useful category.'[16] Likewise, the Bollywood sequel demands careful consideration of the political, economic and cultural differences that make up this category as something quite separate from the Hollywood version.

REMAKING HOLLYWOOD

'I am not trying to criticise the film industry of today . . .
But I cannot help wondering – and often feeling sad –
why so many of the films these days look so monotonous?'
                Former Prime Minister of India, Shri Atal Bihari Vajpayee[17]

'[A]nyone who doesn't follow the West is gone.'
                Ram Gopal Varma, Bollywood producer/director[18]

The names assigned to the major Western and South Asian film industries – Hollywood and Bollywood – echo their similarity, yet there is much to suggest that the relationship between Hollywood and Bollywood is defined less by an even flow of exchange than by a hierarchy of global forces. This is evident, first and foremost, in the ways in which both industries circulate around the world. Unlike Hollywood, Bollywood has been remarkably overlooked in Western film scholarship and criticism. Typically composed of a three-hour 'masala' of song and dance routines, epic spectacle, comedy, melodrama and action sequences, Bollywood films have also tended to be excluded from Western cinemas. As

Jigna Desai observes, the West has tended to view Bollywood productions as 'kitschy and unrefined', with the exception of Satyajit Ray's work, which is safely relegated to the non-culturally specific category of art cinema.[19] Prior to the nomination of *Salaam Bombay!* (Mira Nair, 1988) at the 1989 Academy Awards, the last Bollywood picture to be nominated for an Oscar was *Mother India* (Mehboob Khan) way back in 1957. In the twenty-first century, however, Bollywood's global popularity is on the rise. A number of recent publications point to the increasing popularity of Bollywood in Western popular culture, ranging from Baz Luhrmann's Bollywood-themed play-within-a-film in his *Moulin Rouge!* (2001) to Bollywood-inspired fashion on London high streets.[20] In 2001, the UK tourist board produced a map for visitors identifying various British locations where Bollywood films had been shot.[21] There has also been a resurgence of diasporic filmmakers exploring Indian culture in transnational contexts, such as Gurinder Chadha (*Bhaji on the Beach* [1993], *Bend it like Beckham* [2002] and *Bride and Prejudice* [2004]), Deepa Metha (*Bollywood/Hollywood* [2002] and *Water* [2005]) and Mira Nair (*Salaam Bombay!* [1988] and *Monsoon Wedding* [2002]), whose films have enjoyed considerable success with audiences outside South Asia.

However, this popularity has impacted the relationship between Bollywood and the cultural ethics it has traditionally reflected. Ram Gopal Varma's comment above vocalises a sensibility amongst many Bollywood filmmakers regarding the direction 'New Bollywood' must take if it is to survive in a global environment; but what exactly does Varma mean when he suggests Bollywood must 'follow the West'? In an interview for *Time* magazine, Varma qualifies this statement by asserting that 'following the West, the best of the West, is following originality.' Hardly so when one considers the number of remakes and sequels that pervade Western film production. But what Varma does acknowledge here are the major shifts that have taken place within Hindi commercial cinema throughout the last decade, many of which have sought to align Bollywood with its much more lucrative Western counterpart.

Some of these changes are perceivably beneficial. Many filmmakers have hailed the 'new professionalism' and re-organisation of the Hindi film industry, which has previously tended to base its professional 'contracts' on verbal agreements, but is now becoming much more patterned after Hollywood's rigorously stringent legal system. In addition, Bollywood film production has previously (and notoriously) been funded by the Mumbai underground, which has been the cause of much controversy – for instance, director Rakesh Roshan was shot in 2000 after he allegedly refused mob requests for his son to star in an underworld-financed film.[22] Mafia financiers have also tended to set strict criteria for Bollywood productions to ensure profits, resulting in an overkill of tried-and-test plot formulas. However, following the liberalisation of international trade and commerce and the removal of India's heavy restrictions on global investment, Bollywood is beginning to procure finance from legitimate sources, thus stabilising the film economy and permitting new forms of creative expression to flourish.

Yet what these industrial changes have cost Bollywood in terms of its reflection of and integration with cultural values and national identities is up for debate. Much criticism has been directed towards the steady flow of 'babes, boys, and bikes'[23] into Bollywood films, which have previously tended to adhere to a strict code of modest clothing and an absence of sexual affection. But it is Bollywood's proclivity for remaking Hollywood films that has garnered the most criticism. The comment above by former Prime Minister of India, Shri Atal Bihari Vajpayee, was delivered during his remarks on the latest remake of Hindi classic *Devdas* (Sanjay Leela Bhansali, 2002). Although the Prime Minister gave the film his approval for entry into the 2003 Academy Awards (it failed to achieve a nomination), his comments highlighted the tendency of the Indian film industry to churn out the same old stereotypes and plot formulas. Notably, the Prime Minister does not warn filmmakers against remaking, but simply proposes a different kind of remaking:

> In India we have many great literary works – ancient, medieval and modern. I would urge our filmmakers to be bold and creative and choose powerful themes from the great works of Indian literature.[24]

Clearly, the kind of remaking that is proposed here reinforces cultural ideals; the other kind of remaking implied by Vajpayee – the 'monotonous' remaking of Hollywood films – apparently works to the opposite effect, bleaching out the traditions and ideologies that circulate throughout plot formulas. *Devdas* is indicated in Vajpayee's speech as an example of the kind of remaking that foregrounds cultural distinction. *Devdas* has been remade no less than nine times, and its latest incarnation made history as Bollywood's most expensive film ever, costing over $10 million to produce. Based on the 1917 novel by Bengali writer Sharat Chandra Chatterjee, *Devdas* has been translated on-screen nine times in Bengali, Hindi, Telegu and Malayalam, and has subsequently been popularised over the years as a work of cultural significance – no less than the 'mythological reference point for Hindi melodrama'.[25] *Devdas* fits the description of one of India's 'great literary works', and Vajpayee's call for more adaptations based on such works is clearly a call for productions that enforce Indian cultural values.

Vajpayee's speech is one of few instances in which distinctions are made (albeit implicitly) between kinds of Bollywood remake; more generally, the Bollywood remake tends to be categorised in simple terms as A Very Bad Thing in terms of the representation of Indian culture. Implicit in the criticisms directed at Bollywood remaking is the assumption that, by copying Hollywood,

Bollywood is engaging in a broader activity of cultural hegemony. Amongst the discourses surrounding the practice of film remaking are a wide range of definitions that posit the remake, like the sequel, as a reductive textual process that squanders originality for imitation and commodification. Although recent studies have helpfully shed light on the extra-textual categories of remaking, such as commerce, authorship, critical discourse and cross-cultural dialogue, the Bollywood remake remains entrenched in cliché and disappointment.[26] Yet is 'remaking' the correct term here? What are the precise forms of repetition in this kind of remaking (such as textual, generic, aesthetic), and what are their commercial and cross-cultural contexts?

There is evidence that recent Bollywood 'remakes' do not so much remake or copy Hollywood, but are much more involved in processes of resistance, subversion and globalisation. Consider, for example, Rakesh Roshan's *Koi . . . Mil Gaya* (2003), which portrays a mentally retarded young man, Rohit (played by the director's son, Hrithik Roshan), who continues his late father's work in extra-terrestrial communication by coming in contact with an alien named Jadoo, who gives Rohit superhuman powers. The film is a purported remake of Steven Spielberg's *E. T.* (1982), yet numerous intertexts circulate throughout the production, and on various levels, and in fact the entire production reads much more like a rewriting of Hollywood sci-fi than a regurgitation of Spielberg's film. This is suggested by the following: the theme tune of sci-fi fantasy *The Neverending Story* (Wolfgang Petersen, 1984) resonates throughout Roshan's soundtrack; the musical notes featured in Spielberg's *Close Encounters of the Third Kind* (1977) clearly inspire the melody used in Roshan's film to communicate with beings from outer space; the opening credits crib those of *Star Wars* (George Lucas, 1977); the mediatisation of alien landings echoes *Signs* (M. Night Shyamalan, 2002); Rohit's character, and particularly his relationship with his mother, is starkly reminiscent of *Forrest Gump* (Robert Zemeckis, 1994); after meeting with Jadoo, Rohit's sudden muscularity and sharpened eye vision echo *Spider-Man*; moments from *The Abyss* (James Cameron, 1989), *Flubber* (Les Mayfield, 1997) and a host of other films are also referenced on numerous occasions.[27]

In constructing India's first sci-fi film,[28] Roshan draws upon generic iconographies (and melodies) to contextualise and commercialise his production. Yet this is no standard re-formulation of genre codes; amongst the forms of 'remaking' in *Koi . . . Mil Gaya* are important representations of Indian-ness. Elements of Hinduism are apparent in the presentation of Jadoo as a blue alien – blue being the colour of the god Vishnu, and more generally the signature colour of beings which are capable of fighting evil – who also plays the role of a Hindu god.[29] Rohit repeatedly prays to Lord Krishna, and it is after one such prayer that Jadoo contacts Rohit, suggesting prayer, not technology, as the most effective means of communication. The film's pointed re-alignment of the sci-fi genre with Indian religious values can be seen not simply as creating a bricolage of ideological, generic and textual categories, but as utilising the sci-fi genre as an organising structure within which to vocalise Indian identities and ideologies. Dominic Alessio and Jessica Langer argue that the film's presentation of sci-fi resists Hollywood homogenisation, in so far as the importance of Hindu religion is evident in the film. This, they point out, is never more apparent than in the depiction of a large 'OM-like' spacecraft carrying a Vishnu-like being hovering over the crucifix statue on the roof of Rohit's oppressive Catholic school, which 'is also a signifier of a dominant Hindu nationalistic discourse'.[30] Claiming the film's division of the dominant Indian religious groups, and particularly its reification of Hindu values (such as self-sacrifice) within the plot, as primary markers of this form of signification, Alessio and Langer posit the film as a challenge to the 'hegemony of Hollywood's big blockbuster domination of the SF genre in Bollywood' and, more generally, 'the hegemony of Western cinematic production, both economically and ideologically'.[31] In this light, *Koi . . . Mil Gaya* appears as less a remake than a reflexive commentary on the textual, cultural and industrial relationships between Bollywood and Hollywood, whilst the forms of repetition throughout the film signal an agenda of resistance and cultural signification.

Bollywood's challenges to Hollywood far exceed the rather formalistic, and indeed cultural, dimensions of films like *Koi . . . Mil Gaya*; commercial imperatives are also at work. Claims Desai, Bollywood is now 'a global cinema that consciously positions itself against the hegemony of Hollywood'.[32] Within this statement is an acknowledgement of the ways in which Bollywood is increasingly turning its gaze towards audiences and revenues beyond South Asia. Hollywood offers an important model of the process of globalisation, owning up to 90 per cent of all the films shown in most parts of the world.[33] Whereas Hollywood's transnational media corporations have played a key role in such vast exportations, it is important to note that its films are increasingly organised according to cultural categories rather than generic formulas. As Toby Miller claims in *Global Hollywood 2*, 'the arbitrary interpretations of positioning simplify the meanings of a film in order to appeal to the imaginary impulses of distinct national audiences.'[34] To support this claim, Miller points to *Waiting to Exhale* (Forest Whitaker, 1995), which failed to capture audiences with its original premise of 'chick flick', but fared much better under the banner of 'African-American chick flick'.[35] From such marketing strategies to the slow-but-steady representation of ethnic minorities in big-budget movies, Hollywood is becoming increasingly aware of the importance of being 'global'.

The formulations of repetition and difference in recent Bollywood cinema can be understood in this regard not so much as copying Hollywood but as creating points of distinction and comparison to position Bollywood as both a 'local' cinema, or one that continues to refract Indian identities and cultural values, at the same time as it translates easily to audiences around the globe. In grappling with the two (somewhat contradictory) functions of the global and the local, Bollywood engages in processes of signification and secondariness that can be accessed through a consideration of the sequel's cross-cultural registers. For instance, Roshan's film *Krrish* (2006), the sequel to *Koi . . . Mil Gaya*, extends its predecessor's portrait of hegemonic resistance and Indian identity. *Krrish* accomplishes this by invoking sequelisation as a framework within which to separate more fully the cinematic codes of Bollywood from those of Hollywood, and to render distinct notions of 'Indian-ness' from Western values and identities, at the same time as the film is situated firmly within a 'global' context.

Rather than simply draw upon 'the great works of Indian literature' to achieve these aims, *Krrish* brings together elements of Hindu religion (the main character is named after Lord Krishna), Chinese martial arts, Hollywood films, and a number of elements from ancient and culturally significant Indian texts, *The Mahabharata* and *The Ramayana*. The film focuses on Krishna (also played by Hrithik Roshan), the son of Rohit from *Koi . . . Mil Gaya*. A much more muscular and heroic version of his father, Krishna has also inherited Rohit's superhuman powers, which leads to his transformation into a masked crusader known as Krrish. Krishna's paths cross those of his father when he visits his love interest, Priya (Priyanka Chopra), in Singapore, which is where Rohit apparently died whilst building (and subsequently destroying) a computer that predicts the future. After saving a group of people from a fire, 'Krrish' becomes a media legend and masked superhero, and a reward is offered for the discovery of his identity. Meanwhile, Dr Siddhant Arya (Naseeruddin Shah), the evil scientist for whom Rohit had been building the prophetic computer, has rebuilt the machine for the express purposes of world domination. It also turns out he has been keeping Rohit alive in a virtually vegetative state for the last twenty years, as the computer requires Rohit's heartbeat to function. After killing Dr Arya, saving his father and winning the girl, Krishna returns to India, where he uses his grandfather's old extra-terrestrial computer to say 'thank you' to the alien, Jadoo, who started it all.

Whereas *Koi . . . Mil Gaya* presented India's first sci-fi flick, *Krrish* offers up India's first superhero as a re-imagination of a prominent figure of Hindu religion with overtones of similar superheroes from *The Matrix* (Larry and Andy Wachowski, 1999), *Daredevil* (Mark Steven Johnson, 2003), *Spider-man*, *Superman* (Richard Donner, 1978) and *Batman* (Tim Burton, 1989). The 'local' concerns presented in *Koi . . . Mil Gaya* are repositioned here in a much more international context; filmed in Singapore, Tokyo and Mumbai, *Krrish* also benefited from the input of Hollywood special effects experts Marc Kolbe and Craig Mumma, whose previous work includes *Godzilla* (Roland Emmerich, 1998), *Independence Day* (Roland Emmerich, 1996) and *Sky Captain and the*

World of Tomorrow (Kerry Conran, 2004); the film was choreographed by Tong Ching Siu-Tung, who previously choreographed *Hero* (Yimou Zhang, 2002) and *The House of Flying Daggers* (Yimou Zhang, 2004), both of which appear as influences in the film. The scenery and culture of Singapore feature strongly in the film, no doubt motivated by the Singapore Tourism Board's $10 million 'Film in Singapore Scheme', which funds up to 50 per cent of production costs when films are shot on location in Singapore.[36]

Within this international context are a number of important 'local' dynamics. Krishna's love interest is a Non-Resident Indian (NRI) living in Singapore, and the film's strong emphasis on new technologies – particularly the fortune-telling computer – speaks to the mobility of Indian identities and the modernisation of Indian society that so characterise the twenty-first century. *Krrish* sets out to locate India and its cultures as a dominant feature on the global map, and it does so precisely by invoking the sequel's contextualisation of difference and secondariness to enable both the global and local, or Hollywood and Bollywood, to co-exist. This is implemented at various levels of the film's production. Bollywood has traditionally tended not to produce film tie-ins or merchandise; however, an onslaught of *Krrish* merchandise marks a turn in the tide. The film has also been selected by the Indian Institute of Management (IIM) as a case study for global business practices, amongst them global management of business, global factor of production, global competition, global penetration and market capitalisation. At the same time, however, IIM identifies *Krrish* as 'one of the first Indian movies, which has created a brand called India and propagated Indian cinema style'.[37]

Although *Krrish* pilfers many texts, styles and trends from numerous global intertexts, it perceivably sidesteps any notion of simply 'remaking' Hollywood by successfully localising cultural concerns within a global framework, or by signifying, rather than repeating, the global within the local. As David Morley and Kevin Robins suggest, the local is definitely relative to the global: 'the "local" should be seen as a fluid and relational space, constituted only in and through its relation to the global.'[38] But in the Bollywood 'remake', this kind of relativity is impossible; within the context of mere repetition and imitation, the local copies the global. The sequel, however, highlights points of cultural distinction and difference, and refers to a point of origin that is consistent with the local. For instance, *Krrish*, despite all its references to Hollywood films, locates its textual point of origin in *Koi . . . Mil Gaya*, whilst the reference point for the main character – and thus the film's genre, values and cultural identity – is clearly rooted in Hindu religion.

The figuration of global values in tandem with those of Indian culture in *Krrish* was something of a gamble on Roshan's part, at least as far as dedicated Bollywood audiences are concerned. How would domestic audiences respond to the film's global elements, or indeed the globalising of Indian culture? The film's distribution targeted markets at home with vigour; but abroad, it limped around a handful of theatres. Approximately 150–200 prints of a film are typically released across Indian cinemas at any one time; for *Krrish*, 700 prints were released. In the US, the film played at just fifty-eight cinema theatres – Henry Jenkins observes that the film screened 'not at the local multiplex or even the art house but in small ma-and-pa run theatres which cater to the local south Asian population' – bringing in a total US revenue of just over $1 million.[39] Reviews were mixed. In India, however, critics raved about the film, and box-office figures topped $15 million. If these figures are anything to go by, *Krrish* has proved a much more successful blend of Hollywood and Bollywood than have previous productions, at least with home audiences.

REMEMBERING/REMAKING INDIAN-NESS

'Bollywood films have always provided me with a point of cultural access to the homeland. Keeping up on all things Bollywood has allowed me to navigate my cultural identity by maintaining ties to the most iconic of all Indian cultural values, the Hindi film.'

Sheela Shrinivas[40]

One of the chief objectives of Bollywood's global enterprises is to address diasporic audiences, who, as the above quote by NRI Sheela Shrinivas suggests, revisit and reaffirm their cultural roots through Bollywood. A second demographic targeted by Bollywood's globalisation is South Asian youth, who formed a significant basis of *Krrish*'s merchandising efforts (which focused largely on T-shirts, schoolbags, dolls, activity books and masks), who are apparently 'more likely to seek out group and collective experiences compared to other demographic segments'.[41] Much of Bollywood's presentation of cultural values and identities is therefore carried out according to an agenda of nostalgia and recollection, as if to remind forthcoming generations and NRIs of their roots, and also to embed notions of 'Indian-ness' within an emotional, reflective context. As a number of new films prove, it is the sequel that most often facilitates this kind of nostalgic prompting; claims Arya Aiyappan, 'The recent splurge of sequels setting up new genres in Bollywood has taken the audience for a roller coaster ride down [. . .] memory lane.'[42] In remaking or sequelising Hollywood, then, Bollywood plays an important role not only in constituting 'Indian-ness', but in continuing the ideologies that pervade the cultures of India well into the future.

In considering this notion, it is first important to note the patterns of repetition and 'remaking' that are present not only in Bollywood's formal characteristics, but in its modes of reception and audience response. Says Sumita

Chakravarty, Bollywood is no less than 'a microcosm of the social, political, economic, and cultural life of a nation. It is the contested site where meanings are negotiated, traditions made and remade, identities affirmed or rejected.'[43] Such is the role of Bollywood cinema in Indian popular culture that audiences commonly re-enact film scenes and song performances in a variety of social and cultural situations. The typical Bollywood narrative structure is designed to accommodate such viewing practices, which are also very selective. Lakshmi Srinivas's study of 'active audiences' in India reports viewers routinely turning up for a cinema performance halfway through the film and leaving before it ends, and popping out for groceries during the interval (a standard practice across South Asian cinemas), as well as fastforwarding, rewinding and/or repeating scenes from a film during viewings of films on DVD; conversely, Western audiences tend to watch a film from beginning to end, and do not experience an interval halfway through a screening.[44] In addition to such selective viewing are forms of extremely 'mobile' and active participation. Whereas Western audiences typically watch a cinema screening in relative silence, Srinivas notes a stark contrast amongst Indian audiences, who comment loudly during screenings regarding performances and plot, applaud and cheer at scenes, and also 'talk to characters, give them advice and take sides'.[45] These viewing practices are almost always part of a collective experience; families attend screenings together, and, through such vocal, interactive participation, the audience becomes a collective entity, responding to and discussing the events on screen.

Such interactive participation continues the viewing experience outside the cinema theatre and throughout various aspects of Indian society. Others have noted post-performance repetition amongst Bollywood audiences in the form of weddings that are themed after a particular film scene (or indeed an entire production), songs and dialogue from films that are memorised and repeated as part of social interaction, film costumes that are copied and worn by viewers, and so on. Menon-Broker offers two categories by which to identify the kinds of repetition inherent in Indian reception activity: 'repatterning' and 'reperformance'. According to Menon-Broker, repatterning is a 'style of viewing that allows the film's structure to be broken down into segments that are consumed with limited concern for narrative, plot and causality', whilst reperformance is concerned with imitation and re-enactment, or ' "re-living" the cinema's moments of pleasure [for example] recreating/enacting the songs, the dance, and the costumes in urban public space outside the cinema hall'.[46] Both categories can also be thought of as a kind of cultural dialogue that circulates between audiences and filmmakers. Whereas audiences appropriate and perform elements of Bollywood films throughout a range of social interactions, Bollywood films translate and anticipate these activities and performances according to a stridently formulaic and culturally self-reflexive narrative format.

The forms of participation prevalent throughout Bollywood audiences are an important part of accessing and reconstituting Indian culture, and these forms have arguably developed in harmony with the codes and formulas of Bollywood film. As a relatively new category to emerge in Bollywood in recent years, the sequel offers a number of alternative methods of participation. In particular, the Bollywood sequel serves as a way for audiences not only to reperform cultural values, but also as a remembering scenario by which audiences – particularly NRIs and second-generation Indians – engage in nostalgic forms of interaction that reposition the ideals of 'Indian-ness' within a cultural environment that is rapidly becoming much more 'global'. At once past-bound and future-oriented, the sequel enables such recollective activity to take place in order to redefine the traditional values and qualities of Indian culture, which is especially important in the midst of numerous modernising projects in Indian society. Bollywood may well be benefiting from globalisation, but, as with many developing countries and societies, a major challenge is posed to the diversity of regional Indian mores by the advancement of the global society. The Bollywood sequel perceivably performs the important role of addressing the global transformations that contemporary Indian society is experiencing, at the same time as it reaffirms and reminds of the cultural infrastructure that has so characterised India throughout all its regions, languages and religions for thousands of years.

Lage Raho Munna Bhai (*Munnabhai Second Innings*) (Rajkumar Hirani, 2006),[47] the sequel to *Munnabhai MBBS* (Rajkumar Hirani, 2003), offers such an instance of cultural remembering. The film is largely responsible for the resurgence of popular interest in Mahatma Gandhi (1869–1948), one of India's most prominent historical figures and leader of the Indian independence movement. Attributed with the title of 'Father of the Nation', Gandhi, or 'Bapu', as he is more affectionately known, embodies a number of key Indian principles, amongst them non-violence, spirituality, truth (or 'satyagraha') and humanitarianism. The action of *Munnabhai MBBS* portrays Munna Bhai (Sanjay Dutt), a Mumbai hoodlum, as he studies for India's MBBS degree to become a medical doctor to please his parents, and subsequently develops his own comic medical practices similar to those performed by Robin Williams in *Patch Adams* (Tom Shadyac, 1998). In the sequel, Munna Bhai and his 'sidekick', Circuit (Arshad Warsi), return for more comic action, this time due to a ghostly visit by Mahatma Gandhi (Dilip Prabhavalkar), who persuades Munna Bhai to help other people solve their problems through 'Gandhigiri' – a regional Mumbai colloquialism which refers to the kind of non-violence, or peaceful resistance, espoused by Gandhi throughout his life.[48] 'Gandhigiri' is also used in the film to refer to how Munna Bhai gives up 'dadagiri' – or the use of brutal, physical force to assert a point of view or action – for Gandhigiri. Notably, the film forges a connection between the performance of Bollywood codes – the song and dance number – and Gandhi: Gandhi appears to Munna Bhai each time he performs one of the film's musical numbers. This narrative device is vital in affirming the cultural role of both Bollywood cinema and Gandhi, and implicit in their association is the suggestion that Bollywood and its reper-formance provides access to Gandhi's traditions and teachings. Similarly, Gandhi's teachings inform much of the film's plot. At one point Munna Bhai prompts a neglectful son to respect his father by throwing him a birthday party and buying him a present – a re-enactment of the Hindu belief in paying respect to one's elders. And although Munna Bhai's 'prompting' takes place in the form of hanging the neglectful son out of a skyscraper window by his ankles, Munna Bhai reflects upon his action by paraphrasing a Gandhi maxim: 'violence never works!'

The cultural impact of *Lage Raho Munna Bhai* was massive. According to one newspaper report,

> Thieves who stole goods from a poor man decided to return them after watching this movie. The governments in many states have declared the movie tax-free, so moviegoers will not be charged tax when buying a ticket, and the leader of the Congress party, the ruling party in India, has urged members to watch the film.'[49]

The film also sparked a non-violent protest amongst 2,000 farmers from India's cotton-growing Vidarbha region, who recently experienced a devastating drought-related debt crisis and were refused loans from the region's banks, cul-minating in over 200 suicides. In September 2007 – four weeks after the film's release – protestors garlanded a bank manager with flowers in a direct re-enactment of Gandhigiri, presented in the film in terms of fighting with flowers instead of weapons.[50] Indian mafia don Babloo Srivastava used a similar tactic when arriving at court for a murder case, passing out roses to everyone he met, claiming '[I] hope to be able to spread the message of love and peace by doing what Munnabhai does in the film.'[51] More Munna Bhai-inspired flower-spreading was to be found in Lucknow, a prominent city in Northern India, when local citizens 'protested' at the selling of alcohol at an alcohol store by strewing flowers around the premises.[52] An article in *The Hindu*, India's national newspa-per, hangs much hope on the film's message for future Indian generations:

> It is to be hoped that *Lage Raho Munnabhai*, set in the idiom of today's youth, will motivate them to deepen and accelerate the search for the Gandhi within – before it is too late, for them and for all of us.[53]

Although *Lage Raho Munnabhai* is not the first film to revisit an important his-torical figure – *Rang De Basanti* (*Paint it Yellow*) (Rakesh Omprakash Mehra,

2006) depicts the life of Bhagat Singh, a prominent figure of the Indian independence movement who was executed at the age of twenty-three – it is the
first to use the sequel as a contextualising device by which to juxtapose and
comment upon the divisions within Indian society in terms of past and present.
Specifically, the sequel is used to reposition the values and practices of a
significant historical figure within the context of contemporary Indian society.

Implicit in the film's recontextualisation of Gandhigiri is an indication of
the problems within a nation that is modernising at a rapid rate. The film's
credit sequence conveys this notion by depicting Mumbai as a 'crazy city' that
has come a long way from its pre-industrial origins to become an urban metropolis much like New York or Los Angeles. During this sequence a radio DJ
implicitly contrasts the modern elements of Mumbai city life with those of a
previous era:

> Why don't those 108 [TV] channels wipe away our woes? You, who con-
> nects at the click of a mouse, do you know who lives in the neighbouring
> house? In this era of emails and mobiles, when did you last see your best
> friend's smile? [. . .] Is this the way we wish to live?

The new technologies and modernising projects on display in *Krrish* are coun-
tered in *Lage Raho Munna Bhai* by a reassertion of the importance of family
and social relationships: again, resonances of Gandhigiri. More importantly,
the film's resurrection of Gandhi suggests a need for reconciliation between the
past and future-bound ideologies that underline the transformations within
Indian society. The tensions within Indian society between ethnic, religious and
political groups, and particularly between socio-economic classes, have been
perceived to be exacerbated by the rapidity of the forces of modernisation, and
by exclusion as India moves towards becoming a 'global' nation – the starving
farmers of the Vidarbha region are just one instance of the sectors of Indian
society who have been abandoned in the pursuit of a modernised urban
economy and lifestyle. These troubles are not elaborated upon in *Lage Raho
Munna Bhai*, but acknowledged in subtle shades and as context for the 'mess'
that Gandhi comes to clear up with his message.

Other Bollywood sequels have performed similar methods of cultural
remembering that also reposition the 'local' within the global, and vice versa.
For instance, *International Hera Pheri* (Anees Bazmee, 2009), the forthcoming
sequel to *Phir Hera Pheri* (Neeraj Vora, 2006) and *Hera Pheri* (Priyadarshan,
2000), was originally planned to be shot in a range of locations outside India, in
keeping with the film's (working) title and global theme. However, producer
Feroz Nadiadwala decided that the film's 'local flavour' was central to its cultural integrity, so the film will be shot entirely in Mumbai.[54] Although the film's
'international' sensibility is to be retained, it is significant that localness is

identified here as an important part of the film's depiction of India's location within the global milieu. Another example is offered by Anurag Kashyap's animated sequel,[55] *Return of Hanuman* (2007), which portrays the Hindu god Hanuman, one of the main characters of the ancient Indian epic, the *Ramayana*, as a global superhero. In its rewriting of the *Ramayana*, the film juxtaposes the modern with the mythological – figuring, for instance, the Hindu god Chitragupta surfing the net on his laptop – at the same time as it portrays Hanuman as reperforming *Sholay* (Ramesh Sippy, 1975), which is the biggest blockbuster in Bollywood history. Notably, *Sholay* has acquired a considerable cultural legacy. Some scenes and dialogue from this film – such as the line 'Kitne Aadmi the' ('How many people were there?') and 'Ek Baccha Aur Tum Saat aur Phir Bhi Jaane Diyaa' ('one kid, seven adults, and still you allowed him to go') – have been popularised throughout Indian society to the extent that they resonate 'Indian-ness' and perform vital roles of social interaction. Reperformed in *Return of Hanuman*, the dialogue and scenes from *Sholay* set Indian's cultural (ancient) past and present in conversation; in so doing, the cultural values and traditions that circulate throughout both texts reconfigure 'Indian-ness' in terms of a past-bound identity that speaks to the future. Significantly, the film was the first to receive an Educational Certificate from India's Censor Board, ostensibly because of its message on the issue of global warming, but also because 'the Censor Board [. . .] felt that *Hanuman Returns* [sic] reinforces the belief in our mythological stories thus keeping our tradition and culture alive.'[56] Efforts to recreate Hanuman as a global brand, as well as plans to set-dub a third *Hanuman* instalment in all major international languages, signal the sequel's part in globalising such culturally specific features.[57]

The remembering activities throughout the films noted above treat the sequel as a category that counterpoints the past, present and future to significant cross-cultural effect. The overwhelmingly repetitious forms of reception amongst Indian audiences – which, as Ashish Rajadhyaksha points out, sets Bollywood apart from any other film industry in the world[58] – have traditionally resonated with Bollywood's textual categories and formulas. However, the sequel poses new systems of engagement in terms of its signification of global practices and influences which regional audiences are now experiencing. In this regard, the Bollywood sequel performs a chief role in addressing Indian diasporic audiences, for whom 'cinema viewing constitutes one of the most culturally visible arenas of activity', particularly in terms of re-accessing cultural identities and nostalgically echoing the ethics and customs of their homeland.[59] Discrete from other categories of Bollywood films, the Bollywood sequel facilitates this kind of re-identification specifically because of the binaries it tends to juxtapose and address; pre- versus post-industrial Indian society, global versus local elements, past and present 'Mother India', Gandhi versus a contemporary Mumbai thug. In so doing, Bollywood is additionally reconstituted as possessing its own cinematic codes, styles and categories which are distinct from those of Hollywood; although global inter-texts are present in many Bollywood sequels, they are usually rendered as textual translations of a culturally specific character or custom – the likening of Lord Krishna to a superhero *à la* Superman or Neo, for instance, conveys to Western audiences the popular significance of this important Hindu figure – instead of vacuous retreads.

Whether such sequels continue to balance Indian virtues successfully with global imperatives remains to be seen. Many have already pointed out Bollywood's problematic assertion of 'Indian-ness' which, comprised of numerous regions, tongues and creeds throughout South Asia, can be seen to operate at times to marginalise and exclude those identities and audiences that form this identity beyond its cinematic context. Throughout its globalising endeavours, Bollywood runs a high risk of generating its own hegemony. As Raminder Kaur and Ajay J. Sinsha warn, '[Hollywood] pushes world cultures towards homogenisation, whereas [Bollywood] introduces in those cultures a fragmentary process.'[60] The films examined above show that there is potential for a healthy exploration of the diversity of identities and customs that make up 'Indian-ness' in South Asia and beyond, yet this requires the many cuts and turns of cultural difference to be more fully represented and considered.

CONCLUSIONS

The relationship between Hollywood and Bollywood is a useful case study in examining the sequel's performance in the global economy, yet this relation-ship is not entirely unique. The industrial model that Hollywood has provided for Bollywood is now being echoed throughout a number of globally emerging film industries, some of which have adopted a similar copy-cat label, such as 'Nollywood' (the Nigerian film industry that grew from a few hundred dollars and several eager filmmakers to a $250 million industry in just over a decade), 'Tollywood' (the Teluga film industry, based in the state of Andhra Pradesh in India, now the world's third largest film industry) and 'Pollywood' (the Punjabi-language film industry in India, also known as 'Punjwood'). Wimal Dissanayake also notes the influence of Bollywood on the Sri Lankan com-mercial cinema, which is fast making its mark on the global film scene.[61] Aside from these provocative monikers, many film industries have patterned them-selves after Hollywood's efforts to globalise its industry. As outlined earlier, the sequel is swiftly emerging in this global environment throughout a broad range of cross-cultural dialogues and categories. In particular, the kinds of cultural remembering that inform the Bollywood sequel operate specifically to circulate cultural mores amongst the Indian diaspora by providing a suitable context for the 'global' and 'local' to correspond. As I go on to show, however, the sequel's investments in collective remembering can be regarded in alternative contexts that prove vital not only in understanding the assertion of cultural values in the face of globalisation and homogenisation, but, amidst such rapid global transitions and historical developments, in re-considering our relationship to the past.

NOTES

1. A transcript of this seminar is available at Priya Kapoor, 'FICCI Frames 2007'.
2. http://www.ficci-frames.com/about-us/about-us.htm
3. See Pendakur, *Indian Popular Cinema*, 16.
4. http://www.ibpn.co.uk/creative.asp; Plate, 'Hollywood Faces New Competition'.
5. Hirji, 'When Local Meets Lucre'.
6. http://www.bbc.co.uk/worldservice/arts/highlights/010628_bollywood.shtml
7. http://entertainment.timesonline.co.uk/tol/arts_and_entertainment/film/bollywood/article2665934.ece
8. James, 'France to Sequels'.
9. http://www.china.org.cn/english/features/film/151748.htm
10. Quoted in Bhaskaran, 'Aping Hollywood'.
11. Despite resonances between *Murder* and *Unfaithful* (Adrian Lyne, 2002), Bhatt claims *Double Indemnity* as his source because, in his words, 'there are no copyrights for this film as it was made in [the] 1940's.' See Sherawat, 'Transcription of Press Conference for *Murder*'.
12. Bhaskaran, 'Aping Hollywood'.
13. Ahmed, 'No Bollywood Films for Oscars'. The six films in question are *Koi . . . Mil Gaya* (Rakesh Roshan, 2003), *Gangaajal* (Prakash Jha, 2003), *Janantaram Mamantaram* (Soumitra Ranade, 2003), *Jhankaar Beats* (Sujoy Ghosh, 2003), *Andaaz* (Raj Kanwar, 2003) and *Jogger's Park* (Anant Balani, 2003).
14. http://annenbergfiles.org/2007/08/bollywood_syantani_chatterjee.html
15. Gokulsing and Dissanayake, *Indian Popular Cinema*, 3.
16. Menon-Broker, *A Hall of Mirrors*, 39.
17. http://pib.nic.in/archieve/lreleng/lyr2002/rdec2002/10122002/r1012200216.html
18. Perry, 'The Trailblazer'.
19. Desai, 'Bollywood Abroad', 124.
20. As a good starting point, see Kaur and Sinsha, 'Bollyworld'.
21. Ciecko, 'Theorising Asian Cinema(s)', 18.
22. http://www.time.com/time/magazine/article/0,9171,501020722-320814,00.html
23. http://www.bbc.co.uk/worldservice/arts/highlights/010628_bollywood.shtml
24. http://pib.nic.in/archieve/lreleng/lyr2002/rdec2002/10122002/r1012200216.html
25. Rajadhyaksha and Willemen, *Encyclopaedia of Indian Cinema*, 244.
26. See, for instance, Verevis, *Film Remakes*; Horton and McDougal, *Play It Again, Sam*.
27. Dominic Alessio and Jessica Langer claim that amongst the film's reference to Hollywood sci-fi productions are nods to *Rambo: First Blood Part III* (George P. Cosmatos, 1988), *Back to the Future* (Robert Zemeckis, 1985), *Independence Day* (Roland Emmerich, 1994) and *Apocalypse Now* (Francis Ford Coppola, 1979). See Alessio and Langer, 'Nationalism and Postcolonialism in Indian Science Fiction', 221.

28. http://www.krrishthemovie.com/main.htm
29. See also Alessio and Langer, 'Nationalism and Postcolonialism in Indian Science Fiction', 224.
30. Ibid., 224–6.
31. Ibid., 227.
32. Desai, 'Bollywood Abroad', 115.
33. Miller *et al.*, *Global Hollywood 2*, 9.
34. Ibid., 270.
35. Ibid., 270.
36. http://www.thehindubusinessline.com/bline/2005/07/07/stories/2005070701330400.htm
37. http://news.moneycontrol.com/india/newsarticle/stocksnews.php?cid=1&autono=1554&source=ibnlive.com
38. Morley and Robins, *Space of Identity*, 17.
39. Jenkins, 'Truth, Justice and the South Asian Way'.
40. Shrinivas, 'Does Crossing Over Mean Overstepping Cultural Boundaries?'
41. Srinivas, 'The Active Audience: Spectatorship, Social Relations and the Experience of Cinema in India', 160.
42. http://entertainment.oneindia.in/bollywood/features/don-dhoom-2-071106.html
43. Chakravarty, *National Identity in Indian Popular Cinema 1947–1987*, 32.
44. Srinivas, 'The Active Audience', 165–7.
45. Ibid., 170.
46. Menon-Broker, *A Hall of Mirrors*, 18.
47. The film has had a number of working titles, amongst them *Meets Mahatma Gandhi* and *Carry on Munna Bhai*. The film's producers finally settled on *Munnabhai Second Innings* several months before the film's release.
48. See also Shah, 'Gandhigiri – a Philosophy for our Times'.
49. Sharma, 'How Gandhi Got his Mojo Back'.
50. Ahmed, 'Gandhi-style Protest by Farmers'.
51. 'Munnabhai Effect'.
52. Pradhan, 'Lucknow Citizens go Gandhian on Liquor Merchant'.
53. Shah, 'Gandhigiri – a Philosophy for our Times'.
54. Jha, '*Munnabhai, Hera Pheri* Brand War Hots Up'.
55. Although both the character and concept follow on from Anurag Kashyap's previous animation *Hanuman* (V. G. Samant and Milind Ukey, 2005), which depicted the childhood of Hanuman, *Return of Hanuman* opens with a disclaimer that it is, in fact, not a sequel, leaving audiences and critics a little confused; the film's title, character and plot define the film as a sequel. Thus far, neither Kashyap nor the film's producers have commented on this disclaimer; a third *Hanuman* instalment is slated for release in 2009, and plans to create a series and global brand out of this character seem to contradict the sequel disclaimer. One can only speculate that the disclaimer was intended to enforce the film's 'originality'.
56. Maniar, 'Return of Hanuman is Tax Free'.
57. Sinha, 'Now, Hanuman goes to Manhattan'.
58. Rajadhyaksha, 'Strange Attractions'.
59. Punathambakar, 'We are Like this Only', 3.
60. Kaur and Sinsha, 'Bollyworld', 15.
61. Dissanayake, 'Sri Lanka', 114.

CHAPTER 6

Sequelisation and Secondary Memory: Steven Spielberg's *Artificial Intelligence: A. I.* (2001)

In the introduction to this book I noted a comparison between sequelisation and Sigmund Freud's theory of 'the compulsion to repeat'[1] – which explained patterns of repetitive behaviour as a consequence of repressed trauma – as a helpful way to think about how the film sequel constructs remembering activities and memorialising scenarios by which spectators can access a previous text. However, manifestations of Freud's notions of compulsive repetition and remembering are apparent far beyond the individual spectatorial encounter, and can be found across a range of cultural practices around the world. Cultural theorist Andreas Huyssen has recently pointed out the global 'explosion of memory' discourses in the early years of the twenty-first century, which has led to 'the emergence of a new paradigm of thinking about time and space, history and geography in the twenty-first century'.[2] Might this new paradigm be sequelisation? How far do the relationships between memory, history, re-presentation and repetition within this category address the aims outlined in Huyssen's study? Huyssen argues that this paradigm is most evident throughout the numerous architectural memorials marking urban spaces around the world, whose purpose is to prompt collective remembering of past trauma. Yet many such memory practices and spaces operate to the opposite effect, often prompting more a forgetting than a remembering. Of plans to erect a monument to commemorate 9/11, Huyssen observes:

> How does one imagine a monument to what was already a monument in the first place – a monument to corporate modernism? No surprise that some suggested rebuilding an exact replica of the twin towers. The idea is as absurd as it is intriguing in its logic: the rebuilt twin towers as a monument to forgetting, an erasure of history, an emblem of global capital in a different sense from that of the terrorist imaginary.[3]

In claiming such a monument as 'an erasure of history', Huyssen touches upon a notion that similarly informs the sequel. By creating both a new ending and a retrospective interpretation of a previous production, the sequel encroaches upon the memory of a prior text and infringes upon spectatorial agency to imagine what may have happened next. The sequel makes the past re-present, and in so doing creates a secondary version of the past that is marked by its repetitions of and differences from an 'original'. The relationship between this secondary version of the 'original' and the 'original' itself is shown here to operate in tension. Whilst this tension has been considered previously in terms of the sense of dissatisfaction conjured by the sequel's creation of a new ending, it is perceivable that additional registers of displacement, doubleness and erasure are to be found within the relationship between a sequel and its source that prove vital in considering cultural practices of continuation and repetition in the twenty-first century.

This chapter seeks to position the concept of sequelisation in relation to such activities and categories of memory, repetition and re-presentation in order to understand fully the sequel's broader implications and manifestations in contemporary culture. In particular, the sequel's memory-making registers are compared and contrasted here with what Dominick LaCapra has called 'secondary memory', which seeks to describe second-hand memory and the experiences and efforts to represent the past that arises from this encounter.[4] Huyssen explains secondary memory as a symptom of 'second generation' Holocaust survivors who are compelled to represent their experiences of their parent's Holocaust memories and post-traumatic symptoms.[5] More generally, secondary memory can be regarded as a form of cultural remembering that negotiates and mediates the past through inherited memories. The repetitious and continuous scenarios that emerge from this form of cultural remembering cast a critical light on the sequel's registers of collective remembering.

Steven Spielberg's *Artificial Intelligence: A. I.* is examined closely here to consider the sequel's more complex registers of memory, repetition, erasure and history in three major contexts: cultural memory, the psychological development of memory, and virtual memory. Though not a film sequel in the strict sense of the term (although resonances are to be found with Spielberg's earlier film, *E. T.: The Extra-Terrestrial* [1982]), *A. I.* nonetheless presents the concept of sequelisation in a futuristic setting with much emphasis upon the relationships between past and future, between man and machine, and between the subconscious and consciousness as 'sequels' to each other. The film portrays the creation of a robotic or 'Mecha' child as a living, thinking, dreaming replica of a dead human boy named David. The Mecha David is not unique, but is part of a series of identical dolls which are packaged and sold off to childless families. The David dolls are created to love their 'parents' genuinely, love being 'the key by which they acquire a kind of subconscious'. But, as demonstrated by the robotic David (Haley Joel Osment) on which the film focuses, the Mecha subconscious is shown to be a superimposition of the subconscious of the dead boy after whom the robots are patterned, a subconscious that is dictated to by the subjectivity of its creator, and the robot's own artificial intelligence which reprogrammes desire through old memories.

This creation of a secondary subconscious is chief among the film's rather complex and compelling suggestions of cultural remembering as a collectively reflective process that produces a secondary version of the past. The film's presentation of a virtual subconsciousness is similarly complicated and intricately bound up with the relationships between technology, history, memory and subjectivity. In particular, David's subjectivity is presented as a secondary identity; in exploration of the notion of David's subjectivity as a 'sequel' to that of a human predecessor, I draw upon the theories of psychoanalyst Jacques Lacan, whose work – along with that of Freud – appears to shape the film's cinematographic presentation of the concepts noted above. With overtones of Pinocchio – the puppet who wanted to be a 'real' boy – David's efforts to become real are presented in *A. I.* as a journey towards the psychoanalytic 'Real' as described by Jacques Lacan, and it is this journey that underlines much of the film's suggestive presentation of sequelisation.[6]

A. I. persistently invokes a number of psychoanalytic discourses and responses, showing David's 'mother' at one point on the toilet reading *Freud On Women* while the scene itself is reminiscent of Freud's famous admission of a childhood memory (recounted in *Freud On Women*) of his searching for his mother in a wardrobe and crying until he found her.[7] In Spielberg's scene David opens the bathroom door on his mother and, smiling, says 'I found you.' Whereas Freudian discourses are used to allude to *A. I.*'s cultural and aesthetic engagements, Spielberg's previous flirtations with Oedipal complexes (*The Sugarland Express* [1974], *E. T.*, *Empire of the Sun* [1987], *Hook* [1991]) are noticeably developed in this film into full-blown speculations on the construction of the subconscious and portraits of maternity as a point of origin in an age where the 'original' is purportedly nowhere to be found. As I will demonstrate, the conflict between 'original' and derivative, or sequel, informs the film's portrait of virtual subjectivity. Perhaps more pointed, however, is the film's construction of reflective surfaces and the circle as symbols of David's repetitious psychological development. I go on to discuss the film's representations of the subconscious and subjectivity in terms of the Freudian and Lacanian theories it appears to invoke.

RETURNING TO THE 'REAL'

Used by film theorists in the 1970s to theorise the spectatorial pleasures of the cinema, Lacan's notion of the gaze, at least in his early work, described the process of a child viewing itself in a mirror as a unified conscious self.[8] Regarded as the first act of identification, this act of mirror gazing is essentially a mis-identification because the 'self' is perceived as an image, a fantasy, an 'ideal ego'. In short, the subject (child) is mediated and constructed through the object (mirror). Lacan's definition of 'the mirror stage' is closely associated with the Imaginary, the term given to a primary stage of psychological development defined by the infant's blissful unity with its mother. Lacan determines the Imaginary as a persistent psychological undercurrent by which the ego is constructed, and by which individuals develop and perpetuate a sense of 'self' by identifying with external images. Following this stage is the Symbolic, which is defined by the child's acquisition of language, its experience of loss and separation from its mother, and the child's entrance into what Lacan calls 'the Law of the Father'.[9] These stages have proved fruitful for film theorists seeking to define the process of identification inherent in spectatorship. Drawing parallels between the cinema theatre and the maternal womb, Christian Metz suggested that the cinematic apparatus constructs for the spectator a re-enactment of the Imaginary, while Jean-Louis Baudry emphasised the urgency for a consideration of the Symbolic in terms of the spectator's 'lack' that is perpetuated by the cinematic experience. However, the connections drawn between film spectatorship and psychoanalysis ignored Lacan's third psychic process, the Real, most likely because of its somewhat underdeveloped conceptualisations and elusive, complex conceits. For now, it is enough to say that the Real can be read as a psychic remainder of the Imaginary and the Symbolic by which desire is continually repeated and re-experienced. Although the Real does not refer to reality, it can be understood as the process by which we create reality.

A. I. parallels two narrative strands with equal importance: a father who creates numerous robotic simulacra of his dead son, David, and a mother who 'adopts' a robotic simulacrum of David to fulfil her desire to be a mother again in the event of losing her own son. In both cases, the grief of losing a child propels a parent towards substituting, or replacing, their lost human 'original' with a Mecha 'sequel'. Suffice it to say that the Mecha project is deeply flawed, not least by the rootedness of its design in post-traumatic repetition, but also by the effects of desire, which lead David to kill another robot child. Professor Hobby (William Hurt) creates David to love his 'adoptive' parents, but David only loves his Mommy, and that love is, as Hobby states, 'fuelled by desire'. In turn, David's creation is fuelled by Professor Hobby's desire to re-incarnate his son. Desire is thus conceived of in the film as circular and repetitive, as it is never satisfied. The ramifications of David's design as a machine are that he will always be a child, will always be full of desire, therefore cannot mature, can never acquire a sense of self-unless he becomes human. It is this dilemma – David as a being of pure desire and his circular journey to become, or recover, the Real – that registers much of the desire to remember, recreate and recover in twenty-first-century culture.

The film's presentation of a robotic sequel invokes the notion of the film sequel as an act of re-viewing, or a re-living of a previous spectatorial experience. A major thrust of the following analysis is therefore towards sequelisation as a process that draws upon and extrapolates the 'return' of the Real. Although Lacan's remarks on the Real are sparse and altogether slippery, his suggestions of this as 'the return, the coming back' prompt further examination of the relevancy and development of this notion in contemporary cinema, and have been elaborated at length by Todd McGowan, Elizabeth Cowie, Hal Foster and others to indicate a process of psychic return, a state of pure, regressive, subconscious desire, or *jouissance*.[10] Slavoj Žižek has conducted an interrogation of the Real throughout his works, positing it on the one hand as the underbelly of reality, and on the other as the 'kernel' of trauma that cannot be represented.[11] To me, the Real is implicitly concerned with the repetition of repressed experience that cannot be symbolised. The reason it cannot be symbolised is because all signifiers and symbols lead only to the representation of desire, and not to the object of desire. Lacan's description of the Real as the process by which 'we see ourselves governed by the pleasure principle' motivates my discussion of the Real as comprehensible through the conceptual registers of sequelisation. The pleasure principle's involvement of *jouissance* that is beyond language, and therefore caught up with attempts to represent the unrepresentable – an impossible feat, according to Lacan – seems to me to inform sequelisation, in so far as the sequel intrudes upon our memories of the 'original' to re-represent, perpetuate and rupture that 'unrepresentable' and entirely subjective encounter.

Sequelisation in *A. I.* is a dominating feature of post-global warming, post-apocalyptic America, wherein 'legal sanctions' restrict pregnancies to stabilise international economies, resulting in the creation of Mecha (that do not sleep, eat or deplete natural resources) as servants, workers, lovers, and substitutive offspring for childless parents. Mecha are defined by their 'sequel-ness' as mechanical continuations of mortal predecessors whilst their very existence embodies the sense of 'afterwards-ness' with which this futuristic world is infused. For instance, David is the 'sequel' to Professor Hobby's dead son because he is essentially the consequence, or incarnation, of an intense grief following the death of Hobby's son. Also, David is created in the likeness of the dead boy but possesses an entirely different subjectivity. The trope of the sequel therefore offers a compelling, if not problematic, re-organisation of psychic processes, particularly in terms of its insistence upon the 'return' and compulsion to repeat that underlines the Lacanian Real.

It is my intent, firstly, to consider the inherent modes of desire in sequelisation – the desire to remember, the desire to repeat, the desire to recreate and the desire to return – in the light of the film's meditation on these concepts in the context of mechanised psychological growth. The 'regressive desire' that pervades both the Real and sequelisation, and which is the emotional subtext of Spielberg's film, prompts my interrogation of the Real as based solely on desire; having encountered the 'lack' of the Symbolic, might not the urge of the unconscious towards a primal return be complicit with post-traumatic scenarios, as the film suggests? How far does the sequel deconstruct the process of subjectivity in the act of remembering, and to what end? In order to answer these queries, I go on to consider *A. I.* as a means by which a fuller understanding of both sequelisation and the Real can be achieved.

THE SEQUEL AS ROBOTIC SIMULACRUM

Based on a short story, *Super-Toys Last All Summer Long*, by British novelist Brian Aldiss, *A. I.* has a considerable pre-production history that involves a series of exchanges between Stanley Kubrick and Spielberg. In awe of and influenced by Kubrick's *2001: A Space Odyssey* (1968), Spielberg wrote and directed *Close Encounters of the Third Kind* in 1977. Inspired by Spielberg's *E. T.*, Kubrick purchased the rights to Aldiss's sci-fi novel in 1983. Extensive planning ensued for the film's production, including 1,000 sketches and an attempt to build a robotic child in the same way that Spielberg had created a robotic 'alien' for *E. T.* Kubrick's brother-in-law, Jan Harlan (also his documentarian and executive producer), oversaw the seven-year correspondence between Kubrick and Spielberg, and insisted that Spielberg helm *A. I.* (for which Harlan is credited as executive producer) when Kubrick died in 1999. The result is a conflation of Spielberg's aesthetic fascination with childhood – demonstrated by a body of over fifty films which predominantly recreate the childhood experience, and by the DreamWorks SKG logo, which features a child sitting in the curve of a crescent moon – and a Kubrickian interest in human essence and evolution alongside the emergence of the machine. Although critics largely trashed the film upon its release (mostly for its awkward juxtaposition of Kubrick's typically futuristic cynicism with another dose of Spielberg's family portraits), its currency as a cultural and aesthetic commentary is beginning to be recognised.

Spielberg's interest in families and childhood, as founded in his own painful memories, has been well documented. In Spielberg's own words,

> I use my childhood in all my pictures, and all the time. I go back there to find ideas and stories. My childhood was the most fruitful part of my entire life. All those horrible, traumatic years I spent as a kid became what I do for a living today, or what I draw from creatively today.[12]

Spielberg's twentieth-century works recapture his childhood experience through a variety of portraits of imagination and escape, yet *A. I.* is resolutely self-conscious of 'the mirror of childhood' that is registered in his earlier films.[13] In many ways, the film functions as a post-traumatic iteration – in much the same way as David performs as an incarnation of post-trauma – and self-consciously presents its awareness of that process by imagining David's psychic development as complicit with sequelisation. The film's investments in memory and forgetting also signal much of Spielberg's concerns with preserving eye-witness accounts of traumatic pasts, evidenced by his creation of the Survivors of the Shoah Visual History (SSVH) Foundation in 1994, which was established so 'that history will not be forgotten'.[14] Housing over 45,000 survivor testimonies, the SSVH Foundation emphasises first-hand accounts of a traumatic past as a means by which that past will not be forgotten, and as a means by which the event can be prevented from being displaced or distanced by secondary memory. While the Foundation's archives are extremely beneficial in accessing a major point in history and culture, its existence points to the problems of representing trauma and creating an objective history. These problems are most apparent in *A. I.*, especially in constructing a virtual subjectivity and representing the past.

Spielberg explores the possibilities of a virtual psychological process first and foremost by interrogating conceptions of virtual memory. The film charts David's development from Imaginary to Symbolic to Real through cinematographic and metonymic circularity, and a host of reflective surfaces that suggest the 'mirror stage' of David's development. As suggested earlier, the mirror stage is the point at which a child sees itself in the mirror but does not yet understand that the reflection is a reflection; nor does it comprehend the difference between Self and Other. The film's *mise-en-scène* is constructed entirely with this notion in mind. Having been adopted by Monica (Frances O'Connor) and Henry Swinton (Sam Robards) as a 'replacement' for their comatose son, Martin (Jake Thomas), David's first morning at the Swinton residence is spent watching Monica prepare breakfast, peering from below the stainless steel surface area that reflects – and doubles – his eyes. David's subjectivity at this stage is bound up with Monica. As David never looks at his own image in the mirror, Monica serves as his reflection, his subjectivity. Following a series of reflections is the appearance of the circle at David's first meal with Monica and Henry. An overhead shot of David as he sits directly beneath the circular lighting unit symbolises the 'wholeness' of the Imaginary and the unity that David believes to exist between him and his Mommy. As Lacan indicates, the purpose of the mirror stage is 'to break out of the circle of the *Innenwelt* [inner world] into the *Umwelt* [outer world]', effectively shattering the 'mirror of childhood' in which the Self is unknown.[15] David's complicity at the beginning of the film with the 'circle' of the mirror phase, or *Innenwelt*, is used not only to suggest his 'infantile' development, but also to indicate the complicity of the Mecha Self with a throng of replicated Others. In the arena of artificiality, the Self is a perpetual sequel to Other-ness.

Yet the film deliberately constructs David as virtually developing throughout the three stages of the Imaginary, Symbolic and Real in order to highlight his becoming, by the end, a 'Real' boy, or a boy that permits access to and embodies the Real. David is not born to love his Mommy, but recognises her as such and becomes programmed to love her when she decides to 'hardwire his affections' using Hobby's prescribed imprinting procedure. The scene immediately preceding David's imprinting shows him tucked up in a cocoon-like bed, with hooped strip-lights encircling him from above and below. A circular window above David's head frames an exaggerated virtual crescent moon – unabashedly the DreamWorks logo – which foreshadows the fractured unity that accompanies his entrance into the Symbolic. In this scene Monica watches David in bed, visibly deciding to adopt him for good. This decision is implicitly premised on David's reincarnation of Monica's memories of her son Martin, as David effectively takes his place, once more occupying Martin's bed, clothes and space with a boyish presence. The crescent moon above Monica in this scene appears to be conjured by her decision, appearing throughout subsequent shots to foreshadow the separation, and not the unison, that she puts into effect by solidifying David's love. It is the moment of David's love, his obsessive urgency to win Monica's affections that simultaneously prompts her rejection of him. When Martin comes to, a palpable rivalry emerges between the boys that changes David's love for Monica to obsessive desire. When Martin cunningly advises David that Monica will indeed love him if David creeps into her bedroom in the middle of the night with a pair of scissors and cuts off a lock of her hair, David acquiesces. But he accidentally cuts Monica's eye, and appears to be dangerous, forcing the Swintons to get rid of him.

It is possible to identify the film's suggestion of David's entrance into the Symbolic after the 'mirror phase' by Monica's imprinting, using the words 'cirrus, Socrates, particle, decibel, hurricane, dolphin, tulip, Monica, David, Monica'. The Symbolic 'implies a fixing of the subject' by figuring 'the intervention of the father as [a] third term in the dyadic, imaginary relation of mother and child', which in turn creates 'a rupture' in the psyche of the subject.[16] The 'secondariness' of the Symbolic additionally points to the Self as a creation founded in post-ness. The Symbolic is also governed by the acquisition of language. The word 'Mommy' enters and dominates David's vocabulary upon his imprinting, although Henry remains 'Henry', and David's relationship with him becomes strained. From this point on, moreover, the 'wholeness' of the Imaginary is fractured, and David's reflected image is shattered. David has entered the 'law of the Father', and now that he realises that his Mommy will die and has others to care for and love, his desire for his lost union with her is fortified. As David's object of desire, Monica is figured at this point in concert with the circle. David – head on Monica's lap, eyes pleading – asks his Mommy how long she will live. Here a medium close-up shot captures Monica's reflection in a circular mirror, emphasising her objectivity as a result of David's newly imprinted subjectivity. The circle, then, is additionally the articulation of the 'O' of the 'Other', represented by Monica.

What has occurred at the moment of Monica's imprinting is that David's unconscious has been activated. As Freud argues, the unconscious contains 'impressions' which, forged during childhood, are undiminished by adulthood.[17] Freud's description of the Mystic Writing-Pad as a psychic instrument of memory inscription renders the psychological process of remembering as comparable to a slab whose three surfaces record permanent inscriptions at the same time as 'erasing' undesirable inscriptions.[18] Comparing the two upper slabs of the pad to consciousness and the wax slab to the unconscious, Freud proposes memory as both a *tabula rasa* and as a narrative penned by the author-subject. When pressed by Martin to recall his first memory, David remembers 'a bird with big wings' that is revealed to be a statue outside Professor Hobby's Cybertronics factory building, as seen through a window. The first 'slab' of David's memory, then, is 'penned' by his creator, and the series of words with which Monica programmes him create another layer. From this point on all of David's conscious activity is geared towards becoming a 'real', or human, boy. The play on 'real' throughout the film, however, implies his development as a Real boy, bound by the implications of this process to return to the Imaginary. From the moment of David's decision to become 'real', his unconscious becomes saturated with desires to return to the womb. Because he is built, not born, David's unrecognised, unconscious goal is explicitly to return to the site of his origins, the site of the 'bird with big wings': the Cybertronics factory.

The film indicates the memory process as a superimposition of Real (the real event) and Imaginary (the subjective interpretation). Put differently, David's desire for Monica is conflated with his unconscious desire to return to the Cybertronics factory. Furthermore, the conflation of subjectivities that create his unconscious, or the means by which he creates his own reality, means that to a degree David is his own object of desire, which contributes enormously to the circularity of desire. This dichotomy is explored in early psychoanalytic readings of spectatorship. Reading the 'persistence of the exclusive relation to the mother, desire as a pure effect of lack and endless pursuit, the initial core of the unconscious' of the Imaginary as indicative of the spectatorial experience, Metz determines the Imaginary as 'undoubtedly reactivated by the play of that *other mirror*, the cinema screen, in this respect a veritable psychical substitute' (his emphasis).[19] In other words, the cinema as 'other' becomes a substitute, or surrogate, for the irrevocable Imaginary. Yet both Baudry's observations and Metz's comments are based on a consideration of suture, or a system of shot/reverse shot, that occurs between spectator-subject and film-object. As Kaja Silverman suggests of the shot/reverse shot process,

> the viewer of the cinematic spectacle experiences shot 1 as an imaginary plenitude, unbounded by any gaze, and unmarked by difference. Shot 1 is thus the site of a *jouissance* akin to that of the mirror stage prior to the child's discovery of its separation from the ideal image which it has discovered in the reflecting glass.[20]

By figuring David as both the 'eye-subject' and object within the 'reflecting glass', the film posits the Real as an impossible destination specifically because, at this stage, subjectivity and objectivity are inseparable. David as both 'eye-subject' and mirror is further denoted by a shot during the scene in which Monica abandons David after Martin's hair-cutting scheme. Driving to a woodland area, Monica tells David she has to leave him with Teddy, the super-toy Martin gave to David. As Monica drives away, David's reflection is captured by the circular wing mirror as the car pulls off, making him appear progressively smaller. The reflection, carried off into the distance, reinforces Monica as David's reflection, his narcissistic 'Other'. In this connection, the circular wing mirror frames David as *l'objet petit a*, the little other or 'o', the signifying mark of the desire drive.[21] David is cinematographically imagined as the film's circularity, the signifier of desire, the embodiment of the 'return' underlying the sequel.

In addition to desire and 'return', notions of 'secondariness' and inferiority are also consonant with sequelisation. David is rejected because he is neither Monica and David's 'real' son, nor a 'real' boy. The machine/human or Mecha/Orga axis throughout the film contributes to the sequel's inherent disappointment, otherness and latent artificiality. The film's reference to an earlier text (unmentioned in Aldiss's short story), Carlo Collodi's *Pinocchio*, connects David to his modern textual counterpart in the context of the sequel. At Martin's (scheming) request, Monica reads *Pinocchio* to the two boys. In Collodi's novel the puppet Pinocchio aims to become 'real' in the sense that he desires to be an authentic, original and human. Martin makes the parallels between David and Pinocchio obvious to David in order to undermine his 'eligibility' for Monica's love. The message David receives from this story is that love is coterminous with realness. When Martin wakes from his coma and returns home, David is swiftly demoted from his position as substitute son to Martin's toy. Martin asks what 'super-toy stuff' David can do, if he can walk on the walls or ceiling. David says that he cannot, and asks Martin if he can. 'No,' Martin responds, 'because *I'm real*.' Despite the general advantage of super-toys over humans in many ways – such as intelligence, agility and manual dexterity – the emphasis here is on realness. 'Real', or human, is 'original', and is therefore unquestionably unique and superior.

Yet the division between reality and irreality is so muddied in the film that the notion of 'originality' is shown to be slowly dying. The film adds to this observation by showing a 'Flesh Fair' at which humans gather at an arena – much like a gladiatorial coliseum – to watch Mecha being ritualistically destroyed. Humans, or 'Orga' as they are named in reaction to 'Mecha', are of course 'original', but to validate that originality, Mecha are consistently undermined. 'We are alive', the hostess reminds the crowd, 'and this is a celebration of life.' Mecha are melted with boiling oil, shot from a cannon into rotating blades, and ripped limb from limb. In actuality, the Flesh Fair is not a celebration of life but the demonstration of fears of the 'realness' of Mecha. Because of their 'realness', or accurate representation of human appearance, Mecha appear to pose a threat. To Orga, Mecha signify death, or the death of originality and, thus, the death of humanity.

David's human appearance confuses a number of Orga, and ultimately saves his skin. The host speaker, Lord Johnson-Johnson (Brendan Gleeson), drags David to the centre of the stadium, ready to be burned to death. David cries, 'Don't burn me! I'm David!', echoing the wood in Collodi's novel that later 'becomes' Pinocchio:

> [Master Cherry] grasped the hatchet quickly to peel off the bark and shape the wood. But as he was about to give it the first blow, he stood still with arm uplifted, for he had heard a wee, little voice say in a beseeching tone: 'Please be careful! Do not hit me so hard!'[22]

Collodi's narrative continues to report how Master Cherry gives the piece of wood to his childless friend, Geppetto, who makes himself a marionette named Pinocchio that will dance, fence and turn somersaults. Named after Professor Hobby's son, David is also named after Michelangelo's marble statue 'David', which was (like Pinnochio) sculpted from an odd-shaped material (marble) that had previously been rejected by other artists. Michelangelo's 'David', the Mecha David and indeed Pinocchio are each characterised by rejection. In addition, David and Pinocchio share a desire for originality. David goes so far as to disengage himself from his textual counterpart, crying 'I'm not Pinocchio! Don't let me die! I'm David!', as though the fact of his difference and (false) individuality is a requisite for life.

David's desire to be 'one of kind' is founded, of course, on his desire to be loved by Monica. When Gigolo Joe (Jude Law) tells David that Orga (humans) hate Mecha, David retorts, 'My mommy doesn't hate me! Because I'm special! And unique! Because there's never been anyone like me before, ever!' David, at this point, is the sequel that articulates what other sequels point to in recent years: that despite their derivative condition, they aspire to and claim 'originality' because of particularly charismatic and distinctive traits. For example, one of the innumerable 'cognitive simulacra' in *I, Robot* (Alex Proyas, 2004) insists that he is unique, and that the other robots 'look like me but none of them are me'. In the *Matrix* trilogy (Larry and Andy Wachowski, 1999, 2003, 2003), Neo (an obvious anagram) is 'the one', despite having six Messiah-like 'predecessors', while his antithetical 'double', Agent Smith (Hugo Weaving), has endless 'copies' of himself, or 'me *two*'. The obsession with 'one of a kind' registers the sequel as a symptom of difference. Like the Imaginary, which fuses absence and presence, the sequel is ultimately bound up with difference as a dialogue between history and memory.

SEQUELISING HISTORY

In this connection, the notion of the sequel organises the film's presentation of historical repetition. The racist and fascist sentiments of the Flesh Fair are figured as a continuation of Nazi regimes, whilst the graphic destruction of Mecha is imagined as another Holocaust. 'History', as one of the Mecha asserts, 'repeats itself.' The trauma of the twentieth-century Holocaust is shown to be repeated, but as a sequel, a continuation. It is precisely the film's treatment of historical repetition that sets the sequel apart from repetition and, in so doing, underscores the Real as repetition. As Hal Foster puts it, 'as missed, the real cannot be represented; it can only be repeated, indeed it *must* be repeated.' He goes on to say that 'repetition is not reproduction,' but instead 'serves to *screen* the real understood as traumatic'. However, 'this very need also *points* to the real, and at this point the real *ruptures* the screen of repetition' (his emphasis).[23] David is not a simple Mecha repetition; he 'screens' the traumatic traces of his own circumstances of reproduction. The dialogues between cultural consciousness, historical repetition and psychic *jouissance* in *A. I.* can be read, therefore, as iterations of a cultural anxiety born of past traumas, which are notably played out in the shape of what I call 'prevention-compulsion' in Spielberg's subsequent production, *Minority Report* (2002). The dilemma of the sequel, or the arena of 'post-ness', is indeed the 'impossibility' of the Real, as the urge not only to remember but also to externalise or incarnate the process of memory – the subconscious – leads in the film to a series of problematic re-presentations: for example, the creation of innumerable 'Davids' instead of a variety of 'unique' Mecha children, which ultimately instils in David such a strong desire to be different that he resorts to murder to defend his subjectivity and 'realness'. In Western society, similar problems are apparent in terms of what Huyssen calls 'a hypertrophy of memory', creating an overabundance of pastness and, as evidenced by architecture and art (and film, I would argue), a dichotomy of palimpsest and lacunae.[24] In *A. I.*, the fear of forgetting is so great that images of the past, images of the dead, create an uncanny sense of ever-present absence. Evocations of the future of Western society as we know it thus appear in the film in the context of the struggle between originality and representation, to comprehend the effects of 'post'-ness, or the virtualising of the Real.

As the sequel suggests, the Real is forever displaced from historical repetition, and is wholly distinct from secondary memory. Although secondary memory is commonly used to refer to specific effects of re-presentation imposed by cultural trauma, it is also a technological term, used to denote a computer's long-term memory system. Composed of a three-tiered system of cache (immediate memory), primary memory (main 'functional' memory) and secondary memory, computer memory is a technological configuration of the three-tiered psychic system of Freud's Mystic Writing-pad. David is an expression of both kinds of memory; his virtual subconscious has its origins in computer memory, yet the emotional subtext of his existence is 'second-generation' expression. In many ways, David is an attempt to reconnect with the Real, which is perceivably the major dynamic of 'second-generation' representations: to reveal the Real behind the mask of memory. As Elizabeth Grosz puts it, '[t]he Real . . . is not the same as reality; [for] reality is lived and known through imaginary and symbolic representations.'[25] Yet in attempting to discover the Real, one must contend with the fact that no 'eye-witness' account of the past can ever reveal the Real in its entirety. Secondary representations thus re-organise second-hand memories 'in a certain manner [which] operates in a more satisfactory way, has a positive result, but still leaves out what one does not understand: the Real'.[26]

Spielberg's 'Real' is the Holocaust. Both *Schindler's List* (1993) and *War of the Worlds* (2005) evidence Spielberg's preoccupation with the Holocaust, and *A. I.* indicates a struggle in representing or comprehending the 'real' historical event. In fact, both *A. I.* and *Minority Report* can be read in terms of a self-consciousness of the problems posed by secondary memory, specifically the attempt to come to terms with an event that has shaped Spielberg's cultural identity and historical understanding, but only at the level of second-hand experience. The question posed by both films is how to represent a personal mode of experience within the Real's network of associated secondary memories, or, as Huyssen argues, '[h]ow to represent that which one knows only through representations and from an ever-growing historical distance?'[27] This dilemma is also apparent in *Minority Report*, which in some ways can be read as a 'sequel' to *A. I.* for its engagement with secondary memory.

Like *A. I.*, *Minority Report* portrays the grief of a father, John Anderton (Tom Cruise), who has lost his son. Following the 'vision' of a psychic female Pre-Cognitive (Samantha Morton), John tracks down his son's killer in room number 1006 at a local hotel. Finding the room empty, he rotates the last digit on the door of the room to reveal that it is actually 1009. Turning to the door opposite, John finds the 'real' room 1006, as well as his suspect. One of Spielberg's early encounters with the Holocaust pointedly informs this scene. Relatives of the Spielberg family from Poland and the Ukraine had died during the Holocaust, and some survivors shared their experiences that echo throughout this scene. As Andrew Yule tells it, '[o]nly one aspect of the meeting remained vivid in his mind: one of the group performed a magic trick with his concentration camp tattoo, the "6" twisted round to make a "9".'[28] The evocation of Spielberg's second-hand experience of the Holocaust in this scene – or the portrait of a secondary memory in a scene that portrays the revision of a memory of the future – suggests the Real is only ever 'accessible' as a symbolic interpretation, as a 'sequel' to the event forever complicit with the exigencies of subjectivity and the subconscious.

Nonetheless, the creation of Mecha and the Mecha 'Holocaust' portrayed in *A. I.* index representation politics as a necessary evil in the preservation of subjectivity, culture and originality. Indeed, the 'primitive monsters that could play chess' of the early modern period created by Voltaire, Jacques de Vaucanson and others were not merely designed to duplicate the female ability to give birth or to function as technological sequels, but to recreate and return to the Imaginary by producing sequels in the image of the Mother: the site of all origins. In the twenty-first century, however, that return is informed by the Real as facilitated by the preservation of memory. The Real's 'impossible wholeness of self' is threatened here by the bricolage robots, while the 'lack-of-being' that comes on the heel of maternal unity is reflected by Mecha who are neither alive nor dead.[29] Yet it is this very 'in-between-ness' of Mecha – the fact that they will not die – that indicates their imbrication in memorialisation. As Gigolo Joe predicts, 'when the end comes, all that will be left is us.' Social amnesia is the death of memory, and the death of memory is the end of origins. In the event of impending apocalypse, the most important aspect of humanity in this film appears to be originality, in concert with a clarion call for remembrance.

INCARNATING INNOCENCE

The film's constructions of the Imaginary point to the quest for originality as inseparable from the retrieval of the Mother-as-origin, and as inseparable from the Real. In keeping with this notion, the design of this society is overtly feminised and maternal. When David and Joe are eventually set free from the Flesh Fair, they make a course for Rouge City (a metropolised, post-postmodern sequel to the Moulin Rouge in Paris) in order to find the Blue Fairy. The bridges connecting the island of Rouge City to the mainland pass through the open mouths of large female heads, recalling Lacan's comments on 'the abyss of the feminine organ *from which all life emerges*, the *gulf of the mouth*, in which everything is swallowed up, and no less the image of death in which everything comes to its end' (my emphasis).[30] While the brain of the female Mecha, Sheila (Sabrina Grdevich), at the film's opening is accessed through her open mouth, the heart of (female) Mecha society is found at the other end of the bridge in Rouge City. Buildings shaped as large phalluses were removed to maintain the film's PG-13 rating, though edifices in various forms of the female body (and named 'Mildred') abound. This is apparently the home of the virtual 'mother', the place where, as Joe puts it, 'the ones who made us are always looking for the ones who made them'. Essentially the desert of the Real, Rouge City features numerous representations of fetishised females specifically to underscore the absence of the maternal figure, and is paved therefore with disunity, artificial 'sequels' and the 'lack' of Realness. The excessive presence of the virtual mother and the absence of the 'real' mother indicate at this point the displacement of originality by 'secondary' originality, which, although 'immortal', retains only a remembered trace of the Real, and never the Real itself.

David's condition and the world around him suggest the Real as a resistance against futurity, a regressive return that results not in the reconstruction of infantilism but in mechanical reproduction, cryogeny and an apocalypse of reality. Frozen in time, David is the unconscious incarnate, a being entirely 'fuelled by desire' but infinitely unable to satisfy that desire. David may further be perceived as innocence incarnate, the articulated suspension of a pre-Oedipal era from which all adult desires originate. As Freud puts it, '[o]ur childhood memories show us our earliest years not as they were but as they appeared at the later periods when the memories were aroused.'[31] Essentially composed of phantasies, these memories project adult desires upon infantile experiences. Urges of adulthood are interpreted by Freud as giving shape to unintelligible childhood encounters, yet it is further conceivable that infantile memories – suspended forever in the perpetual summer of the unconscious – are projected by an adult subject in the form of wishes and dreams. Charged with 'screen memories', the unconscious seeks 'to get itself represented by a subject who is still unaware of the fact that he is representing to himself the very scene of the unconscious where he is'.[32] Projected desires, as David signifies, are memories scripted upon the unconscious that are replayed throughout maturity by adult phantasies. In David's case, desire and memory are one. His 'love' is no more than the dichotomous repetition of repressed 'memories' (such as the 'bird with big wings', which is revealed to be synonymous with the Blue Fairy) that are configured as desires, and vice versa. Thus, David's journey to the Blue Fairy culminates in an unconscious return both to the place of his origins – underlined by Professor Hobby's admission, 'I guess that makes me your Blue Fairy' – and to the destination of his dream. The playing out of David's imprinted 'memories' suggests the sequel as the perpetuation of remembering, which is essentially rooted in the present tense. However, the modes of duplication in the world of *A. I.* have created a ruptured sense of presence, and as a consequence a 'superimposed' order of pastness and futurity has replaced present-ness. The portrait of 'Man-hattan' as 'the end of the world' suggests this most strongly, for the city is entirely submerged under water – 'full of weeping' – and appears to be drowning in its own reflections.

After encountering Dr Know in Rouge City, Joe, Teddy and David make their getaway in an amphibi-copter to Manhattan. As they fly past the decaying flame of the Statue of Liberty (the only part of the statue that is not submerged), Manhattan's skyline appears as a dystopic relic flooded by tears, an oceanic terrain with echoes of Kevin Costner's *Waterworld* (1995). David's destination features colossal statues of lions that 'weep' into the ocean below. This is the realm of the Imaginary, the desert of the Real flooded by recreations of and returns to the mirror phase, resulting in uncanny manifestations of narcissism (Mecha), and an apocalyptic realisation that the 'mother', or, more specifically, the maternal womb, cannot be recreated or re-entered. Landing inside the lion-posted Cybertronics building, David finds a door inscribed with the refrain from W. B. Yeats's apocalyptic poem, *The Stolen Child*. Therein David finds 'another who is me', another 'David', his identical simulacral twin.[33] David stares rigidly at his *doppelgänger*, yet the other 'David' does not flinch at his uncanny clone. Freud's notions of the uncanny or 'double' self as a 'harbinger of death' seem to be played out here, for David's immediate response is aggressive fear that there exists a rival for his mommy's affections.[34] 'You can't have her,' David whispers, before swinging a steel lamp at his opponent's head and bashing his motherboard 'brains' in. An overhead shot captures David, still swinging at thin air, beneath a circular lighting structure similar to the one at the Swinton residence, but with a difference: this time the circle is not whole. It is composed of two crescents, not quite joining in the middle, signalling the double fracture of the Imaginary (emphasising the meeting of the two Davids and the consequence of this encounter). The double 'C' further harks back to the clinic at the film's opening in which Martin was contained during his five-year coma. As Monica enters the clinic the camera pauses momentarily on the door sign that reads 'Cryogenics'. The 'C' in 'Cryogenics' resembles a crescent moon, and beside it another crescent, facing the opposite way, pre-empts the double crescent figured in the double Davids scene. The moon denotes the perpetuation of childhood or the perpetuation of the memory of childhood, which is in turn suggested as the origin of all desire.

In the next room of the Cybertronics factory David finds rows of unprogrammed 'Davids' hanging along the walls. Finished Davids, as well as

Darlenes, are packed in boxes that are headlined with the caption 'At Last A Love Of Your Own'. Echoing Ripley's horrifying discovery in *Alien: Resurrection* (Jean-Pierre Jeunet, 1997), whereby she finds a series of botched attempts to 'revive' her genetically (including a grotesquely deformed twin, whom she kills), the mechanical sequels seriously undermine David's aspiration to be 'one of a kind'. 'You're the *first* of a kind,' Professor Hobby reasons, yet the simulacra articulate the originals' irreplaceability and, in contrast, the utter insignificance of the sequel.

The mystery behind David's 'bird with big wings' memory is explained by an inchoate David-doll that faces a window behind which stands the bird-like Cybertronics effigy. Although David's Blue Fairy is yet to be found at this point, a shot capturing David as he presses his head inside the unfinished face of the doll configures David himself as the Blue Fairy, for blue lights behind the eye sockets of the doll light up David's eyes as he peers through towards the window. Moreover, the palimpsest created by David and his undeveloped twin stresses David as both original and sequel, his own shot/reverse shot, a 'link' in a series of manufactured images. As foreshadowed by shots of David through pleated glass, the palimpsestuousness of the David-doll shot suggests David's residence in immortal youth, an existence wherein Joe's (final) comment 'I am . . . I was' is not possible. David's condition is not founded on a perpetual Imaginary as was intended, but instead is the materialisation of an infinite Real, a continually recycling apocalypse. This is because David is nothing more than someone else's memory; his own memories are palimpsests upon a text that has already been penned. Panning across a veritable shrine of photographs of David and his father, an earlier shot shows a large photo of David (at the age that he is cloned) on Professor Hobby's desk with a plaque that reads 'In Loving Memory of David'. By creating a simulacrum that is essentially outside time and thus will not mature or die, Professor Hobby incarnates the memory of his son without recourse to mortality. David is programmed not only to love, but also never to forget.

Perhaps to indicate the triadic phases of psychological construction that are each initiated by and concomitant with the womb state, David is submerged underwater no less than three times throughout the film. The first time, David accidentally falls into the Swinton's outdoor pool, dragging Martin with him. When Martin is rescued, David is left on the pool floor, arms outstretched, abandoned before he is finally and conclusively abandoned by the Swinton family. The second occasion of submersion occurs after David's acquaintance with his double. Sitting storeys above the ocean in Manhattan, David hurls himself into the sea in what appears to be a suicide attempt. Here he finds New York's theme park, Coney Park, underwater, replete with a *Pinocchio* set and – as luck would have it – a Blue Fairy statue. Again, the presence of the circle dominates in the form of a gigantic ferris wheel beside the Blue Fairy that will eventually trap David underwater. At this point, however, David catches a glimpse of the Blue Fairy before Joe swoops to his rescue. When Joe is plucked from the amphibi-copter by the police, David and Teddy begin their final descent in the vehicle towards the Blue Fairy. The narcissistic overtones at this point are obvious, reinforced by a slow superimposition of David's reflection and the underwater Blue Fairy statue against the amphibi-copter glass. However, when David gazes at the surface of the water (or, indeed, any reflective surface), the reflection he sees staring back at him is not his own face, but the Other, the object of his desire. Hence (in part) David's reaction to his 'other' in Professor Hobby's study. The shattered glass in this earlier scene is congruent with the 'shattering' of the Imaginary, the first of a dyadic 'shattering' of the mirror phase that accompanies David's two-fold journey to his origins: to discover Professor Hobby, and to find the Blue Fairy, who emulates Walter Benjamin's comments on the 'Angel of History' whose face is turned to the past, and also to the future.[35] For indeed the Blue Fairy shatters in a later scene and, after the re-dawning of the Ice Age, the world of which David is the sole 'living' memory is in a state of splinter, a post-apocalyptic secondary Real.

When David and Teddy are rescued from their sunken 'cage' by robots, it is apparent that New York, and indeed the world, has been encased in ice. New York at this point evokes Rem Koolhaas's description of 'Manhattanism' as 'a factory of manmade experience, where the real and natural [have] ceased to exist'.[36] For as the robots inform David, mankind is no more; David is the sole 'enduring memory' of human beings. At this point architectural icons of New York (such as the Chrysler building) peer above ice dunes, reduced to shattered pieces that signify the deconstructed subjectivity that accompanies post-ness.

THE SEQUEL AND THE DOUBLE

The film's representation of New York as a shattered, post-traumatic space is retrospectively concomitant with post-9/11 discourse and, in this context, with the modes of 'doubling' and sequelisation that have occurred throughout the film. Audiences in Australia, Germany and the United Kingdom viewed the film 48 hours after 9/11 (at its 13 September 2001 release). As I recall, the film seemed to capture the world's emotional landscape at that moment, charged with uncertainty and, as Jean Baudrillard later commented, 'symbolic significance'. In the context of 9/11, David's destruction of his twin pertains to 'the rhetoric of the mirror', and to Baudrillard's conviction that 'only the doubling of the sign truly puts an end to what it designates.'[37] Focusing – perhaps rather coldly – on the facelessness and doubled identity of the twin towers, Baudrillard's comments reflect the uncanny ramifications of the 9/11 tragedy. Gregory T. Esplin's observations are worth repeating at length:

> The uncanny is reflected even in the details of the World Trade Center's destruction: everything related to the incident seems [to] come in doubles. It occurred on the date in which the number one is repeated twice: 11. The United States President in '01 was George Bush. Not the first one, but the second: Bush II . . . A feeling of eerie repetition also surrounds September 11, since this was the second time Islamic fundamentalists attacked the WTC, the first being the 1993 truck bombing of the North Tower which left six dead but failed to bring down the structure.[38]

A. I.'s engagement with the 'double-ness' of the World Trade Center – and, inadvertently, with 9/11 – is reflected in the enduring presence of the twin towers amidst New York's decaying structures. The towers function here symbolically to register the apocalypse of this world caused by the proliferation of uncanny representations or replicas of a lost original. At the end of the world, the Real is the existence of the double.

By the film's end, David has become the signifier of this lost original, or of the human race. David functions at this point as 'a traumatic-apocalyptic inscription' upon the cinematic palimpsest of New York, and, for audiences witnessing the film's pre-9/11 release in New York, serves as the 'letter' Lacan describes as arriving 'in reverse form'.[39] David is the memory of that trauma 'posted' from the future, returning to his destination in past-ness. The film's cinematography confirms this notion, for David's first appearance in the film is photographed in such a way as to liken him to the slender robots that rescue him in the future. As such, David is a memory sent to the past from a catastrophic state of post-ness in order to screen the moment of trauma. David's construction thus suggests the 'sequel' as a symbol of post-trauma, an attempt to get over the past, inscribing new identities, change and cultural progress on a culture weighted with memories of the Holocaust.

In this light, the Real appears to be complicit with notions of trauma and apocalypse. In Berger's words, '[a]pocalypse and trauma . . . both refer to shatterings of existing structures of *identity* and *language*, and both effect their own erasures from memory and must be reconstructed by means of their traces, remains, survivors, and ghosts: their symptoms'[40] (my emphasis). The Real as an unrepresentable remainder correlates with this reading as the re-enactment of a subconscious past throughout perpetuity. It is in this manner that David achieves the wish he has harboured for two millennia. One of the robots that save David recounts a project devised to recreate mankind with samples of human DNA (as in Spielberg's *Jurassic Park* [1993]), and informs David that they also attempted to retrieve a memory trace of human existence. As a result, they discovered that space-time stored information about every event that had ever occurred. The lock of hair that David successfully retrieved from Monica's head is still held in Teddy's pocket and, using this sample, the robots are able to achieve David's wish. That is, however, until Monica falls asleep, for the experiment conducted by the robots proved that 'resurrectees' stayed alive only as long as they were conscious. David's return to his childhood is a potently psychic event, for the Swinton residence and Monica are reconstructed according to David's memories, yet each seems different to him. Once again he tells Monica 'I found you,' and their entire day together is essentially a reconstruction of David's memories: making Monica coffee, just the way she likes it ('you never forget, do you?'), painting his memories of the Flesh Fair, Gigolo Joe and the amphibi-copter, and celebrating his birthday (recalling the event at Martin's birthday, which prompted Monica's abandonment of David). What is being suggested at this point is that the reconstruction of David's memories results in a forgetting, or screening, of the trauma of Monica's abandonment, in tandem with the full exposure of the Real. David is essentially a post-apocalyptic inscription in so far as he is coded to re-present and re-live the past, and therefore both embodies and screens past-ness. The trope of the sequel functions in much the same manner. By infringing upon the memory of the 'original' and continuing or adding to that memory, sequelisation perpetuates the act of remembering, which is an act grounded in the present. David dies at the end of the film when he returns to the origins of his memory, when the Real is made possible, yet the suggestion is that his death is a kind of life, or a return to the virtual subconscious.

CONCLUSIONS

The notion of the Real as both a remainder of and an urge to repeat the Imaginary informs the film's construction of a virtual subconscious, as the virtual is removed from human reality and is entirely preoccupied with the sense of absence and re-construction. Moreover, the repetition of the Real appears in David's case to create, at a very subconscious level, every experience and urge as a repetition of the 'thing itself', of his object of desire, which, as I have demonstrated, is essentially himself. David's repetitious perpetuation of his own subjectivity – as complex a notion as it appears – creates narrative trajectories of interrelated events and identities that are ultimately past-bound. This is because David is programmed to be past-bound; he is the sequel that persistently looks back at the past whilst reconstructing that past in the future. The *fort/da* (gone/there) dichotomy underscoring Freud's thesis of the pleasure principle – and the memory of his mother in the wardrobe – is very much part of the sequel's investment in reconstruction, yet the sequel's self-reflexive engagement with reconstruction and memory as entirely subjective scenarios interrogate contemporary memory politics – evidenced by 'public memory' spaces – by repositioning the subject in remembering. David's virtual subjectivity and memory are secondary in so far as they continue the memories of his creator and 'original', which also frame David's own memories. The symbolic domination of the circle, then, serves to indicate the process of the Real in the virtual landscape as neither a straightforward shot/reverse shot dialogue nor a projection of desire, but as the continual repetition of memory, the origin or 'kernel' of which lies in the terrain of the Imaginary.

It is precisely the composition of memories by an entity that is just that – a living memory – that underscores *A. I.*'s treatment of subjectivity and sequelisation. The chief connection between sequelisation and the Real lies in their inherent investments in memory as a remainder of a moment in the past. In terms of the Real, the remainder is the moment that the infant is faced with its otherness in the mirror. Sequelisation plays in this field of memory stratagems by creating a kind of superimposition of reconstructed memorialisations and subjectivities within the framework of re-presentation. Indeed, just as the sequel is a composite of old and new, or Self and Other, Mecha are portrayed in the film as 'bricolage' assemblages of old and new technologies, styles and identities. The film juxtaposes concepts of mimesis, repetition and sequelisation to posit the threat of artificiality – demonstrated by the Flesh Fair – as premised on difference, not sameness.

More broadly, the sequel appears to problematise the experience, or memory, of the original. Sequels draw upon the 'afterward-ness' or reception of the original, only to re-interpret and orchestrate spectators' memories of that original. On what she calls 'post-performance reception' in theatre, Susan Bennett writes that an audience's main 'interpretive activity' takes place immediately after a performance – either by discussion, attending further performances, or reading reviews and source texts – and that these activities are 'likely to enhance the experience of that production in the individual's memory'.[41] Likewise, the sequel functions as the belated ending of the 'original', as a protracted reconstruction of the original experience. Like David, who is programmed to be past-bound and operates as a sequel that persistently looks back at the past whilst reconstructing that past in the future, the film sequel prescribes meaning, fills in the gaps, and re-opens the post-performance reception process of engaging with the original in a familiar yet unfamiliar way. Also like David, the sequel is rejected because it impinges upon the post-performance moment, infringes upon the memory of the original, and prescribes a memory in replacement of that memory. The sequel invokes presence, while the original is happily fixed in the past. The 'restructuring of past syntheses' that occurs in the event of the sequel is, in this light, a reorganisation of memory.[42]

NOTES

1. Freud, 'Beyond the Pleasure Principle', 30.
2. Huyssen, *Present Pasts*, 4.
3. Ibid., 159.
4. LaCapra, *History and Memory After Auschwitz*, 20–1.
5. Huyssen, *Present Pasts*, 135.
6. Lacan *The Four Fundamental Concepts of Psychoanalysis*, ix, 53, 68–9, 116–18, 205–6, 279–80. See also Žižek, *The Sublime Object of Ideology*, 162–4, 173–5; Shepherdson, 'A Pound of Flesh', 73; McGowan and Kunkle (eds) *Lacan and Contemporary Film*, xvi–xix, 24–7, 95–6, 112; Walsh, 'Returns in the Real'.
7. Freud, 'Excerpts from Freud's Letters to Fliess', 55.
8. Baudry, 'The Apparatus'; Metz, *The Imaginary Signifier*; Mulvey, 'Visual Pleasure and Narrative Cinema'.
9. Lacan, 'The Mirror Stage as Formative of the Function of the I as Revealed in Psychoanalytic Experience'.
10. McGowan, 'Looking for the Gaze'; Foster, *The Return of the Real*; Cowie, *Representing the Woman*; Fuery, *New Developments in Film Theory*, 6–20.
11. See Žižek, *Enjoy Your Symptom! Jacques Lacan in Hollywood and Out*; Žižek, *Everything You Always Wanted to Know About Lacan*; Butler and Stephens, *Slavoj Žižek*.
12. Quoted in Yule, *Steven Spielberg*, i.
13. Metz, *The Imaginary Signifier*, 253.
14. www.vhf.org
15. Lacan, 'The Mirror Stage as Formative of the Function of the I as Revealed in Psychoanalytic Experience', 5.
16. Cowie, *Representing the Woman*, 98.
17. Freud, 'A Note on the Mystic Writing-Pad', 213.
18. Ibid., 227.
19. Metz, *The Imaginary Signifier*, 250.
20. Silverman, 'Suture', 219.
21. Lacan, *The Four Fundamental Concepts of Psychoanalysis*, 282.
22. Collodi, *Pinocchio*, 3.
23. Foster, *The Return of the Real*, 132, Lacan, *The Four Fundamental Concepts of Psychoanalysis*, 50.
24. Huyssen, *Present Pasts*, 4.
25. Grosz, *Jacques Lacan*, 34.
26. Quoted in Lemaire, *Jacques Lacan*, 116.
27. Huyssen, *Present Pasts*, 136.
28. Quoted in Yule, *Steven Spielberg*, 6.
29. Lacan, 'The Instance of the Letter in the Unconscious or Reason since Freud', 203.
30. Lacan, *The Seminar of Jacques Lacan, Book II*, 164.
31. Freud, 'Screen Memories', 322.
32. Baudry, 'The Apparatus', 317.
33. Lacan, *The Four Fundamental Concepts of Psychoanalysis*, 116.
34. Freud, 'The Uncanny', 235.
35. Benjamin, 'Theses on the Philosophy of History', 259.
36. Koolhaas, *Delirious New York*, 10.
37. Baudrillard, *The Spirit of Terrorism and Requiem for the Twin Towers*, 41, 43, 44.
38. Esplin, 'Double or Nothing'.

39. Berger, *After the End*, 26; Lacan, 'Seminar on "The Purloined Letter" ', 52.
40. Berger, *After the End*, 19.
41. Bennett, *Theatre Audiences*, 164.
42. Freud, 'The Uncanny', 217–52.

References

Aarseth, Espen (1997) *Cybertext: Perspectives on Ergodic Literature*. Baltimore, MD: Johns Hopkins University Press.

Aarseth, Espen (2006) 'The Culture and Business of Cross-Media Productions', *Popular Communication*, vol. 4, no. 3, pp. 201–11.

Abel, Richard (1994) *The Ciné Goes to Town: French Cinema, 1896–1914*. Berkeley, CA: University of California Press.

Ahmed, Zubair (2003) 'No Bollywood Films for Oscars', http://news.bbc.co.uk/1/hi/entertainment/film/3153098.stm

Ahmed, Zubair (2006) 'Gandhi-style Protest by Farmers', http://news.bbc.co.uk/1/hi/world/south_asia/6044476.stm

Alessio, Dominic and Jessica Langer (2007) 'Nationalism and Postcolonialism in Indian Science Fiction: Bollywood's *Koi . . . Mil Gaya* (2003)', *New Cinemas: Journal of Contemporary Film*, vol. 5, no. 3, pp. 217–29.

Altman, Rick (1999) *Film/Genre*. London: British Film Institute.

Anderson, Chris (2007) *The Long Tail: How Endless Choice Is Creating Unlimited Demand*. London: Random House.

Anderson, John (2007) 'We Called it a Festival, but it Became a Market', *Guardian Unlimited*, January 19, http://film.guardian.co.uk/features/featurepages/0,,1993650,00.html

Andrews, Amanda (2006) 'Pirates Tale Captures Fans to Become £1bn Treasure Trove', *The Times Online*, July 3, http://business.timesonline.co.uk/article/0,,9071-2253552,00.html

Apperley, Tom (2004) 'Getting Stuck on Level One: Designing a Research Methodology Appropriate to Xbox', http://tomsphd.blogspot.com/2004/08/getting-stuck-on-level-one-designing.html

Applebaum, Stephen (1998) 'Scare Stories: Wes Craven Interview', *The Independent*, http://findarticles.com/p/articles/mi_qn4158/is_19980425/ai_n14159415

Barthes, Roland (1974) *S/Z*. Trans. Richard Miller. New York: Noonday.

Baudrillard, Jean (1994) *Simulacra and Simulation*. Trans. Sheila Faria Glaser. Ann Arbor, MI: University of Michigan Press.

Baudrillard, Jean (2002) *The Spirit of Terrorism and Requiem for the Twin Towers*. Trans. Chris Turner. London: Verso.

Baudry, Jean-Louis (1986 [1975]) 'The Apparatus: Metapsychological Approaches to the Impression of Reality in the Cinema', in Rosen (ed.), *Narrative, Apparatus, Ideology*, pp. 299–318.

Benjamin, Walter (1992) 'Theses on the Philosophy of History', in Hannah Arendt (ed.), *Illuminations*. Trans. Harry Zohn. London: Fontana, pp. 245–55.

Bennett, Susan (1997) *Theatre Audiences: A Theory of Production and Reception*. Second Edition. London: Routledge.

Berger, James (1999) *After the End: Representations of Post-Apocalypse*. Minneapolis, MI: University of Minnesota Press.

Berliner, Todd (2001) 'The Pleasures of Disappointment: Sequels and *The Godfather, Part II*', *Journal of Film and Video*, vol. 53, nos. 2–3 (Summer/Fall), pp. 107–23.

Bhaskaran, Gautaman (2003) 'Aping Hollywood', *The Hindu*, August 22, http://www.hinduonnet.com/thehindu/fr/2003/08/22/stories/2003082201380200htm

Biguenet, John (1998) 'Double Takes: The Role of Allusion in Cinema', in Horton and McDougal (eds), *Play It Again, Sam*, pp. 131–46.

Biskind, Peter (2004) *Down and Dirty Pictures: Miramax, Sundance, and the Rise of Independent Film*. London: Simon & Schuster.

Brown, Richard (2005) 'Film and Postcards – Cross Media Symbiosis in Early Bamforth Films', in Vanessa Toulmin and Simon Popple (eds), *Visual Delights – Two*: *Exhibition and Reception*. 2 vols. Eastleigh: John Libbey, pp. 236–56.

Budra, Paul (1998) 'Recurring Monsters: Why Freddy, Michael, and Jason Keep Coming Back', in Budra and Schellenberg (eds), *Part Two*, pp. 189–99.

Budra, Paul and Betty A. Schellenberg (1998a) 'Introduction', in Budra and Schellenberg (eds), *Part Two*, pp. 3–18.

Budra, Paul and Betty A. Schellenberg (eds) (1998b) *Part Two: Reflections on the Sequel*. Toronto: University of Toronto Press.

Butler, Rex and Scott Stephens (eds) (2005) *Slavoj Žižek: Interrogating the Real*. London: Continuum.

Canby, Vincent (1974) ' "*Godfather, Part II*" is Hard to Define', *The New York Times*, December 13, p. 58.

Canby, Vincent (1980) ' "*The Empire Strikes Back*" Strikes a Bland Note', *The New York Times*, June 15, p. D25.

Carroll, Noël (1982) 'The Future of Allusion: Hollywood in the Seventies (and Beyond)', *October*, vol. 20, pp. 151–81.

Casetti, Francesco (1999) *Theories of Cinema 1945–1995*. Austin, TX: University of Texas Press.

Castle, Terry (1986) *Masquerade and Civilization: Carnivalesque in 18th Century English Culture and Fiction*. London: Methuen.

Castle, Terry (2000) 'Phantasmagoria and Modern Reverie', in Gelder (ed.), *The Horror Reader*, pp. 29–49.

Chakravarty, Sumita (1993) *National Identity in Indian Popular Cinema 1947–1987*. Austin, TX: University of Texas Press.

Ciecko, Anne T. (2006a) 'Theorizing Asian Cinema(s)', in Ciecko (ed.), *Contemporary Asian Cinema*, pp. 13–30.

Ciecko, Anne T. (ed.) (2006b) *Contemporary Asian Cinema: Popular Culture in a Global Frame*. Oxford: Berg.

Clover, Carol J. (1992) *Men, Women, and Chainsaws: Gender in the Modern Horror Film*. Princeton: Princeton University Press.

Clover, Carol J. (2000) 'Her Body, Himself' (extract), in Gelder (ed.), *The Horror Reader*, pp. 294–311.

Collodi, Carlo (1996) *Pinocchio*. Trans. E. Harden. London: Puffin.

Cook, David A. (1996) *A History of Narrative Film*. Third Edition. London: W. W. Norton.

Cowie, Elizabeth (1996) *Representing the Woman: Cinema and Psychoanalysis*. Minneapolis, MN: University of Minnesota Press.

Crawford, Shawn (1991) *No Time to Be Idle: The Serial Novel and Popular Imagination*. Washington, DC: Washington Press.

Creed, Barbara (1993) *The Monstrous Feminine: Film, Feminism, Psychoanalysis*. London: Routledge.

Decherney, Peter (2007) 'Copyright Dupes: Piracy and New Media in Edison v. Lubin (1903)', *Film History*, vol. 19, pp. 109–24.

Delamater, Jerome (1998) ' "Once More, from the Top": Musicals the Second Time Around', in Horton and McDougal (eds), *Play It Again, Sam*, pp. 80–94.

Deleuze, Gilles (1994) *Difference and Repetition*. Trans. Paul Patton. London: Athlone.

Desai, Jigna (2006) 'Bollywood Abroad: South Asian Diasporic Cosmopolitanism and Indian Cinema', in Rajan and Sharma (eds), *New Cosmopolitanisms*, pp. 116–37.

Dika, Vera (1990) *Games of Terror: 'Halloween', 'Friday the 13th', and the Films of the Stalker Cycle*. Madison, NJ: Fairleigh Dickinson University Press.

Dissanayake, Wimal (2006) 'Sri Lanka: Art, Commerce, Cultural Modernity', in Ciecko (ed.), *Contemporary Asian Cinema*, pp. 108–19.

Dobler, Thomas and Sven Jockel (2006) 'The Event Movie: Marketing Filmed Entertainment for Transnational Media Corporations', *International Journal on Media Management*, vol. 8, no. 2, pp. 84–91.

Druxman, Michael B. (1975) *Make It Again, Sam: A Survey of Movie Remakes*. Cranbury, NJ: A. S. Barnes.

Durham, Carolyn A. (1998) *Double Takes: Culture and Gender in French Films and Their American Remakes*. Hanover, NH: University Press of New England.

Dyer, Richard (2006) *Pastiche*. London: Routledge.

Eco, Umberto (1990) *The Limits of Interpretation*. Bloomington, IN: Indiana University Press.

Eco, Umberto (1997), 'Innovation and Repetition: Between Modern and Post-Modern Aesthetics', *Daedalus*, vol. 114, no. 4, pp. 161–84.

Edgers, Geoff (2004) 'Out of the Realm of Imagination', *Boston Globe*, March 21, http://www.boston.com/news/globe/living/articles/2004/03/21/out_of_the_realm_of_imagination/?page=1

Elsaesser, Thomas (1998) 'Fantasy Island: Dream Logic as Production Logic', in Elsaesser and Hoffmann (eds), *Cinema Futures*, pp. 143–58.

Elsaesser, Thomas (2005) *European Cinema Face to Face With Hollywood*. Amsterdam: Amsterdam University Press.

Elsaesser, Thomas and Kay Hoffmann (eds) (1998) *Cinema Futures: Cain, Abel, or Cable? The Screen Arts in the Digital Age*. Amsterdam: Amsterdam University Press.

Epstein, Edward Jay (2006) 'The End of Originality, or Why Michael Bay's *The Island* Failed at the Box Office', *Slate Magazine*, http://www.slate.com/id/2135544/

Esplin, Gregory T. (2005) 'Double or Nothing: The Uncanny State of Post-9/11 America', *Philament: An Online Journal of the Arts and Culture*, vol. 6, http://www.arts.usyd.edu.au/publications/philament/issue6_pdf/ESPLIN_Double%20or%20Nothing.pdf

Ezra, Elizabeth (2000) *Georges Méliès*. Manchester: Manchester University Press.

Fell, John L. (1983a) 'Motive, Mischief and Melodrama: The State of Film Narrative in 1907', in Fell (ed.), *Film Before Griffith*, pp. 272–83.

Fell, John L. (ed.) (1983b) *Film Before Griffith*. Berkeley, CA: University of California Press.

Fielding, Raymond (1983) 'Hale's Tours: Ultrarealism in the Pre-1910 Motion Picture', in Fell (ed.), *Film Before Griffith*, pp. 116–30.

Fischer, Lucy (1996) *Cinematernity: Film, Motherhood, Genre*. Princeton: Princeton University Press.

Forrest, Jennifer and Leonard R. Koos (eds) (2002) *Dead Ringers: The Remake in Theory and Practice*. Albany, NY: State University of New York Press.

Foster, Hal (1996) *The Return of the Real: The Avant-Garde as the End of the Century*. Cambridge, MA: MIT Press.

Frazer, John (1979) *Artificially Arranged Scenes: The Films of Georges Méliès*. Boston, MA: G. K. Hall.

Freud, Sigmund (1992 [1902]) 'Excerpts from Freud's Letters to Fliess', in Elisabeth Young-Breuhl (ed.), *Freud On Women: A Reader*. London: Hogarth.

Freud, Sigmund (1995 [1899]) 'Screen Memories', in James Strachey (ed. and trans.), *The Standard Edition of the Complete Psychological Works*. London: Hogarth, vol. 3, pp. 301–22.

Freud, Sigmund (1995 [1919]) 'The Uncanny', in James Strachey (ed. and trans.), *The Standard Edition of the Complete Psychological Works*. London: Hogarth, vol. 17, pp. 217–52.

Freud, Sigmund (1995 [1920]) 'Beyond the Pleasure Principle', in James Strachey (ed. and trans.), *The Standard Edition of the Complete Psychological Works*. London: Hogarth, vol. 19, pp. 19–30.

Freud, Sigmund (1995 [1922]) 'Medusa's Head', in James Strachey (ed. and trans.), *The Standard Edition of the Complete Psychological Works*. London: Hogarth, vol. 18, p. 273.

Freud, Sigmund (1995 [1925]) 'A Note on the Mystic Writing-Pad' in James Strachey (ed. and trans), *The Standard Edition of the Complete Psychological Works*. London: Hogarth, vol. 10, pp. 227–32.

Fuery, Patrick (2000) *New Developments in Film Theory*. London: Macmillan.

Gaines, Jane M. (2006) 'Early Cinema's Heyday of Copying: The Too Many Copies of *L'Arroseur arrosé* (*The Waterer Watered*)', *Cultural Studies*, vol. 20, nos. 2–3 (March/May), pp. 227–44.

Gelder, Ken (ed.) (2000) *The Horror Reader*. London: Routledge.

Genette, Gérard (1997) *Palimpsests: Literature in the Second Degree*. Lincoln, NE: University of Nebraska Press.

Gerhart, Mary (1992) *Genre Choices, Gender Questions*. London: University of Oklahoma Press.

Gerow, A. A. (1996) 'Swarming Ants and Elusive Villains: *Zigomar* and the Problem of Cinema in 1910s Japan', *CineMagaziNet!*, vol. 1 (Autumn), http://www.cmn.hs.h.kyoto-u.ac.jp/NO1/SUBJECT1/ZIGOMAR.HTM

Gokulsing, K. Moti and Wimal Dissanayake (2003) *Indian Popular Cinema: A Narrative of Cultural Change*. Second Edition. Stoke on Trent: Trentham.

Goldberg, Andy (2006) 'Snow, Swag, Sparkle Challenge Sundance's Indie Spirit', January 26, *M&C*, http://movies.monstersandcritics.com/features/article_1089315.php/Snow_swag_sparkle_challenge_Sundances_indie_spirit

Gooch, Joshua (2007) 'Making a Go of It: Paternity and Prohibition in the Films of Wes Anderson', *Cinema Journal*, vol. 47, no. 1 (Fall), pp. 26–48.

Grant, Barry Keith (1986a) 'Introduction', in Grant (ed.), *Film Genre Reader*, pp. ix–xvi.

Grant, Barry Keith (ed.) (1986b) *Film Genre Reader*. Austin, TX: University of Texas Press.

Greenberg, Harvey R. 'Raiders of the Lost Text: Remaking as Contested Homage in *Always*', in Horton and McDougal (eds), *Play It Again, Sam*, pp. 115–30.

Greenspun, Roger (1972) 'Something Happened on the Way to the Sequel; Roundtree Returns in "Shaft's Big Score"', *The New York Times*, June 22, p. 47.

Grosz, Elizabeth (1990) *Jacques Lacan: A Feminist Introduction*. Sydney: Allen & Unwin Australia.

Gunning, Tom (1986) 'The Cinema of Attractions: Early Film, Its Spectator, and the Avant-Garde', *Wide Angle*, vol. 8, pp. 63–70.

Gunning, Tom (2000) *The Films of Fritz Lang: Allegories of Vision and Modernity*. London: British Film Institute.

Gunning, Tom (2004) 'The Intertextuality of Early Cinema: A Prologue to *Fantômas*', in Robert Stam and Alexandra Raengo (eds), *A Companion to Literature and Film*. Oxford: Blackwell, pp. 127–43.

Halbwachs, Maurice (1992) *On Collective Memory*. Ed. and trans. Lewis A. Coser. Chicago: University of Chicago Press.

Hammond, Paul (1974) *Marvellous Méliès*. London: Gordon Fraser Gallery.

Hancock, David (2004) *Screen Digest Cinema Intelligence Briefing Report*. London: Screen Digest.

Hansen, Miriam (1994) *Babel and Babylon: Spectatorship in American Silent Film*. Cambridge, MA: Harvard University Press.

Harmetz, Aljean (1985) 'The Sequel Becomes the New Bankable Film Star', *The New York Times*, July 8, p. 15.

Harraway, Clare (2000) *Re-citing Marlowe: Approaches to the Drama*. Aldershot: Ashgate.

Harries, Dan (2002) 'Film Parody and the Resuscitation of Genre', in Neale (ed.), *Genre and Contemporary Hollywood*, pp. 281–93.

Harris, Paul (2007) 'Killer Made his own Horror Film for the YouTube Generation', *Daily Mail*, April 20, http://www.dailymail.co.uk/pages/live/articles/news/worldnews.html?in_article_id=449604&in_page_id=1811#StartComments

'Here Come the Sons and Daughters' (1974) *The New York Times*, June 30, p. 15.

Higgins, Scott (2007) *Harnessing the Technicolor Rainbow: Color Design in the 1930s*. Austin, TX: University of Texas Press.

Hills, Matt (2005) *The Pleasures of Horror*. London: Continuum.

Hirji, Faiza (2005) 'When Local Meets Lucre: Commerce, Culture and Imperialism in Bollywood Cinema', *Global Media Journal*, vol. 4, no. 7, http://lass.calumet.purdue.edu/cca/gmj/fa05/graduatefa05/gmj-fa05gradref-hirji.htm

Hoberman, James (1985) 'Ten Years that Shook the World', *American Film*, vol. 10, pp. 34–59.

Holmlund, Christine (2004) 'Introduction: from the Margins to the Mainstream', in Holmlund and Wyatt (eds), *Contemporary American Independent Film*, pp. 1–17.

Holmlund, Christine and Justin Wyatt (eds) (2004) *Contemporary American Independent Film: From the Margins to the Mainstream*. London: Routledge.

Horowitz, Josh (2007) 'Jack Nicholson Talks!', *MTV.Com*, November 5, http://www.mtv.com/movies/news/articles/1573487/story.jhtml

Horton, Andrew and Stuart Y. McDougal (eds) (1998) *Play It Again, Sam: Retakes on Remakes*. Berkeley, CA: University of California Press.

Huang, Martin W. (2004) 'Introduction', in Martin W. Huang (ed.), *Snakes' Legs: Sequels, Continuations, Rewritings, and Chinese Fiction*. Honolulu: University of Hawai'i Press, pp. 1–18.

Hughes, Linda K. and Michael Lund (1991) *The Victorian Serial*. Charlottesville: University Press of Virginia.

Hunter, J. Paul (1997) 'Serious Reflections on Farther Adventures: Resistances to Closure in Eighteenth-Century English Novels', in Albert J. Rivero (ed.), *Augustan Subjects: Essays in Honor of Martin C. Battestin*. Newark, DE: University of Delaware Press, pp. 276–94.

Hutcheon, Linda (1986) 'Postmodern Paratextuality and History', *Texte*, vols 5–6, pp. 301–12.

Huyssen, Andreas (2003) *Present Pasts: Urban Palimpsests and the Politics of Memory*. Stanford, CA: Stanford University Press.

Iampolski, Mikhail (1998) *The Memory of Tiresias: Intertextuality and Film*. Trans. Harsha Ram. Berkeley, CA: University of California Press.

Iser, Wolfgang (1978) *The Act of Reading: A Theory of Aesthetic Response*. London: Routledge & Kegan Paul.

James, Alison (2001) 'France to Sequels: *Moi Aussi*', *Variety*, September 4, http://www.variety.com/article/VR1117852204?categoryid=13&cs=1

Jameson, Fredric (1991) *Postmodernism, or, The Cultural Logic of Late Capitalism*. London: Verso.

Jenkins, Henry (1992) *Textual Poachers: Television Fans and Participatory Culture*. London: Routledge.

Jenkins, Henry (2004) 'Interactive Audiences? The Collective Intelligence of Media Fans', http://web.mit.edu/cms/People/henry3/collective%20intelligence.html

Jenkins, Henry (2006a) 'The *Snakes on a Plane* Phenomenon', *Confessions of an Aca/Fan: The Official Weblog of Henry Jenkins*, June 21, http://henryjenkins.org/2006/06/the_snakes_on_a_plane_phenomen.html

Jenkins, Henry (2006b) 'Truth, Justice and the South Asian Way', *Confessions of an Aca/Fan: The Official Weblog of Henry Jenkins*, July 6, http://www.henryjenkins.org/2006/07/truth_justice_and_the_south_as.html

Jenkins, Philip (2002) 'Catch Me Before I Kill More: Seriality as Modern Monstrosity', *Cultural Analysis*, vol. 3, pp. 1–17.

Jha, Subhash K. (2007) '*Munnabhai, Hera Pheri* Brand War Hots Up', *Hindustan Times*, October 8, http://www.hindustantimes.com/StoryPage/StoryPage.aspx?id=8130b7da-ab42-4c06-a008465823b8a46c&MatchID1=4660&TeamID1=5&TeamID2=2&MatchType1=2&SeriesID1=1172&PrimaryID=4660&Headline=EMMunnabhai%2fEM%2c+EMHera%2fEM+EMPheri%2fEM+brand+war+hots+up

Jowett, Garth (1974) 'The First Motion Picture Audiences', *Journal of Popular Film*, vol. 3 (Winter), pp. 43–52.

Kapoor, Priya (2007) 'FICCI Frames 2007: Movie Remakes and Sequels: Revisiting the Past or Intellectual Bankruptcy?', March 28, http://www.exchange4media.com/FICCI/2007/ficci_fullstory07.asp?news_id=2543

Kaur, Raminder and Ajay J. Sinsha (2005) 'Bollyworld: An Introduction to Popular Indian Cinema through a Transnational Lens', in Raminder Kaur and Ajay J. Sinsha (eds), *Bollyworld: Popular Indian Cinema through a Transnational Lens*. London: Sage, pp. 11–34.

Kawin, Bruce F. (1972) *Telling It Again and Again: Repetition in Literature and Film*. Ithaca, NY: Cornell University Press.

King, Geoff (2000) *Spectacular Narratives: Hollywood in the Age of the Blockbuster*. London: I. B. Tauris.

King, Geoff (2005) *American Independent Cinema*. London: I. B. Tauris.

Klemesrud, Judy (1975) 'Film Notes: From Sequel Mania to Disappearing De Niro', *The New York Times*, Oct 5, p. 139.

Koolhaas, Rem (1994) *Delirious New York: A Retroactive Manifesto for Manhattan*. Rotterdam: 010.

Krebs, Albin (1976) 'Fritz Lang, Film Director Noted for "*M*", Dead at 85', *The New York Times*, August 3, p. 28.

Lacan, Jacques (1981) *The Four Fundamental Concepts of Psychoanalysis*. Trans. Alan Sheridan. London: W. W. Norton.

Lacan, Jacques (1988) *The Seminar of Jacques Lacan, Book II: The Ego in Freud's Theory and in the Technique of Psychoanalysis, 1954–55*. Trans. Sylvana Tomaselli. New York: W. W. Norton.

Lacan, Jacques (1988 [1955]) 'Seminar on "The Purloined Letter"', trans. Jeffrey Mehlman, in John P. Muller and William J. Richardson (eds), *The Purloined Poe: Lacan, Derrida & Psychoanalytic Reading*. Baltimore: John Hopkins University Press.

Lacan, Jacques (2000 [1966]) 'The Instance of the Letter in the Unconscious or Reason since Freud', in Julie Rivkin and Michael Ryan (eds), *Literary Theory: An Anthology*. Oxford: Blackwell, pp. 190–205.

Lacan, Jacques (2001 [1977]) 'The Mirror Stage as Formative of the Function of the I as Revealed in Psychoanalytic Experience', in *Écrits: A Selection*. Trans. Alan Sheridan. London: Routledge, pp. 1–7.

LaCapra, Dominick (1998) *History and Memory After Auschwitz*. Ithaca, NY: Cornell University Press.

Landow, George (1992) *Hypertext: The Convergence of Contemporary Critical Theory and Technology*. Baltimore, MD: Johns Hopkins University Press.

Lebo, Harlan (1997) *The Godfather Legacy: The Untold Story of the Making of the Classic Godfather Trilogy Featuring Never-Before-Published Production Stills*. New York: Fireside.

Leggatt, Alexander (1998) 'Killing the Hero: Tamburlaine and Falstaff', in Budra and Schellenberg (eds), *Part Two*, pp. 53–67.

Lemaire, Anika (1977) *Jacques Lacan*. Trans. David Macey. London: Routledge.

Levy, Emanuel (1999) *Cinema of Outsiders: The Rise of American Independent Film*. New York: New York University Press.

Lewis, John (2005) '*"Mother Oh God Mother . . ."*: Analysing the "Horror" of Single Mothers in Contemporary Hollywood Horror', *Scope*, vol. 2, http://www.scope.nottingham.ac.uk/article.php?issue=2&id=68

Leyda, Jay (1968) 'A Note on Progress', *Film Quarterly*, vol. 21, no. 4 (Summer), pp. 28–33.

Liestøl, Gunnar (1994) 'Wittgenstein, Genette, and the Reader's Narrative in Hypertext', in George Landow (ed.), *Hyper/Text/Theory*. Baltimore, MD: Johns Hopkins University Press, pp. 87–120.

Lowenstein, Adam (2005) *Shocking Representation: Historical Trauma, National Cinema, and the Modern Horror Film*. New York: Columbia University Press.

Lukow, Gregory and Steven Ricci (1984) 'The "Audience" goes "Public": Intertextuality, Genre and the Responsibilities of Film Literacy', *On Film*, vol. 12, pp. 28–36.

Lütticken, Sven (2004) 'Planet of the Remakes', *New Left Review*, vol. 25 (Jan/Feb), pp. 103–19.

Macdonald, Scott (2006) *A Critical Cinema 5: Interviews with Independent Filmmakers*. Berkeley, CA: University of California Press.

McGonigal, Jane (2003) 'A Real Little Game: The Performance of Belief in Pervasive Play', http://www.avantgame.com/MCGONIGAL%20A%20Real%20Little%20Game%20DiGRA%202003.pdf

McGowan, Todd (2003) 'Looking for the Gaze: Lacanian Film Theory and its Vicissitudes', *Cinema Journal*, vol. 42, no. 3 (Spring), pp. 27–47.

McGowan, Todd and Sheila Kunkle (eds) (2004) *Lacan and Contemporary Film*. New York: Other.

McLarty, Lianne (1998) '"I'll be back": Hollywood, Sequelization, and History', in Budra and Schellenberg (eds), *Part 2*, pp. 200–17.

Malaney, M. A. (1920) 'Rev. *Excuse My Dust*'. *Moving Picture World*. March 20, p. 1157.

Maltby, Richard (2003) *Hollywood Cinema*. Second Edition. London: Blackwell.

Maniar, Parag (2007) 'Return of Hanuman is Tax Free', *The Times of India*, December 24, http://timesofindia.indiatimes.com/India_Buzz/Hanuman_Returns_is_tax-free/articleshow/2645377.cms

Manovich, Lev (2002) *The Language of New Media*. Cambridge, MA: MIT Press.

Manvell, Roger (2007) '*Doktor Mabuse der Spieler; Das Testament des Dr. Mabuse*', http://www.filmreference.com/Films-De-Dr/Doktor-Mabuse-der-Spieler-Das-Testament-des-Dr-Mabuse.html

Mayshark, Jesse Fox (2007) *Post-Pop Cinema: The Search for Meaning in New American Film*. London: Praeger.

Mazdon, Lucy (2004) 'Introduction', *Journal of Romance Studies* (Special Issue on Film Remakes) vol. 4, no. 1, pp. 1–11.

Mekas, Jonas (2004) 'Independence for Independents', in Holmlund and Wyatt (eds), *Contemporary American Independent Film*, pp. 30–4.

Menon, Prathamesh (2003) 'Bollywood Undressed', http://www.student.city.ac.uk/~ra831/group8/prash.htm

Menon-Broker, Aditi (2004) *A Hall of Mirrors: Repetition and Recycling in Hindi Commercial Cinema*. Unpublished PhD thesis, Northwestern University.

Metz, Christian (1986 [1968]) *The Imaginary Signifier* (Excerpts), in Rosen (ed.), *Narrative, Apparatus, Ideology*, pp. 244–80.

Miller, Toby, Nitin Govil, John McMurria, Richard Maxwell and Ting Wang (2005) *Global Hollywood 2*. London: British Film Institute.

Miller, Tom (1999) 'Struggling With Godzilla: Unraveling the Symbolism in Toho's Sci/Fi Films', *Kaiju-Fan*, http://www.historyvortex.org/GodzillaSymbolism.html

Morley, David and Kevin Robins (1997) *Space of Identity*. London: Routledge.

Morris, Robert K. (1972) *Continuance and Change: The Contemporary British Novel*. Carbondale, IL: Southern Illinois University Press.

Mulvey, Laura (1999 [1975]) 'Visual Pleasure and Narrative Cinema', in Leo Braudy and Marshall Cohen (eds), *Film Theory and Criticism: Introductory Readings*. Fifth Edition. New York: Oxford University Press, pp. 833–44.

Munnabhai Effect: Guns to roses' (2006) *Express India*, September 27, http://cities.expressindia.com/fullstory.php?newsid=203119

Musser, Charles (1990 [1984]) 'The Nickelodeon Era Begins: Establishing the Framework for Hollywood's Mode of Representation', in Thomas Elsaesser (ed.), *Early Cinema: Space, Frame, Narrative*. London: British Film Institute, pp. 256–73.

Napier, Susan J. (1993) 'Panic Sites: The Japanese Imagination of Disaster from *Godzilla* to *Akira*', *Journal of Japanese Studies*, vol. 19, no. 2 (Summer), pp. 327–35.

Naremore, James (1995) 'American Film Noir: The History of an Idea', *Film Quarterly*, vol. 49, no. 2 (Winter), pp. 12–29.

Ndalianis, Angela (1999) ' "Evil Will Walk Once More": Phantasmagoria – the Stalker Film as Interactive Movie', in Greg M. Smith (ed.), *On a Silver Platter: CD-Roms and the Promises of a New Technology*. New York: New York University Press, pp. 87–112.

Neale, Steve (1990) 'Questions of Genre', *Screen*, vol. 31, no. 1 (Spring), pp. 45–66.

Neale, Steve (ed.) (2002) *Genre and Contemporary Hollywood*. London: British Film Institute.

Nietzsche, Friedrich (1968) *The Will To Power*. Trans. Walter Kaufman and R. J. Hollingdale. New York: Vintage.

Noriega, Chon (1987) 'Godzilla and the Japanese Nightmare: When "Them!" Is U.S.', *Cinema Journal*, vol. 27, no. 1 (Autumn), pp. 63–77.

'Notes Written on the Screen' (1916) *The New York Times*, June 18, p. X5.

'Now – The $10,000 Sequel to *The Diamond from the Sky*' (1916), December 9, *Motion Picture News*, vol. 14, no. 23, p. 3501.

Nowlan, Robert A. and Gwendolyn W. Nowlan (2000) *Cinema Sequels and Remakes 1903–1987*. Jefferson, NC: McFarland.

Nugent, Frank S. (1936) 'Consider the Sequel; Inspired by Ancestor-Worship, They Yet May Lead to Serials for Adults', *The New York Times*, May 31, p. x3.

Null, Bradley (1998) 'An Interview with Shane Meadows', *FilmCritic.com*, http://www. filmcritic.com/misc/emporium.nsf/reviews/An-Interview-with-Shane-Meadows

O'Hehir, Andrew (2006) 'Beyond the Multiplex', *Salon.com*. http://www.salon.com/ent/ movies/review/2006/01/26/btm/print.html.

'Online Fan Sites, Songs Inspire *Snakes on a Plane* Reshoots' (2006), *Pan and Scan: The DVD Blog*, March 24, http://www.panandscan.com/news/show/Web_Video/New_Line/ Snakes_on_a_Plane/Online_Fan_Sites,_Songs_Inspire_Snakes_on_a_Plane_Reshoots/495

Pearce, Craig and Baz Luhrmann (1996) *William Shakespeare's 'Romeo and Juliet': The Contemporary Film, The Classic Play*. New York: Laurel Leaf.

Pendakur, Manjunath (2003) *Indian Popular Cinema: Industry, Ideology, and Consciousness*. Cresskill, NJ: Hampton.

Perkins, Claire (2008) 'Remaking and the Film Trilogy: Whit Stillman's Authorial Triptych', *Velvet Light Trap*, vol. 61 (Spring), pp. 14–25.

Perry, Alex (2003) 'The Trailblazer: Interview with Ram Gopal Varma', *Time*, Oct. 20, http://www.time.com/time/asia/covers/501031027/int_varma.html

Pinedo, Isabel C. (1997) *Recreational Terror: Women and the Pleasures of Horror Film Viewing*. Albany, NY: State University of New York Press.

Plasse, Sabina Dana (2007) '*Everything's Cool* at Sundance', *Sun Valley Guide* (Summer), http://www.svguide.com/s07/everythingscool.htm

Plate, Tom (2002) 'Hollywood Faces New Competition: World Film Industry Is Globalization at Its Best', *UCLA International Institute*, http://www.international.ucla.edu/article.asp? parentid=2059

Popple, Simon and Joe Kember (2004) *Early Cinema from Factory Gate to Dream Factory*. London: Wallflower.

Pradhan, Sharat (2006) 'Lucknow Citizens go Gandhian on Liquor Merchant', *Rediff India Abroad*, September 21, http://www.rediff.com/news/2006/sep/21sharat.htm

Punathambakar, Aswin (2003) 'We are Like this Only: Desis and Hindi Films in the Diaspora'. Unpublished MA Thesis, Massachusetts Institute of Technology.

Quinn, Michael (2001) 'Distribution, the Transient Audience, and the Transition to the Feature Film', *Cinema Journal*, vol. 40, no. 2 (Winter), pp. 35–56.

Rajadhyaksha, Ashish (1996) 'Strange Attractions', *Sight and Sound*, vol. 6, no. 8 (August), pp. 28–31.

Rajadhyaksha, Ashish and Paul Willemen (1994) *Encyclopaedia of Indian Cinema*. London: British Film Institute.

Rajan, Gita and Shailja Sharma (eds) (2006) *New Cosmopolitanisms: South Asians in the US*. Stanford, CA: Standford University Press.

Ramsaye, Terry (1964) *A Million and One Nights: A History of the Motion Picture*. Third Edition. London: Frank Cass.

Ressler, Robert (1993) *Whoever Fights Monsters: A Brilliant FBI Detective's Career-Long War against Serial Killers*. New York: St. Martin's.

Rogin, Michael (1985) ' "The Sword Became a Flashing Vision": D. W. Griffith's *The Birth of a Nation*'. *Representations* (Special Issue: American Culture Between the Civil War and World War I), no. 9 (Winter), pp. 150–95.

Rombes, Nicholas (2005a) 'Introduction', in Rombes (ed.), *New Punk Cinema*, pp. 1–20.

Rombes, Nicholas (ed.) (2005b) *New Punk Cinema*. Edinburgh: Edinburgh University Press.

Rosen, Philip (ed.) (1986) *Narrative, Apparatus, Ideology: A Film Theory Reader*. New York: Columbia University Press.

Ryan, Marie-Laure (2001) *Narrative as Virtual Reality. Immersion and Interactivity in Literature and Electronic Media*. Baltimore, MD: Johns Hopkins University Press.

Sanders, Peter (2007) 'Coming Soon: A New Take On the Old Double Bill', *Wall Street Journal*, September 24, http://online.wsj.com/public/article/SB119059131017936814-OZZOI_tuNSFSpeesiCSjM_Wl0xc_20080923.html

Schivelbusch, Wolfgang (1977) *The Railway Journey: Trains and Travel in the 19th Century*. Trans. Anselm Hollo. Oxford: Basil Blackwell.

Scholes, Robert (1985) *Textual Power: Literary Theory and the Teaching of English*. New Haven, CT: Yale University Press.

Schwartz, Vanessa R. (1998) *Spectacular Realities: Early Mass Culture in Fin-de-Siècle Paris*. Berkeley, CA: University of California Press.

Sciretta, Peter (2007) 'Craven Talks *Scream 4*', *Slash Film*, February 27, http://www.slashfilm.com/2007/02/27/wes-craven-talks-scream-4/

Seidl, Monika (2003) *Revisiting Classics: Retroactive Performativity as a New Way of Seeing Adaptations of Classics. A Theory and Two Case Studies* (manuscript, Habilitationsschrift).

Seltzer, Mark (2000) 'The Serial Killer as a Type of Person' [Extract], in Gelder (ed.), *The Horror Reader*, pp. 97–107.

Shah, Mihir (2006) 'Gandhigiri – a Philosophy for our Times', *The Hindu*, September 28, http://www.hinduonnet.com/2006/09/28/stories/2006092802241000.htm

Shapiro, Eben (1998) 'On MTV, Studios Find No Such Thing as a Free Plug', *Wall Street Journal*, May 29, http://www.stayfreemagazine.org/ml/readings/MTV.pdf

Sharma, Swati Gauri (2006) 'How Gandhi Got his Mojo Back', *Boston Globe*, October 13, http://www.boston.com/news/globe/editorial_opinion/oped/articles/2006/10/13/how_gandhi_got_his_mojo_back/

Shepherdson, Charles (1997) 'A Pound of Flesh: Lacan's Reading of the Visible and the Invisible', *Diacritics*, vol. 27, no. 4, pp. 70–86.

Sherawat, Mallika (2004) 'Transcription of Press Conference for *Murder*', March 25, http://www.idlebrain.com/news/functions/pressmeet-murder.html

Shrinivas, Sheela (2003) 'Does Crossing Over Mean Overstepping Cultural Boundaries? *Monsoon Wedding*', http://reviews.media-culture.org.au/modules.php?name=News&file=article&sid=1873

Silverman, Kaja (1986 [1983]) 'Suture' [Excerpts], in Rosen (ed.), *Narrative, Apparatus, Ideology*, pp. 219–35.

Simonet, Thomas (1987) 'Conglomerates and Content: Remakes, Sequels, and Series in The New Hollywood', in Bruce A. Austin (ed.), *Current Research in Film: Audiences, Economics, and Law*, Vol. 3. Norwood, NJ: Ablex, pp. 154–62.

Singer, Ben (1997) 'Serials', in Geoffrey Nowell-Smith (ed.), *The Oxford History of World Cinema*. Oxford: Oxford University Press, pp. 105–11.

Singer, Ben (2001) *Melodrama and Modernity: Early Sensational Cinema and its Contexts*. New York: Columbia University Press.

Sinha, Ashish (2007) 'Now, Hanuman goes to Manhattan', *Rediff India Abroad*, December 11, http://www.rediff.com/money/2007/dec/11hanu.htm

Smith, Murray (1998) 'Modernism and the Avant-Gardes', in John Hill and Pamela Church Gibson (eds), *The Oxford Guide to Film Studies*. Oxford: Oxford University Press, pp. 395–412.

'Special Service Section on Ruth Roland in *The Tiger's Tail*' (1919) *Motion Picture News*, April 26, p. 2663.

Srinivas, Lakshmi (2002) 'The Active Audience: Spectatorship, Social Relations and the Experience of Cinema in India', *Media, Culture & Society*, vol. 24, pp. 155–73.

Sturken, Marita (1997) *Tangled Memories: The Vietnam War, the AIDS Epidemic, and the Politics of Remembering*. Berkeley, CA: University of California Press.

Thompson, Kristin (1985) *Exporting Entertainment: America in the World Film Market, 1907–34*. London: British Film Institute.

Thussu, Daya (2004) 'Taming the Dragon and the Elephant: Murdoch's Media in Asia', http://www.wacc.org.uk/wacc/publications/media_development/2004_4/taming_the_dragon_and_the_elephant_murdoch_s_media_in_asia

Tietchen, Todd F. (1998) 'Samples and Copycats: the Cultural Implications of the Postmodern Slasher in Contemporary American Film', *Journal of Popular Film and Television*, vol. 26, no. 3, pp. 98–107.

Tithecott, Richard (1997) *Of Men and Monsters: Jeffrey Dahmer and the Construction of the Serial Killer*. Madison, WI: University of Wisconsin Press.

Toulmin, Stephen (1985) *The Return to Cosmology: Postmodern Science and the Theology of Nature*. Berkeley, CA: University of California Press.

Traill, H. D. (1970 [1892]) *The New Fiction and Other Essays*. Port Washington, NY: Kennikat.

Tucker, Ken (2004) 'The Life Examined with Wes Anderson', *New York Magazine*, December 13, http://nymag.com/nymetro/movies/features/10643/

Tudor, Andrew (2001) 'Why Horror? The Peculiar Pleasures of a Popular Genre', in Mark Jancovich (ed.), *The Horror Film Reader*. London: Routledge, pp. 47–56.

Tudor, Andrew (2002) 'From Paranoia to Postmodernism? The Horror Movies in Late Modern Society', in Neale (ed.), *Genre and Contemporary Hollywood*, pp. 105–16.

Twitchell, James (1992) *Carnival Culture: The Trashing of Taste in America*. New York: Columbia University Press.

Tzioumakis, Yannis (2006) *American Independent Cinema: An Introduction*. Edinburgh: Edinburgh University Press.

Verevis, Constantine (2005) *Film Remakes*. Edinburgh: Edinburgh University Press.

Walsh, Michael (1994) 'Returns in the Real: Lacan and the Future of Psychoanalysis in Film Studies', *Post Script*, vol. 14, nos. 1–2 (Winter–Spring), pp. 22–32.

Wee, Valerie (2006) 'Resurrecting and Updating the Teen Slasher: The Case of *Scream*', *Journal of Popular Film and Television*, vol. 34, no. 2 (Summer), pp. 50–61.

West, Jackson (2007) 'Lonelygirl15 Creators Announce Spinoff', *NewTeeVee.com*, April 17, http://newteevee.com/2007/04/17/lonelygirl15-creators-announce-spinoff/

Whitehead, Mark (2003) *Slasher Movies*. Vermont: Trafalgar Square.

Yule, Andrew (1996) *Steven Spielberg: Father of the Man*. London: Little, Brown.

Zimmermann, Patricia R. (2005) 'Digital Deployment(s)', in Holmlund and Wyatt (eds), *Contemporary American Independent Film*, pp. 245–64.

Žižek, Slavoj (1989) *The Sublime Object of Ideology*. London: Verso.

Žižek, Slavoj (1991) *Looking Awry: An Introduction to Jacques Lacan Through Popular Culture*. Cambridge: MIT Press.

Žižek, Slavoj (1992) *Everything You Always Wanted to Know About Lacan (But Were Afraid to Ask Hitchcock)*. London: Verso.

Žižek, Slavoj (2001) *Enjoy Your Symptom! Jacques Lacan in Hollywood and Out*. London: Routledge.

Žižek, Slavoj (2002) *Welcome to the Desert of the Real*. London: Routledge.

Index